MW01626376

RUN
FOR THE LOVE OF LIFE

RUN

FOR THE LOVE OF LIFE

What I learned while running more than 10 000 miles through some of the harshest landscapes on Earth.

Erica Terblanche

Published by Quickfox Publishing,
PO Box 50660 West Beach 7449
Cape Town, South Africa
www.quickfox.co.za | info@quickfox.co.za

Run For The Love of Life
ISBN Paperback: 978-0-620-95677-2
ISBN Ebook: 978-0-620-95678-9

First edition

Editor: Michelle Bovey-Wood
Cover design: Jacques Marais and Vanessa Wilson
Cover photographs © RacingThePlanet
Typesetting and production: Quickfox Publishing
Printed by: XMD, Cape Town, South Africa

DISCLAIMERS

Credits

All attempts to credit appropriate texts and authors have been made. Should you find permission or reference to your text has been omitted in error, please email contact@thrive-guru.com so that this can be rectified as soon as possible.

Identity protection

The story, as recounted by the author, is her personal and true perspective of events as they occurred and is not meant in any way to harm or defame. All attempts were made to conceal the identity of previous romantic partners through the use of pseudonyms and the deployment of deliberate vagueness with respect to any identifying characteristics.

This book is dedicated to my mom, for her unconditional love and for teaching me to dare and to do.

ACKNOWLEDGEMENTS

This being my first novel, the list of those to whom I am deeply grateful is a long one, as I seek to acknowledge the people who first saw the writer's spark in me and fanned it:

My 8th Grade Afrikaans teacher, Mr Hattingh, who looked me dead in the eye and said: "To be a writer is to be the conscience of the nation," and so sowed the seed of what I hoped to become.

All of the people through the many years who encouraged me to "Write!" with the urgency that plagued me, until I did: Marilise Erasmus; David Clark; Kelly Campbell; Lizelle Barkhuizen; Sharon Stokes; Cindy Sullivan; Andrew Alberico; Gillian Banks; Roslyn Zuha; Ruth Levitan; Liz Murphy; Tracey Sanders; Juliette Young and Aurelia Venclovaite. Thank you for being my flame-bearers.

All of my family and friends who backed me on the journey of writing *RUN* – especially Elaine Mills for the many writing sessions together, Catherine Glennie for Monday write club, Ettie Flax for your support and your sketches, Kirsten Pansegrouw for reading the first draft, and Katerina Pishiris for persevering through the many drafts, and for your enduring encouragement.

Much thanks also to all of the people who invested their time and energy in writing reviews for *RUN*. These reviews are so incredibly valuable and precious to me. Just reading them makes me grateful that I keep company with such amazing human beings.

Jacques Marais, arguably South Africa's top adventure photographer; and Simone Sharpe, my social media guru: Thank you for investing yourself, heart, body and soul, into this project, and for your genuine, warm-hearted, all-in support in getting *RUN* out into the world.

Vanessa Wilson at Quickfox Publishing, thank you, too, for hearing and believing in the voice of *RUN* very early on. Thank you for encouraging me right from the start, and for everything you and Adele have done to get my book published in the most professional, top-quality form possible. I could not have wished for a better agent-publisher duo than you and Michelle Bovey-Wood. I am truly proud to publish under your label because I know that it is synonymous with excellence.

The greatest thanks go to my editor, Michelle Bovey-Wood. As Stephen King says: "To write is human, to edit divine." I have been blessed with the genius, honesty and courage of a gifted editor, whose advice shaped *RUN* until it became a story with soul. Michelle, thank you for your wise guidance, your meticulous editing and, above all, for going so many extra miles to get my book published and noticed. I will forever be grateful for the professional leap of faith you took to back me and for carrying me through by the strength of your belief and intuition.

And to my love, Helen Grace Seyler, and to my mom, Dolores Terblanche, who read and edited every single one of the many drafts. Thank you for your rigorous guidance and honesty, and for never once failing to believe that *RUN* would be a success. For your enduring love and support there are not enough words of thanks.

And to God, in whom I believe and who gave me the courage, gifts and inspiration I needed to persevere to the end – in everything.

CONTENTS

FOREWORD

When first approached with the manuscript for *RUN for the Love of Life*, I expected nothing more than another ego-soaked chronical listing yet another super-athlete's sporting achievements, extolling the virtues of exercise and reminding me that I am little better than a sack of dough that spends too many hours sitting behind my desk, glaring at a flickering screen. How wrong I was – and never have I been happier to be so.

Yes, Erica Terblanche is a super-athlete – in fact, her feats extend beyond the realm of what most of us mere mortals can comprehend: Choosing to run thousands of kilometres through the world's hottest deserts and across the some of its most hostile landscapes – simply, as the title suggests, for the love it – speaks to not only an extraordinary strength of body but an indomitable spirit. It is this spirit that is evocatively captured within the pages of this book, as the reader is led by the hand through a life journey that is bravely honest, heartbreaking, humorous at times, awe-inspiring, and infinitely compelling.

Above all else, *RUN* is one extraordinary woman's love letter: To her sport, to those she has loved, to the wonders of the natural world, and to the woman she has eventually become.

Guided by the generous addition of a QR Code that offers access to Erica's unique Couch to 10km in 10 Weeks running programme, I feel compelled to take the first few steps. Even if it means learning to walk before I can run, Erica's passion is infectious. I may never be able to follow in her footsteps, but the resilience and strength put forth in this book is an exhortation to us all to suck on the marrow of life and all it has to offer.

Michelle Bovey-Wood
Writer, editor, media specialist
Managing Director of BWRC Resourcing & Consulting

FROM THE AUTHOR

What I have learned by running thousands of miles – many of them through the desert – is the importance of believing in oneself and dreaming big. It is through the process of such dreaming that one uncovers an elemental secret of life: Every worthwhile accomplishment starts first as a small seed of hope.

I have written this book as an invitation to you to rekindle your dreams. My wish is that as you are swept along on this journey that you simply BEGIN to do that which you have perhaps been wanting and waiting to do for so long.

RUN for the Love of Life pays homage to that which we can achieve if we strike out towards a worthwhile goal and consistently and diligently stay with our practice, one small, patient step at a time. It is a story of struggle and becoming; of love and love lost; of grace and forgiveness, and of coming home. It is a book about never giving up and about becoming the best that we can be.

You will read tales of long-distance running adventures in the harshest and most awe-inspiring natural landscapes in the world – the Sahara, the Atacama, the Namib, the Grand Canyon and the Kalahari, among others. But you will also observe what emerges at the outer edges of human endurance: Unwavering commitment, perseverance through pain and tedium, inescapable humility and prayers at the cliff-edge of quitting. This book speaks to the victory of the human spirit over adversity – and of the camaraderie and love that makes us stay the course against all odds.

In the end, these are stories about far more than just running: They are examples of how our share of challenge and pain shape and refine us; how, over time, the grit in the shell becomes the pearl. They are stories of how our dreams can come true, with hard work and conscious and consistent effort, while facing all of the risks, difficulties and stresses of trying.

My intention is to inspire you to take that first step – in running or in whatever journey is uniquely your own. It is as simple as that – one step, and then the next – and you will find that eventually, every following step will take care of itself.

Erica Terblanche

"I am not trying to tell you that everything is going to be easy from now on. In fact, running takes dedication, discipline, and determination. But if you show up, you will find a level of happiness, peace, and self-sufficiency greater than you may have ever known. Run Club inspired me to MOVE. This book will do the same for you. It has the power to change your life."

– Vernon Pieterse

Graduate of Thrive Run Club's Couch to 10km in 10 Weeks programme, 2018

"Make up your mind that no matter what comes your way, no matter how difficult, no matter how unfair, you will do more than simply survive. You will thrive in spite of it."

JOEL OSTEEN

1

CHOOSE A PATH WITH HEART, SAHARA DESERT, 2009

"All paths are the same. They lead nowhere. Does this path have a heart?
If it does, the path is good; if it doesn't, it is of no use.
One makes for a joyful journey. The other will make a curse of your life.
One makes you strong, the other weakens you."

CARLOS CASTANEDA

The greater the darkness, the brighter the stars.

And so, too, it is with suffering: The greater the sorrow, the greater the opportunity for us to grow – if we choose it.

Like everyone, I have known my share of suffering, and one thing I do know is that the deeper the dark well we fall down, the stronger we get as we climb, one slow hand over the other, back towards the bright-blue sky overhead.

Hope is a long rope.

It can draw us up, even out of the deepest well – as long as we keep hoping and keep moving towards the light. I mean physically moving. It is by the sheer act of moving our bodies – whether swimming; dancing; running; surfing; hiking; gardening; stretching in long, slow ohms, or whatever other way one chooses, that we are able to process our grief and come out the other side, salt-caked and sweating, shattered and thoroughly cleansed, inside and out; and feeling suddenly light, as if we have dropped a bag full of suffering and old ghosts.

On 10 September 2009, I hit one of the lowest points of my then-39 years of life. We walked down Holborn Street in London. Behind us loomed the macabre gingerbread brick-stack of the High Court, and behind it the sky shone brilliant-blue. A good summer day like any other. The pavement seemed a dim blur through my tears. My now-ex-wife walked beside me. Billy was silent, cold and grey as a stone.

We had just stood together at a wooden, barred counter atop polished floors. "Sign here," the clerk had said. It seemed so indecent – ending everything in as trifling a manner as buying stamps at the post office. We had signed. It was over. Almost seven years, thousands of kilometres of adventure, all of the love that had gone before and all of the high dreams that had once stretched ahead of us, and all the meaning that those had given to our lives. All gone.

The divorce papers were filed. On the same day, a man-and-a-van arrived, and then it was done. All that remained was the pain and the emptiness; the flashes of relief mixed up with grief; the fragile exhilaration of new freedom, and then, again, the loss like a severed limb.

For reasons unknown to the machinery of my rational mind, in the aftermath of my divorce I was compelled towards the Sahara Desert with the same urgency that a drowning man thrashes for the blue surface.

The Sahara of which I had read stood in my mind's eye as a place of miracles, of illumination, a place for wandering and healing, a place where one could climb out of the narrow coffin of rumination. It was the Bedouin desert of the Sufi poets, Rumi and Hafiz, where poems blew barefoot across the vast sands. It was a magical place where a willing pilgrim could be hollowed out, purged and purified, and where prophets tuned into the great voice of God.

To get through the pain of our divorce, I needed to cut deep, right to my marrow, where I hid a lifetime of aching for things gone wrong and things done wrong. Perhaps it was redemption I sought as much as healing. And one thing was certain: A glossy-brochured camel safari, complete with a train of bearers and table-buckling, belly-bulging buffets for breakfast, lunch and dinner were not going to do that holy work! Oh no! My heart was clear: I needed to run the Sahara Desert. I wanted to run bearing all of my belongings on my back, carrying scarcely enough food and sunscreen for seven days and a thin sleeping mat, and to disappear into all of that barrenness.

I could never have imagined that I would encounter an experience so extraordinary that in seven short days it would heal my heart in a way that seems impossible, even now.

And so, on the eve of 23 October 2009, I stood at the Lufthansa check-in desk in Heathrow Airport, waiting to board a plane to Cairo. I had entered one of the toughest endurance races on the planet, a seven-day, 250km run across the Sahara – the hottest desert on Earth – all while carrying everything I could need for the duration of the race, bar water[1].

The race formed part of the RacingThePlanet series, which hosts races in some of the most inhospitable places on Earth, including the Sahara, the Atacama, the Gobi and Antarctica, each respectively the hottest, driest, windiest and coldest deserts in the world.

It seemed impossible, yet, somehow, I was absolutely sure that I was going to get through it.

In the beginning

I came to running via endurance sport and comparatively late in life, at the age of 30, while working 80-hour weeks, as an ambitious new recruit at one of South Africa's major banks in Johannesburg. There was no semblance of an athlete within me, but there was an appetite for adventure that had throbbed hard within since early childhood. I had been waiting for just the right moment to find an outlet.

I grew up on a far-flung South African farm, on the endless maize- and wheat-covered flatlands of the then-Orange Free State. After school, I would roam the wild, open veld, free and barefoot among the animals and beneath the endless African sky. From the very beginning, Nature weaved herself into my heart and my bones.

1 In addition to seven days' worth of food, I carried toiletries; a sleeping bag; one set of clean clothes; two pairs of socks; a hat; a thin foam mattress; a medicine kit; a compass; eating utensils; a headlight; spare batteries; sunscreen; trekking poles; sandals and a pencil and paper for when inspiration struck.

When I turned 12, my family moved to George, at the foot of the Outeniqua Mountains, in the epicentre of the Garden Route, with its spectacular network of hiking trails. I joined a local hiking club and hiked almost every multi-day hiking trail in South Africa. In the gentle rhythm of the long-distance trails, shoed in heavy, Dubbin-polished hiking boots and carrying a rudimentary steel-frame backpack, I escaped much of the teenage angst that besets many in the throes of growing up. It was my first taste of how spending time in nature could profoundly redirect a young person's destiny.

Those hiking adventures changed my life and sowed a seed that would lie dormant in my heart, just waiting for the right time to shoot roots and push through to disrupt my sedentary, workaholic adult life.

Long before distance running, my first real foray into endurance sport came in 2001, in the form of adventure racing.

A few days after my 30th birthday, and several months after completing my full-time MBA, I watched my television screen one evening with my jaw hanging open as adventure racing teams bashed their way through a Fijian forest in the dead of night. I instinctively knew that I had found my sport. From what I could see, it offered an unparalleled way to get back into the unchartered wilderness.

Adventure racing had just taken off in South Africa, and I convinced three friends from my MBA course to join my team. I signed us up for our first 24-hour race in a place called Little Switzerland, in the foothills of the Drakensberg Mountains.

On that first night of racing across mountains bathed in moonlight, I fell so deeply in love that I married the sport at once and found myself a permanent team. I was the sport's ardent bride for five years, and I devoted all of my free time, money, dreams and energy to mastering myself at the edge of the outermost boundaries of human perseverance.

The longest distance races would sometimes last for five days and five nights. We would race continuously with no more than two hours' sleep here and there, and then often only deep into the third or fourth night. The course directors sent us running, cycling, kayaking and bundu-bashing across unchartered wilderness terrain, over winter mountains and through rain and sleet. We got lost in deep, dark cavernous ravines, rock-climbed up and down vertical rock faces at night – sometimes wearing lifejackets as we ascended beneath waterfalls. We completed biking legs, often carrying and dragging our bikes through the unnavigable undergrowth, and down river gorges so steep that we had to use climbing rope. And there was always water – a lot of it, and dangerous, too. We could be found swimming across raging, swollen rivers in flood, or kayaking for hours at night along crocodile-infested rivers, or on the wild caps of a heaving ocean. And we did all of that in a state of delirious sleep deprivation, having not closed our eyes for 72 hours or more. Hallucinating and tripping hard while shooting a raging Grade 4 river in driving rain in the black of night is no joke.

These descriptions are not superlative.[2] They are as accurate as they are extreme. Those races pushed me to the outer limits of my ability. It was there, in that golden doorway of complete exhaustion, that I discovered that there is no limit. Through endurance racing, I learned a great and irrefutable metaphysical truth: At the edge of physical failure, at the point of "I cannot take another step," there is an endless reservoir of available energy – if your heart is in what you are doing.

Against all the odds of a late career start, I became an athlete and achieved the pinnacle of success in the sport by racing for three years for Team Cyanosis, South Africa's top, unbeaten team, and representing South Africa at the 2006 Adventure Racing World Championships in New Zealand.

Then, as abruptly as I started, I left adventure racing and the southern tip of Africa to follow Billy, my wife-to-be, to the United Kingdom. She was eager, young, and restless, and she needed to spread her own wings in both work and sport.

In return for uprooting my life in South Africa, Billy agreed to join me on a six-month bicycle-tour through South-East Asia, where I could gather some sunlight before relocating to the Northern Hemisphere and facing the long, grey winters that I so dreaded.

---

2 I kept a faithful record of every adventure race, from my very first to my very last to capture the otherworldly realities of adventure racing and the people who live for it. Perhaps I will write about it one day.

Ten thousand kilometres later, we had cycled from Singapore to Hong Kong.[3] The journey had changed us and without consciously realising it, somewhere between the cycling and our intercontinental relocation, our relationship had begun to show distressing cracks. Still, we got married anyway. Hope against incorrigible hope.

For our first three years in London, we worked hard to rebuild our lives on a new continent, and we travelled a great deal, exploring the cultural opulence of Europe. But apart from a few fun runs and obstacle races that Billy and I did together, my adventure racing days had seemingly ended.

Perhaps it was predictable that after my marriage ended, I would long to race again. But then I needed to go it alone, without a team or the pressure or the weight of too much stuff. I wanted to lose myself in the wide, hot expanses of the great Sahara Desert, in a desolate sparseness so vast that it would burn away all of the sorrow and the UK winter from my bones and scour out all of the pain that I no longer wanted to lug around in my life. There was no simpler or more elegant way to do it than to run.

Getting to Egypt

Three weeks prior to my departure for the desert, my physiotherapist had forbidden me to run. During my divorce I had developed such bad inflammation of the tibial band in my left leg (ITB) that I was unable to run more than 100m without collapsing in pain. Every runner dreads ITB inflammation because it often takes months to heal and requires a complete break from running. For any runner, that is the most abhorrent of prescriptions.

A good friend advised me that in the metaphysical world, my injury signified that I was stuck and that I didn't know how to move forward. I waved her analysis away, not believing too much in what hadn't been validated by science. But now, years later, I have come to realise that the body never lies – it is a faithful record of one's emotional life.

3 We biked an average of 89km a day, for 150 continuous days, starting from Singapore, via Malaysia, Cambodia, Thailand, Laos, Vietnam, into the south-west of communist, rural China and on to Hong Kong. Visit www.bikingasia.blogspot.com

From the outset, I was resolute about racing in the Sahara. I avoided my physiotherapist and sought the advice of an osteopath, who worked on my psoas – the muscle that connects the legs to the spine and holds the key to our emotional wellbeing and ability to relax.

Three days before the race, I was still unable to run, yet at the final treatment, my osteopath said: "Just go! Follow your heart; your will is strong – your body will cope."

I phoned my mom from the check-in queue at Heathrow and told her that I was too injured to run. "Don't worry. I will just walk the whole thing," I told her.

Once at the front of the Lufthansa check-in queue, the lady at the counter said in a judicious tone: "Madam, you have no visa for Cairo."

Leafing through a 600-page visa regulation manual, she pointed to page 365 as proof. "Sorry, Miss, I have to confiscate your ticket. You will not be allowed to board this flight."

Her words fell like lead in the pit of my stomach. She took my ticket and shut the counter. In shock and feeling nauseous, I emptied my savings account and booked an Emirates Business Class ticket for the obscene amount of £1 200. The flight was leaving in just over two hours from Gatwick Airport.

I sped from train to train and raced as fast as I could from Heathrow, but as I drew into Gatwick, my flight closed. All of my savings down the drain. One of the gate attendants felt my desperation and offered me a lifeline: "There is a cheap flight to Cairo with Air Austria at 6am, via Vienna. It gets you to Cairo by 3.30pm tomorrow. It is the last one for the day.

That flight would get me to Cairo too late to meet the RacingThePlanet buses, which were scheduled to leave at 10am in the morning. It was nearly midnight, and the busyness of Gatwick had subsided. I sat on the cold airport floor outside a closed coffee shop with my back against the wall and my backpack between my feet. I had no ticket, still no visa, and no way of travelling the 400km into the desert once I arrived in Egypt. All I had was my race entry and the name of the hotel in Cairo where the racers were overnighting.

With nothing left to lose, I phoned the Cairo hotel. The concierge passed me on to someone who was involved with the race logistics – a man who was courteous but spoke little English. He listened patiently as I explained my predicament – no ticket, no visa, no bus.

All he said, in a tone of absolute conviction, was: "Madam, you come!"

I hung every gamble on the authority in his voice, maxed out my credit card for the Air Austria ticket, turfed all of my check-in luggage so as to evade the visa issue at check-in, and at 6am made my way on to the flight illegally via the unmanned check-in terminal.

An hour later in Vienna, we briefly disembarked and reboarded for the last leg to Cairo. The lady at the Departure gate leafed through my passport and frowned. She was trying to remember page 365 of that awful visa bible. I held my breath and prayed. The queue was long, and the passengers were red-eyed and impatient, so she waved me through.

Once on the flight, I caught my breath and tried to ignore the reality that I was an illegal passenger on my way to Egypt. Instead, I made a list of all the happy thoughts that I wanted to carry into the desert which would, like magic carpets, buoy me through the difficult moments.

There is nothing as heavy as a dark thought, and on long-distance runs, they are as energy-depleting and ultimately as fatal as shoes that are one size too small. The quickest way through into the light is to displace negative thinking with bright thoughts. I scribbled down five statements that lit up my entire parasympathetic nervous system. Underneath each were factual proof-points to feed my rational mind – just in case it got into naysaying.

1. I have the innate potential to do this.
   - ✓ My life force is very strong – my osteo says I have healing powers.
   - ✓ Billy thinks that I am the most mentally strong person in the world.
   - ✓ I have years and years of adventure racing muscle memory to draw on.
2. I am in a good place right now.
   - ✓ I am fit and lean.
   - ✓ My body feels soft, relaxed and strong from all of the yoga. The tension is gone.
   - ✓ My diaphragm has completely opened. My chi has flooded back so much that my lips tingle.

   - ✓ I have strategies for calming my mind: Tapping and breathing.
   - ✓ My backpack weighs only 7.5kg wet.[4]
3. I have so much love in my life – and love gives me wings.
   - ✓ My mom, my dad and my sister love me.
   - ✓ I have a lot of new friends who are all rooting for me.
   - ✓ I have many old friends who mean the world to me.
4. I love what I am about to do.
   - ✓ I love the desert.
   - ✓ I love running.
   - ✓ I love the wild.
   - ✓ I love minimalism. Only a small backpack, sunscreen and a bit of food for seven days.
   - ✓ I love simplicity and clarity.
   - ✓ I love the journey for itself.
   - ✓ I love the prospect of making new friends.
5. I can write a thousand poems in the desert.
6. And something wonderful can happen.

Now, many years later, and after much formal education in Psychology and Positive Psychology, I understand why my simple list was so powerful. It was created on the building blocks of the things that make our lives worthwhile: Love and connection; meaning and purpose; the holding of worthwhile goals; a sense of agency and self-belief and being engaged in doing something one loves for its own sake.

At the most critical moments, this little list would enable me to reach states of awe and appreciation – the emotional states of high performance that help to block out the energy thieves of resentment, fear, worry and stress. Every success and failure start with a thought.

"Ten minutes to landing," the flight captain announced.

My stomach twisted into a knot. I was facing almost certain deportation, or perhaps worse. As we descended the stairs to the tarmac, a small airport vehicle, siren blaring, raced towards us. A soldier and air hostess

4 Wet-weight refers to pack-weight including water – usually one to two litres.

leaped off, and before I knew it, me and my sparse hand luggage were tucked between them as we careened to the terminal. Neither official said a word. Once there, they marched me double-quick to what I thought may be detention cells.

I was wrong: I was marched straight into the Platinum Member Lounge, where I was offered a lavish spread of exotic snacks and teas, asked to complete the visa form and to pay US$100. Then a transport shuttle was arranged to ferry me to my hotel. As I stepped out of the shuttle, I was escorted to a minibus carrying camera equipment for the race, and within an hour, I found myself out of Cairo's chaotic traffic and in the mesmerising vastness of the endless desert.

The sun set blood-red and pink over the whiteness. The driver stopped for evening prayer. All was still and quiet. The driver then rolled up his mat and set off once again, as if beset with a death wish. We flew along the sandy road, touching ground only here and there, and by 9pm, we had caught up with the transfer buses.

I said a prayer of thanks to God, to the universe, and to my anonymous benefactor who had implored: "Madam, just come!" and to the efficiencies of the third world where one could still find a way through the red tape. In the darkness, I boarded the bus of sleeping racers.

By the time we got to camp, it was past midnight, hours after the intended arrival time. One of the buses had broken down and the racers were tired and hungry. Tensions ran high, and within the hour everyone had gone to bed.

Still wired from my battle to get to Egypt, I sought a quiet moment at the fireside. Three Bedouin men sat in silence, watching the flames and the steam slowly rising from a worn metal kettle. There was not a breath of wind; only stars and stillness.

"Welcome;" said one of the young men and pointed to a low camp seat. "Tea?"

I accepted and we drank in silence. After a while, they introduced themselves as Mohammed, Mahmud and Hassan. Mahmud had the face of a desert angel after the rain: Smooth skin, a wide mouth, not a sign of a frown or a wrinkle, a broad forehead and chin in perfect symmetry, large hazelnut-brown eyes and the most gracious of manners. I thanked them for the tea and prepared to retire to my tent where my fellow tentmates were already fast asleep.

"You are welcome," Mahmud said in a voice so gentle that it felt like Rumi was speaking from the star-washed sands. I felt a stirring of love where all of the sorrow lived, and I realised that the Sahara had begun its healing work.

Day 1 – A surprising start

34.3km: 4 hours, 43 minutes

In the morning, I was given a cursory kit check, and within five minutes, I was lined up at the start with 133 racers from 23 countries. The long wait was over. Months of preparation had come down to that one single moment in time. The drummers rolled out the final 10 seconds … Three, two, one … And we were off!

I had no great expectations as I shuffled off the startline alongside the mid-fielders. I had meant to walk because of my injury, but I soon realised that my ITB tolerated the shuffle. I increased the pace and slowly began to overtake my fellow racers, one by one.

The total distance of each stage was broken up into 10–15km stretches between checkpoints, where volunteers had set up simple gazebos and water-refill points. We were each allowed a precious two litres of water, which would then need to see us through to the next refill point. In 50°C heat, that just about met our enormous hydration needs of 12–15 litres a day.

As far as the eye could see, the Sahara was a vast ocean of yellow sand and patches of shimmering-hot, salt-white rock beds. The temperature climbed aggressively. By 10am, 20km into the race, the ambient temperature had reached 48°C. I shuffled along, disoriented and dizzy from the assault of heat and dazzling light, and the sensation of my bare skin being cooked alive.

At 30km, I found the shadow-side of a large rock – the only shelter for miles and miles in every direction. Out of desperation, I slipped on the long-sleeve, white, UV-protective shirt I had packed – not out of volition, but because it was designated mandatory gear. The relief of not having the sun beating directly on my skin was akin to bathing in freshly sliced cucumbers. For the first time, I palpably understood the large swathes of cloth and the elaborate headdresses of the Bedouins.

I had never before been in that kind of heat, but the drive for survival, and the creativity that relies on instinct, kicked in. I slipped on a pair of white, cotton gloves that I had packed for protection against sunburn, and I wet them with water from my water bottle. When the heat became overwhelming, I intermittently cupped my gloved hands around my ears. The breeze stirred by my running passed over the wet cotton, acting like my very own air-conditioning system and cooling the ambient temperature by as much as 2–3°C. Who knows from where my ancient brain fished that idea? I suspect it could have been from watching the great African elephants flap their capillary-rich ears to cool themselves.

By 30km, there was not another soul in sight. In every direction stretched endless space, silence and the great privilege of solitude.

There is a stillness and simplicity that comes from running in the desert – a pervasive feeling that there is enough time and reason to feel at peace. It was a feeling that had at its base the simplest and deepest happiness. I stood still for a long time to absorb the silence. Then I fashioned a little sand heap and balanced my camera for a few, memorable selfies to mark the moment.

Mid-way through my selfie shoot, one of the RacingThePlanet Land Rovers came roaring out of the distance. When the vehicle drew near, the passenger rolled down the window and hollered: "Erica! What are you doing?! Run! You are first lady home!" It was Mary Gadams, a formidable visionary and the owner of RacingThePlanet.

I stared after the car as it sped away in the direction of the finish line. "It can't be," I thought. I collected my camera and picked up my pace. There was still no sign of my ITB. Extraordinary.

I crossed the line in 4 hours, 43 minutes as the first lady home and in a solid 15th position overall out of 133 racers. That afforded me the gift of many hours before the others began to arrive. I cherished that quiet time and used it to do slow, soft yoga inside our empty tent, followed by 10 minutes of stilling my mind: Just breathing, thinking nothing. Just being.

"Erica?" Mahmud ducked his head into the tent. He held out a cup of sweet, black tea.

"Welcome," he said, flashing a dazzling smile. I don't know why, but his presence loosened the tight gauze around my broken heart more than any other person in the race.

One by one, racers came over the finish line and staggered to their tents. Our camp of 15 Bedouin tents, housing eight racers each, was arranged in a semi-circle, each tent facing inwards. Over the next seven days, the people in my tent became closer than family. Each of us, in our own way, was going through a life-changing experience, which we shared intimately while waking and racing and struggling and eating and sleeping in such close quarters. In those harsh conditions, the veneer quickly washed away beneath sweaty brows.

At sunset, I clambered high up on to one of the white sandstone sentinels that guarded our camp. I sat there in the vastness until the sun set golden across the infinite horizon. I waited until the stars emerged, one after the other, and eventually covered me in a cascade of shimmering diamonds. I sat there long after everyone had gone to sleep and felt a universe of peace settling over me.

Racing the Sahara was like falling in love for the first time, and no race after it would ever quite compare. There was no competitive pressure, nor a benchmark of prior performance to which I had to live up. I was anonymous and had no expectations of myself, other than finishing the race – even if it meant I had to walk the entire course. I had no idea what to expect, nor any sense of how profound seven days of running through the desert could be.

For these reasons, running the Sahara in October 2009 would remain the purest and most spiritual race in which I would participate over my next 10 years of competitive endurance running. I would only return to that blissful way of running in my late 40s when I raced again purely for the joy of it, forgoing any notions of podiums and winning.

Day 2 – Run with your heart

44km: 6 hours, 15 minutes

On the morning of Stage 2 it rained. Mahmud sat with us at breakfast. His eyes shone with a special light as he watched the rain sifting like a soft, blue veil over the sands. As far as the eye could see, the white desert dropped away into a splendour of nothingness and silence. Snow-white rock formations mushroomed here and there across the vastness. Later, I would write in my journal about my growing sense of awe: "*Here every rock is stacked in prayer, reaching high towards the heavens in reverence. This also is my church.*"

The desert felt young, gentle and mistakenly disarming. In reality, ahead of us lay 44km of knee-deep sand and extreme heat. The rain passed swiftly, and in its place the desert cranked up the temperature. By 8am, the mercury boiled at the 40°C mark, with the added challenge of chest-oppressing humidity.

I welcomed the heat. It awoke in me some strange and powerful cellular reaction of joy, and a feeling of being held. There in the desert, the heat was reliable, a constant. It was something I could trust. Heat made me feel safe.

But the heat had a dark side, too. In the desert, a human being ideally needs one litre of water for every hour of exertion, and in those temperatures, one will die within two days without water. The Sahara is beautiful – the wispy dunes appear soft to the gaze, and the sky so wide, blue and beautiful that it can break your heart. It is a great deception: The desert can kill in an instant. One wrong turn away from the lifeline of the little pink RacingThePlanet route flags, one moment of lost concentration, or a few hapless hours in the wrong direction without shade or water could end a racer's life.

Minutes before we set off, I practised a few yoga downward dogs and warrior poses, while reminding myself how yoga had literally unlocked my body, and with it, my running performance. There is nothing quite like yoga to release a runner's stiffness. There was no sign of the ITB. It seemed that I had run and stretched myself out of my injury.

Standing at the startline, I noticed the softness and suppleness in my body – my psoas felt long and relaxed. Only 115 racers lined up alongside me. The first day in the desert had already claimed 17 runners.

As soon as we tore away from the startline, the field quickly diffused; small, insignificant dots of colour disappearing into the vastness.

At the front of the pack, we picked up the line of pink flags and began shuffling towards the horizon. It seemed far less taxing to shuffle-run across the sand than to walk. I had never before run in deep sand for those distances, and most certainly not like a laden pack animal. Instinct is extraordinary. I imagined myself as a little desert gecko, and I kept my steps as light and as quick as possible, hovering across the dunes, while keeping my feet flat, splay-footed and at an angle to the directional drift of the sand.

Gecko tactics or not, in that terrain I had to dig deep. Not even an hour into the stage, it felt like a searing-hot iron had been thrust into my spine. A sharp, neural tension shot through my body and set my neck on fire as I strained hard against my backpack, which pulled down on my bruised shoulders, as heavy as an obelisk. The more I strained and pushed, the worse the pain grew. My mind wanted to enter into the fight, but then I remembered Billy and my mom, and my sister and my friends, and those thoughts triggered a spill of gratitude. Then I deliberately fetched some more thoughts from my 'magic carpet' list, which lifted my physiology out of the pain and the downward spiral of thoughts that came with it. My steps began to lighten, and the pain abated further.

In that moment, my body grasped that the desert is a place that punishes resistance. I did three rounds of breathing exercises and muttered a mantra: "Just let go, relax, relax easy …"

A comfort came over me, a sense of my body cooling down, despite the fact that the temperature was rising relentlessly. And it came on the wing of sweet surrender – to the heat, to the distance, to the moment, and to time itself.

"No fight," I added to the mantra.

My body relaxed completely. All of the push and tension drained out and a sensation of bliss washed over me. It was in that moment that I realised the secret to running in environments that pose great challenge and discomfort: It is to run the way a lover kisses their beloved: Gently and without force.

My heart opened. I stuck out my chest to physically lead the way with my actual heart organ. My spine immediately straightened and my shoulders dropped. A powerful, thick, inveterate current of energy coursed through the full length of my being.

"Yes! That's it! Don't run with the limit of your arms and your legs – run with your heart," was the great metaphysical secret that rang through my body as clear as birdsong.

The secret of long-distance running is to run with heart.

What I remember of the remaining 34km is a great sense of body ease, akin to euphoria. I had run myself into a runner's high.

In that high state, one can fall in love in one single moment, because the heart is open and full.

There among the high, windswept dunes, I met Luke Carmichael, a gentle and good-looking young man from the United Kingdom. Trotting side by side, a mutual affection arose between us as easily as a breath. We ran in silence, our feet sinking deep into the hot sand, sweating and breathing hard, with only the shimmering heat and the blinding silence of the desert and each other's footfall for company. In that moment, we were the only two people in the universe.

I arrived at the finish line of the second stage alongside Luke, as the first lady of the day in a time of 6 hours, 15 minutes, and more than an hour before Christina Dotson, in second place. The gap between us widened a little every day, which bought me the precious advantage of running at ease. I didn't need to push hard, so I could settle into a deep calm and enjoy the extraordinary beauty of the desert.

By the time night fell, the last competitors had made it over the line after more than 12 hours of relentless superhuman effort. Nine more racers had thrown in the towel from heat exhaustion and fatigue, bringing the total number of withdrawals to 26. It was the highest ever number of losses in a RacingThePlanet race.

That evening, racers descended on the cyber tent like soul-starved zombies. RacingThePlanet had set up 12 anti-break, sand-proof, desert-worthy laptops for us to receive messages from home – manna from Heaven. Over the course of the race, I received 83 messages from people I loved, from people who were watching and cheering and appreciating the magical experience from afar.

I counted my treasures: Wonderful messages from my sister and my mom and dad, precious messages from friends across the world, and from work colleagues. Some messages stirred up old regrets and longings – and that was good. Unlike in the crush of daily life, there was time and space in the desert to be with those feelings, to welcome them as guests and to sit with them to hear their messages, and when done, to finally see them go.

There were many messages from Billy, written with humour, tenderness and all of the warm familiarity of two people who had shared a life and shaped their own exclusive language for almost a decade. It buoyed me and cut me in equal measures. Billy was my adventure soulmate. We had been inseparable. In our eight years together, we had barely spent 20 days apart.

Billy had risen above the pain of our divorce and reached out to me as a racer, and out of a deep respect for the ritual of endurance that we both loved and shared; my inimitable Adventure Billy who always said: "Yes!" to every single mad adventure I ever proposed.

To my surprise, there were also three precious messages from Princess Anastacia.

Princess Anastacia and Billy, and the transformative power of love

Princess Anastacia came before Billy, and she was my first true love.

She was a child when we met – 19 years old, as gentle as an angel, and just as innocent. We both were.

"You are my little piece of magic in the world," I used to tell her when she would hover her hand just so, above my forehead, and sooth every heartache I had ever known. Princess Anastacia directly mainlined love into my heart-vein, as if she could see the inner recesses of my soul and couldn't help but rush to heal me.

She was the quintessential lady: Regal, elegant and mysterious, with long, shiny black hair, dark, almond eyes and perfect skin – as warm as molasses. She never lost her sense of self on my muddy wilderness adventures. She always remained intractably dressed in purple thigh-high boots, tailored mini-skirts, or suchlike. On hikes, she insisted on wearing her dainty, glittering-blue, high-heeled sandals, which sometimes got stuck on the rungs of my 4x4 rooftop tent. She was Cinderella and somehow, I was the prince that she would follow to the far ends of the Earth.

It was 1996. I was 25 years old. We were so young then and full of bravery and hope – and equal measures of youthful stupidity. If I had only understood that she was rare and that I would never quite find love like hers again for decades to come, I would have taken greater care.

"Dad, I am coming to visit. I am bringing someone," I had said on the phone. Perhaps because I didn't offer a name, my dad instinctively knew to mentally prepare himself for whatever was to come. By the time we arrived, he had put away a generous glass of whiskey.

I was bringing home a girl and I had no idea how my father would react. I imagined the worst.

We walked in the door. My palms were clammy.

Princess Anastacia wore a low-cut African dress and entered the room with the decorum of a beauty queen. Her eyes shone with innocence and apprehension. She dazzled my dad with a white-toothed, full-lipped smile and asked for the bathroom.

Once out of earshot, my father and I locked eyes.

Finally, he cleared his throat, and of a thousand things he could say, he said: "Well, Lokkie," (my parents' nickname for me) "she truly has spectacular breasts."

I had never loved my dad more than in that moment, for his full and wholehearted acceptance of Princess Anastacia, and for the kindness with which he held the difficult road I had walked in discovering that I preferred women. My dad said: "Yes," to it all. As the years went by, my father said of Princess Anastacia: "Take good care of her. A good woman is hard to find." But I was too young and foolish to heed his advice.

Princess Anastacia and I were together for almost seven years before the wilderness and the bright lights of the city pulled us in different directions. She wanted to spend our summer holidays in Sandton City, in the glittering retail heart of Johannesburg, selling clothing to help especially over-sized women feel gorgeous. I wanted to river-raft the Grade 5 rapids of rural Swaziland.

One night, I lay behind her back, and in the dark betrayed her with a fervent prayer for an adventure buddy who would trek into the wilderness with me. Not even three months later, Billy rode into my life on a mountain bike: Smart, shy, athletic, long-limbed, blonde and golden-tanned, with a ravenous appetite for adventure – exactly as I had requested.

Billy and I spent a great deal of time together, running and riding under the hot African sun. She was seemingly completely straight. "I would never fall for a woman," she pronounced loudly to anyone within earshot.

It seemed safe and innocent. But as the days became months, we both began to slip from our moral centres toward each other. What we dream of is far more dangerous and creative than we can imagine. Long before the reality of our daydreams arrive, we create the scaffolding for it. Our most intense longings fill the blank pages of energetic possibility, and the universe flows towards it, like water towards gravity.

Six months later, I left Princess Anastacia for Billy. I was a hard-edged asshole.

I was 32, and Billy, a tender 25, had never been with a woman. Well-intended, but unskilled, we fumbled our way into our relationship and eventually into marriage. Along with 33% of marriages in the UK since 1975[5], we would eventually flounder on the sharp rocks of irreconcilable conflict that followed our honeymoon phase.

In the discordant final year of our marriage, I started attending weekly Buddhist meditation sessions – for resolution and to find a brief reprieve from the pain Billy and I were unwittingly inflicting upon each other. The teachings were profound. "Even an ant wishes to be happy. Fishing is fun, but not so much for the fish, or the worm. Every creature has an equal right to happiness," my teacher would say.

And I really got that. Deeply.

Those teachings brought about a fundamental change in the way I saw everything. I understood with great clarity that all beings are equal – shoulder-to-shoulder in the web of life. It is a great foolishness to imagine oneself in any way better than, superior or inferior, to another. It is a mirage. There is only life and being.

The shift in how I was in the world came too late for Billy and me, but it was not too late for the rest of my life and for the better ripples I would leave in the world. The loss of love is an astute teacher.

"*... the difficult times we fear might ruin us are the very ones that can break us open and help us blossom into who we were meant to be,*" wrote Elizabeth Lesser in her seminal work, *Broken Open.*[6] In my life I have learned that the mistakes we make can become the most luminous of lighthouses along the way – as long as we learn and grow for the better.

As human beings, we are hard-wired for connection and turn towards love, like sunflowers turn to the sun. Some months after my divorce, and still wading in a half-light of loss and grief, I hesitantly ventured on to a

---

5 www.ons.gov.uk (Accessed: 13 July 2021)

6 Lesser, E. *Broken Open*, Villard, 14 June 2005.

dating site – mostly to make new friends. The week before I left for the Sahara, I met woke, vegan Sarah.

We found immediate resonance in each other's love for Nature and an appreciation for the Spartan life. She was a gardener by occupation and a devoted Buddhist. Her gentleness drew me into a brief and kindred exchange. And so it came about that in the Sahara Desert, I wore her elephant necklace as a lucky charm. We all need someone to run for. We all need love.

She messaged me during the race: *"Hi Erica, follower of the Night Plow. I am so excited! You are the leading woman! Even with a wounded leg! Bravo, my friend! You are my hero and inspiration! Remember the elephants! 'The elephant can walk on the tips of its toes along near-vertical mountain paths; It can move in silence without leaving a trace; Although it moves at a stately pace, it can do so faster than any.' Heathcote Williams. Be the elephant, my friend."*

I kept every one of the 83 messages, and even now, 10 years later, I occasionally leaf through them with great gratitude for the love that came to me there in that hot desert. They remind me to run with heart – our hearts are more powerful than our bodies and far more reliable than our will. The antidote of tiredness is wholeheartedness.

Day 3 – The day the sky melted

42.5km: 6 hours, 21 minutes

On Day 3, we started the 42.5km stage in great spirits. Our bodies and minds had begun to acclimatise to the exertion and heat. Racing had become our daily routine. In place of fatigue, there was a new kind of energy, a clean burn in our mitochondria because we had shed the pollutants of modern living and had each leaned down by at least a kilogram or two.

The 113 remaining racers ascended the high, golden dunes. We dotted the ridges like a line of brightly coloured ants, insignificant in the expanse, filling the universe with our striving and hope against a sky of intense cobalt blue. The mercury crept upwards – to 43°C, then 45°C, eventually to a blistering 50°C.

The field thinned out until I was utterly alone, and I settled into a hypnotic rhythm. At one point, I became aware of an overwhelming silence. It filled all of the Earth with its immensity, and as far and wide as the eye could see was only space, endless vast space, and my shadow on the sand.

Shuffle, shuffle, shuffle, shuffle. The sound of my footfall scraped across the shimmering sand.

The sky had turned from blue to molten lead, and it seemed as if the entire universe was melting in the delirious heat and dripping from the sky in slow, hot, gun-metal streaks.

High on the heat, I thundered into camp after 6 hours, 21 minutes of running, a whole two hours ahead of Teresa Lam of Hong Kong, who was duelling with Christina Dotson for second place.

All afternoon we rested in our Bedouin tents while the remaining racers trickled across the finish line well into the dusk.

That evening, I waited until the stars poured out of Atum's sack, the Egyptian's universal source, creator of the universe, as he trailed and completed the darkening sky. Once everyone had gone to sleep, I walked far beyond the camp into the star-showered stillness. For an hour or more I moved from one slow and deliberate yoga pose into the next, thinking nothing, wishing nothing – just watching as one shooting star after another fell from the sky. I felt awake and rejuvenated in the very core of my being, despite the past three days of physical exertion. Perhaps that is where exertion takes us: To a place of deep contentment and inner quiet. Perhaps that is where the healing happens – in the place of surrender where one is too tired to fight.

I joined the Bedouin brothers at their fire and sat in silence. They had little English and I, no Arabic, but we made do with sign language and the sheer desire to hear each other.

Hassan explained that he was excited because he was preparing to get married. Mohammed pointed to the outer edge of the Plow constellation: "Duhbe and Merak." He drew a straight line with his finger from them to the North Star, Polaris: "Al Jidi." I shared that I had lost love and that I was there in the desert to heal my heart. They nodded their quiet empathy.

Mahmud told me about his university studies in Cairo and his great love affair with the desert: "I don't mind how. Every winter I find a way to come to the desert. It is where I am home."

And that is what bonded all of us on that race. No matter whether we were racers, organisers, camp-builders, supporters or owners of Racing ThePlanet, we were a tribe united in our inextinguishable love for the great, big, magical desert, and who we became there.

Day 4 – A single hard-baked date

40.5km: 6 hours, 12 minutes

On Day 4 of the race, we followed the Route of the Nomads. I was feeling stronger and lighter with every day that passed, and I had altogether begun to overlook the fact that I was in a race. It wasn't just because I was winning and that I had the comfortable cumulative four-hour lead over the next female, but something magical was happening to me out there. The further we travelled and the lighter my frame became, the less I felt tethered to the world.

Perhaps this is why the yogis, the Christians, Hindus, Muslims and most seekers on a spiritual path, observe a practice of fasting. In altered physical states, there is a doorway into the spiritual, to the place where one begins to get a sense of that which is invisible to the eye.

The first 20km of the route cut across a lunar landscape of desert sand and rocky outcrops and then on to a small plateau. It was veined in long lines of rose quartz and strewn with black and brown pebbles.

As I crested the plateau, my entire being became aware that the little stones were alive with a thick, hot energy of their own. I picked up a hot, brown pebble and stood there for a moment, feeling the vibration of its life, of all the universe in it, and the old volcanic heat at its core and before all things. The stone lay on my palm. Some might say it was the heat that got to me, but I swear that in all of that great silence, I felt its sonorous hum; a singing stone.

Its vibration right there reattuned me to the spirit that lives in everything – in every tree and stone, every river and mountain. In that moment I realised just how very much I had fallen asleep to Nature's palpable life energy, and I had grown a little numb from living so immersed in city noise, bright lights and deadening concrete.

I pocketed the stone and ran light and easy across the vast plateaux.

About 20km into the run, I came upon a vast stretch of hard-packed, white sand and spotted what looked like another lone, brown stone – lost in all of the whiteness.

It was a palm date, almost too hot to touch, baked into a sweet toffee under the scorching sun. I put it in my mouth and almost passed out with delight. It was possibly the sweetest of sweet things I had ever tasted in my life.

In scarcity, we find the secret of true abundance. Antoine de Saint-Exupéry once said that everything a man needs can be found in a single drop of water. The desert was teaching me appreciation; to experience the magic and lifegiving force, even in the smallest of things. The emptier my cup, the more it ran over.

After 40.5km, and 6 hours, 12 minutes, I ran into camp to the sound of Bedouins fervently beating the finish-line drums – a job customarily performed by the race marshals. Perhaps it was because of that very first evening around the fire drinking tea together, but for some reason, those highly-attuned desert nomads came out every afternoon from where they were tending to camp duties to cheer me across the finish line.

That afternoon, Hassan took the thick, silver ring from his finger and made me a necklace. "For good luck," he said, and hung the spider-engraved gift around my neck. In Egypt, the spider represents the goddess of weaving, hunting and war. I believe they hoped for me to not just win the race, but to win in life, and to find a new spouse and make a family. Nothing seemed more important to them than that, and whether or not I had children.

Later, Mahmud came to the tent bearing tea and a small plastic bag, which he handed to me without ceremony. "It is a desert rose[7] from the Western Desert. I found it when I was a young boy."

The bag contained an artfully shaped natural stone that resembled a many-petaled rose. Mahmud explained that it was for a clear mind, for power and energy in the body, and for good fortune in love.

---

7 Selenite desert rose is a crystal prized for carrying a gentle, calming and rejuvenating energy. It is used to relieve stress while enhancing willpower and clarity of the mind, and cleansing the energy of the body.

"It is very strong for the heart." He didn't need to say more. His gift was for my healing.

Mahmud and I continue to touch base on Facebook every few months. He always asks when I will come back to my desert home. Perhaps I will return one day; and I hope there will be children to go with me.

Day 5 – The long day

87km: 14 hours, 48 minutes

We had run a cumulative distance of 160km over four days in brutal conditions. We were wired down to our leanest running frames. Our Day-One, pink, sunburned skin had leathered into brown, and fierce resolve chiselled every face at the startline of the fifth day. Ahead of us lay the ultimate mental and physical challenge of the Long Day: Almost 90km in one go.

The Long Day is a defining feature of all seven-day stage races. It requires participants to run the equivalent of nearly 100km in extreme heat on unforgiving terrain, while carrying everything you need for seven days – and that after having completed four, or sometimes five, marathons back-to-back on preceding days.

The Long Day is a scarce and precious opportunity. It is much more a mental, emotional and spiritual challenge than it is a physical test. We fear and look forward to the Long Day in equal measure. It is what we dread. It is what we go for – the chance to test our mettle; to sift for gold.

A Long Day in the desert is an alchemist that tempers, purifies and forges one through the heat and limits of one's own exhaustion. It leaves one a little humbler, cleared of mental clutter, simplified. All of the debris and weight of old things is stripped away by the burning, so that we come out the other side brightly polished and more open.

Since the 1980s, many socio-cultural scholars have pondered the rapid growth and increasing difficulty of endurance events, and there are as many theories as theorists. Le Brenton[8] suggests that participants of truly extreme

8 Le Brenton, D. Playing Symbolically with Death in Extreme Sports, *Body & Society*, (1):1–11, 6 March 2000.

events seek a feeling of aliveness and a way to approximate the sacred in a society in which values are in crisis.

Atkinson[9] suggests that endurance sport is a meaning-seeking response to the middle-class malaise that has arisen from our successful transition out of our struggle for survival.

Yet others, like Hanold,[10] propose that endurance-sport participation helps us to construct a positive social identity.

There may be some truth in all of these theories. Since the end of World War II in 1945, we have entered a golden age[11] of relative safety and prosperity, greater than any time before in human history. My sense is that in western societies where the majority has entered the middle class, and where we are no longer preoccupied with surviving famine, war, malaria and stemming neonatal deaths, we turn to endurance sports to provide us with a calamity – an equivalent set of challenging conditions against which to test ourselves, and within which to build resources of resilience and grit – the kind we sorely needed to weather global pandemics like COVID-19.

One thing is certain: When racers finally cross the finish line of the Long Day, they have the strongest sense that they will be able to endure and get through anything in life.

Finally, the Long Day was upon us. The doorway into the unknown opened wide. We huddled around the breakfast fires, the atmosphere frothed up into an electric cocktail of great trepidation mixed with hope, elation, excitement and warm-hearted camaraderie.

A total of 92 runners gathered at the startline at 6am. The countdown ended with the bang of a drum, and with it every man and every woman's race began with one step, and then another towards the endless horizon.

I set off at 9am, together with the top 15 runners.

We had all day, all night and half of the next day to get home – 33 hours of grace. Before us stretched the seemingly infinite landscape and the

---

9 Atkinson, M. Triathlon, suffering and exciting significance, *Leisure Studies,* 27(2):165–180, April 2008.

10 Hanold, M.T. Beyond the Marathon: (De)Construction of Female Ultrarunning Bodies, *Sociology of Sport Journal,* 27, 160–177, 2010.

11 Globally more people die of suicide every year (1.4%) than from war (0.2%), homicide (0.72%) and terrorism (0.05%) put together. The biggest two killers are cardiovascular disease (32%) and cancer (17%). *Global Burden of Disease Study*, 2017. Institute for Health Metrics and Evaluation (IHME), www.healthdata.org (Accessed: 5 July 2021)

wealth of ample time within which to be fully engaged in just one, single, all-consuming activity. As the kilometres and hours stacked up, each of us, in our own way, entered a state of flow – a congruent singularity of focus and complete contentment at doing for hours that which we loved to do for the sake of it – running. We ran for the love of running and for the love of life.

Mary Gadams had designed a masterful course of raw beauty and stark variation. The first section of the day led us across a featureless, vast moonscape. Our pack of 15 late-starters ran strong and fast. Together, we accessed the pure euphoria of lightness and motion, taking extreme pleasure in the journey and in our able bodies, high on the sheer delight of moving forward so swiftly.

It is remarkable how the mind recalibrates to accommodate for increased distance. On the previous marathon-distance days, fatigue had set in at 30km, and the finish line at 40 or 44km hadn't come a moment too soon. On the Long Day, having mentally prepared for more than double the distance, 40km came swiftly and painlessly.

We dropped off the high plateau and into the village of El Ris, the first sign of civilisation since the start of the race five days earlier. Children ran to greet us. I was running alongside James Elston from the UK. He was setting a swift pace, perhaps a clip above my comfort zone, but I hung on, both of us intent on chasing down as much distance as possible before sunset.

At the 50km mark, we entered an oasis straight out of Aladdin's *Arabian Nights*: A lush verge of date-heavy palm trees and shade, and the sweet smell of groundwater seeping to the surface. I stopped to gather a few handfuls of dates beneath the trees, so glad for the extra few calories of sustenance. At that point of the race, most racers were on the sparsest of rations and had already shed most of their own body fat reserves. We were on the thin, red line of optimal energy burn.

James ran on. I had enjoyed his company, but once alone, I felt my breath and stride expanding, my back broadening and my spine lengthening. My body reached into the solitude, and there I found a renewed energy of awareness and witnessing: A beautiful oneness. My focus doubled.

The course led us away from the colour and bustle of the oasis into the magical landscape of the Sahara dunes. Their soft, S-shaped rims swished up and up into the sapphire-blue sky. The wind streaked across the dunes' spines and plumed long, powdery tails of golden sand into the air.

I stopped and just stood there in the blaze of the sun and all of that exquisite silence.

Inside me opened reverence as large as the desert, for I understood that what my eyes were witnessing was sacred, and that my heart, too, had opened to that sense of Something Greater – that which at some point in our life communicates to us all. The desert tuned in my ear to hear.

The longer we stayed in the desert, the more acutely attuned our five animal senses became. Coming down from the high dunes, I smelled water. It had a sweet, rich scent. It was as if I could tip my tongue into the wind and taste its wetness. And true enough, as I came through the ocean of sand nearing Checkpoint 5, I could make out a small, round cement structure – a dam. It was fed by a perennial desert spring and was large enough for 20 thirsty camels to gather around it.

The sweetness of the water saturated the dry air. The local nomads invited me to swim. It was as unthinkable as it was irresistible. Not caring that race time was ticking, I slid into the coldness. My skin broke out in goosebumps of sheer physical pleasure. I felt immeasurably rich, like an Egyptian queen bathing, knowing all the while in my bones how precious every drop of water in the desert is. Every day, I had witnessed that the only thing that stood between us and death were the two litres of water made available to us at every RacingThePlanet checkpoint.

I had five to six hours of running ahead of me, and set off from the dam refreshed and invigorated, alone in the vastness of the black desert to meet sunset among the black, volcanic flumes and scattering of black stones. There was not a single soul in sight. All of the Earth was mine.

Shuffle-shuffle-shuffle.

A few moments before the sun touched the skyline, a voice called from the wilderness. High up on a rock, Zandy, the masterful RacingThePlanet photographer, had perched himself at the ready for sunset.

"Run!" he yelled.

I doubled my pace to the spot where his lens, my silhouette and the giant red orb of the desert sun aligned perfectly for a moment of photographic genius.

Zandy hollered with delight.

Noticing how engrossed he was in his craft, and how his clothes hung from his thin frame like a sack, I yelled: "Do you have water and something to eat?"

"No!" he laughed, "I don't need anything. I eat photos and sunsets!"

I left him there in his bliss, running into my own, and into the deepening dusk.

But the sprint had cost me. Soon after I left Zandy, my knee buckled in a debilitating jolt of pain. My ITB flared up for the first time during the race. I bit down hard and staggered on as best as I could.

Ahead of me lay 35km of night running, and I calmed myself by thoughts of good fortune that I had managed to come that far without pain. I was already in the second half of the Long Day. It was going to be okay. I just needed to put one foot in front of the other.

Darkness fell and the pain became unbearable, but I didn't entertain a single thought of stopping. By the grace of God, I started catching up to the racers that had left on the 6am shift. They helped me to forget.

I passed my tentmate, Anita, who had for the past five days brought up the rear of the race, spending more than 16 hours a day out in the brutal conditions, barely getting three or four hours to eat, recover and sleep before starting all over again on the next day's ordeal. Anita wanted nothing more in the world than to finish the Long Day.

When I passed her, she was in great pain and exhausted, but she remained completely resolute: "I'm finishing this thing, even if it kills me." Her heart was still in it, long after her body had failed.

Soon after, I caught up with the oldest participant in the race, 70-year-old, tough-as-nails Jennifer Murray and her daughter, Christy Powell, who had joined the race as a birthday surprise for her mom. They were also my tentmates, and I knew just how deep Jennifer had to dig, for she had not been able to eat for the past three days. She was on her final wire, but refused to quit.

As night deepened, I passed the inspiring team of Jesse Yoo, Tom Adair and blind teammate Ron Hackett from Canada. Together, they had run a cumulative 220km across some of the toughest terrain in the world, defying all limitations of running without sight.

Then came the all-girl team of supermodel goddess and seven-summit record-holder Annabel Bond and her two gorgeous girlfriends, Lucy Tang and Cecil Ward. They were singing, telling jokes and making such merriment under the desert stars that I completely forgot about my ITB for a while.

The desert sky had turned velvety-black by the time I caught up with the front woman, Venetia Price of the UK. She had set off three hours ahead of me at 6am.

"Only 20km to go," I said as I limped up to her and slowed to walk.

"I'll run with you," she offered in a spirit of great camaraderie, and upped her pace. It made all the difference.

Just before midnight, we crossed the finish line together, overjoyed and ululating because the Long Day was finally done. The race was in the bag. All that remained was to wait for racers to arrive one by one; to stagger across the finish line, physically broken but more whole than they had ever felt in their lives.

Day 6 – A day for rest

We awoke to the spectacular sight of the Black Desert dropping away in every direction. We had nothing to do all day but rest and wait. The hours passed as smoothly as a trickle of sand.

For most of the day, I sat away from camp on a high dune, watching, listening and filling myself up with the silence and space, so that I could take it home to London as a talisman against the noise and the rush and the forgetting.

In the desert, acoustics are long and drawn out. One feels the wind coming over the dunes long before one hears it. Sound travels slowly and patiently to find the willing cup of one's ears, for there are not many listeners. It is a thing of great beauty.

All day, we sat around and cheered the drumbeats that would announce another warrior safely home. By 2pm, all of the racers had arrived, except for Anita. Reports from the field were that she was 3km from camp. She had only one hour left before the Long Day 33-hour cut-off, and she still had to negotiate a difficult last section over high dunes and deep sand. The odds of her finishing in time grew slimmer by the minute.

Soon there were only 10 minutes left. Then five.

When word came that Anita was about to come into view from the final dune section, every racer and all of the camp staff gathered at the finish line. When she came into the final strait, we roared with such irrepressible and raw joy at her victory that my body covered in goose bumps, despite the unbearable heat.

Anita stumbled across the finish line with a mere three minutes to spare, crying with joy, and then somehow managed to leap for the sky. Out of all the racers: The persevering; the blistered; the injured; the old; the blind; the struggling and the frontline sprinters, Anita was the hero. Despite great odds stacked against her, she had refused to give up. She had fully committed her body to the pain, discomfort and fear. She was at peace that the trying in itself was victory enough.

Day 7 – The final sprint home

On the final morning of the race, Mahmud stood with me at the breakfast fires. He sharpened my journal pencil with his knife. I thanked him, and he responded with his customary: "You are welcome."

A sadness lay between us. Who knew what life would hold and whether our paths would ever cross again? He brought me a parting gift of 3kg of tightly-parcelled desert dates and bade me farewell. He turned and disappeared into the busyness of breaking down and packing up the last desert camp of the race. And just like that, it was over.

It is perhaps true that desert partings are the saddest of all. I am not sure why – and maybe because life there exists on a sharp and precarious edge of bad odds, and maybe, too, because one's heart is more open in a place that inspires such awe and gratitude for the smallest of things – a drop of water.

We were ferried out of the desert in a fleet of 4x4s to our buses. The Bedouin camp workers waved. The great, big, droning buses carried us back to civilisation. As we travelled away from the heart of the desert, the pristine dunes became torn by roads, pockmarked by rubbish, and later by buildings, until they finally succumbed under the heavy foot of the sprawling city of Cairo. Four hours later, we arrived at the tourist-stomped Pyramids of Giza.

We ran a final victory lap of 3km from the buses to the official finish line at the foot of the Great Pyramids. Despite the commercial cacophony, it was possibly the most spectacular finish venue any race could ever boast.

I ran alongside winning male, Paolo Barghini, who had subsisted on 1.5kg of ghee for seven days. An Italian running machine, he was a man who would years later become a good friend. He bore the Italian flag, and I carried aloft the South African flag. It was a special moment, and one I couldn't have imagined in my wildest dreams. I had completed the race a good 12 hours ahead of my nearest competitor.

Because of my pre-race visa disaster and the rescheduled timing of my return flight, I was unable to stay for the official prizegiving ceremony one day hence. I was glad for it – grateful to escape the come-down, when we would trade the vast magical desert for the segregation and confinement of a five-star hotel, each in our own rooms, and the disconnect that I knew would come.

Right there at the foot of the Giza Pyramids, Mary Gadams awarded me an enormous silver Wimbledon-tennis-sized winner's plate for First Female Home.

It all happened in a flash. Within minutes of saying my goodbyes to Anita and all of my tentmates and fellow racers, I was in a taxi to the Cairo airport – unshowered, desert-raw, undone from seven days in the wilderness, and changed in ways I had not yet fully understood.

On the plane, I took my seat next to a Swedish couple, Clause and Catherine from Gotland. Catherine leaned over and asked about my spectacular trophy. Only then did I burst into tears. I wept and wept, completely stripped of all the layers that conceal us, my heart blown wide open and cleared out. Out poured all of the grief of losing Billy, mixed up with gratitude for everything that had happened in the desert; for the race and for the desert itself; for the Bedouin brothers, and for Mahmud and the knowing that all of it would be in my bones and soul forever.

I sent Mary Gadams an email of thanks and ended the note with what I had learned from the race: *"Don't run with your legs; don't run with your arms; don't run with the limits of your body. The best way yet is to run gently – run with your heart."* I believe that she read it out at the awards ceremony as a farewell note to my fellow racers who had become as close as family.

That race made me understand that every difficulty in our life presents an opportunity. Labelling struggle as good or bad confuses the issue. If I had not got divorced, and had not suffered for it, I would never have discovered the magical desert or gone on to run the way I did for years to come. The Sahara race had begun a life-long affair with long-distance running that would enrich my life in ways I could never have foreseen.

Within a week of arriving back in the UK, I had signed up for the RacingThePlanet 250km race across the Atacama Desert in Peru.

The path was set, and my heart was wholly in it.

"Anything is one of a million paths. Look at every path closely and deliberately, and ask, 'Does this path have a heart?'"

CARLOS CASTANEDA

2

BEYOND COCOA LEAVES AND SALINE DRIPS, ATACAMA DESERT, CHILE, 2010

"Some races are stars, some are stones, but in the end, they are all rocks, and we build upon them."

CHRISSIE WELLINGTON

I would never have said that I was motivated by winning. Perhaps because I never imagined that I could. But once I had a drink from the champion's chalice in the Sahara, I wanted another sip – and that made all the difference. The open-hearted euphoria of running through the white desert was replaced by narrower and sharper emotion. It was a tension – acidic in the blood and heavy in the feet.

As a returning RacingThePlanet champion, I had foregone the privilege of anonymity. In the starting shoots of the Atacama Desert race were three former RacingThePlanet female champions and two formidable challengers, including Dianne Hogan-Murphy, who had won the Gobi March in 2009. To boot, I was racing side by side with fellow South African Ryan Sandes, the rising trail-runner extraordinaire. A double win for our country was a real possibility. I felt pressure as heavy on my chest as the effects of the thinning Andes air.

My lungs were used to coastal pressures, not the ailing breathlessness that comes at high altitudes. While climbing Kilimanjaro some years before, I had vomited my way to a near-miss summit. Our buses from San Pedro had already climbed well above 3 000m to the startline, and headaches and a vague queasiness had taken hold. My face was also slightly swollen. It was the first sign of high-altitude oedema and worse things to come.

When given the chance, I love taking the front seat on a transfer bus – first and foremost to avoid motion sickness, but also because I can see into the distance and get a sense of the terrain we will be crossing during the race. It gives me an opportunity to quiz the bus driver on all of the secrets of the location – especially about what wild animals still roam there, and what edible plants and roots one may find, and where to find water in the wild.

Our bus driver had the look of a weathered guerrilla fighter – moustachioed, burly, gnarled, and geared for flirtation, as if every opportunity were potentially his last. Scraping together our meanings, we communicated in the universal language of hand signals, wild gestures and meaningful eye contact. We laughed and he winked a lot, with a hunter's glint in his eye.

All too used to the tell-tale signs in coastal folk who arrive on that high ledge of the world, he recognised that I was feeling unwell. Perhaps motivated by our brief flirtation, or perhaps out of a simple, uncomplicated kindness, moments before the start of the race, he appeared with a plastic bag of dried leaves and pointed at my cheeks.

I gestured: "Stuff my cheeks full? Thank you so much!"

I should have at least tried to gather some more information about the substance, or how best to administer the medicine, but there was no time. We were lining up for the countdown.

Searching at the precipice

Years before, during an exploratory phase in my youth, inspired by Aldous Huxley's *Doors of Perception*[12], I had taken peyote, the Native American Indian ceremonial substance that induces altered states in pursuit of greater consciousness and wisdom. I had prepared for days, read up on mescalito, fasted, and stated upfront the questions I wanted answered – about the nature of death and God and time. I was young, courageous and willing to try risky pathways to find answers. I was hunting for short cuts.

12 Huxley, A. *The Doors of Perception*, Chatto & Windus, 1954.

The peyote had induced the most extraordinary visual experience. When I had looked towards the sky, I had been presented with universe upon universe of starry constellations that rotated clockwise, and the next one counter-clockwise, and the next one clockwise, and so on, into eternity. I can't explain the phenomenon, yet seeing it so clearly made me comprehend a truth about the unfathomable, incalculable nature of eternity – that our universe is one of complete boundlessness, and that our life energy is circular and eternal. These understandings arose outside of my own mind. I have no science to back this, but my belief that this is true is unshakable.

Seeking the edge and looking for the boundaries has been my life-long fascination. Because the outermost boundaries are mutable and can be transited, they provide a doorway into the beyond. Endurance running offers a path to the edge, a way to get to a place that one recognises as the end, only to find that one is able to go beyond. This happens over and over again at 5km, at 30km, at 60km, at 80km, at 150km, and at 208km, or however far one goes.

Over and over again, one comes through the pain into an altered wonderland of acute sensory perception, renewed physical resource and euphoria. We call it runner's high, and science explains its occurrence as the effect of a complex mix of feel-good hormones, including serotonin, dopamine and endorphins.

But I believe that there is more to it than a mere cocktail of hormones. Running is an honest pathway. Every illumination is earned. There are no sudden insights; it comes slowly as one's body and mind adjust to the discipline of sustained training. The wisdom builds one kilometre at a time. And then suddenly, on a random day like any other, one finds that one can run far enough and easy enough for clarity to arrive like a fresh breeze. It arrives in the form of a blue-sky-clear mind, and often creative insight and solutions that arrive unbidden.

Einstein, Edison, Nietzsche and the Greek philosophers all had strict physical training regimens. It is said that in his day, 2000BC, Socrates was the fittest man in Athens. In ancient times, people seemed to have a greater sense of, and honoured, the body-mind connection. Jesus, Mohammed and the prophets, Jeremiah and Moses, walked into the desert to receive their divine illuminations.

I once had a life coach who said that no matter how messed up and deranged her mind felt at the beginning of a run – like messy spaghetti bolognaise – at the end of as little as 5km, every strand would have untangled and then neatly arranged themselves in little, white music-bar rows of clarity.

But high up there in the Andes, my mind didn't feel clear. I experienced the unwelcome guest of competitive pressure and all of the monkey-mind chatter that goes with it.

Day 1 – Disaster

36km

There were 145 of us from 40 countries lined up under the start banner, milling together, hugging, laughing and wishing each other well. Trail runners are like that. We are a family, united by our love of moving freely, often preferring to run alone along wild and far-flung trails. There, we were all together in our pack, smelling of nervous sweat. Around us, the endless mountains dropped away into a purple abyss.

Quiet and focused, Ryan Sandes seemed to stand aside from the merriment. He had recently won two of the four-series RacingThePlanet 250km desert races and was aiming for his third victory.

I hugged every racer in reach, stuffed my cheeks with the entire pack of cocoa leaves, and beat my chest 10 times for luck and courage.

We were done with waiting. We pushed towards the line, muscles tense, spring-loaded, and our hearts thumping hard. The countdown … Ten, nine, eight, seven, six, five … a deep breath … a few runners ululating … four, three, two, one!

Volcanic dust billowed beneath our feet as we tore off. Runners jostled for position, and soon we were a thin line strung out across the high-altitude trail. It felt like we were running along the spine of the Earth.

Some runners were frowning and pushing hard, unable to control the natural urge to sprint for the finish line. In long-distance running, this is sheer foolishness. The sport favours the patient and the shrewd; those who hold back and preserve precious energy; those who plan and execute every step with precision, always looking for the next hard patch in the shifty dune sands, or a friendly foot-clearing among sharp rocks, always taking the inside corner of every curved trail to shave off a few centimetres of track. It is a beautiful discipline of sustained focus. Meditative and addictive.

My feet stepped quick and sure. I felt strong and was pushing ahead among the top 30 runners. A good start. The thin, green juice from the softening leaves tasted bitter on my tongue. I ran alongside runners from Switzerland, the UK and the US. Everybody's country flag was stitched smartly on to their shirtsleeves. We ran proud.

Ahead of us lay six days of running 250km at high altitude, in temperatures pushing well over 40°C, across the razor-sharp salt flats of Chile, and alongside the undulating volcanic folds of Death Valley, which is known to be the most inhospitable place on Earth.

I supressed any visions of next days and next stages, and chained my focus to my step, and then the next, knowing that all mental motivation depended on shrinking the mammoth task ahead and breaking it down to only that leg. I kept my thoughts only on the distance to the next water station, where volunteers would hustle to fill my bottles and pour cool, crisp water over my already overheating head, and shout encouragement as they hustled us out of transition.

My laser focus didn't last long.

On approximately the fifth kilometre, I remember a Swiss runner introducing himself and asking for my name. I was stumped. My name? Nothing. Complete vacuous mind. Empty like a question unasked.

The Earth tilted on its side.

My last memory is one of accelerating wildly out of my steady, conservative pace. The support crew at the water stations recounted how I went sprinting into the checkpoints like an Olympian in the 100m event, tearing past in high spirits, refusing water refills and using my water allocation to bathe instead, before swiftly overtaking the entire field of runners, until I found myself on the heels of the top five men.

I have no recollection of that feat, but I distinctly recall the sudden and awful awakening when all of the leaf-induced power left my body as swiftly as it had entered it.

Critically dehydrated, I fell down on all fours under a viscous sun, vomiting green bile and cramping. Somehow, I mustered the energy to stand, and through sheer force of will, I staggered the final stretch to camp and collapsed in a miserable heap at the medical tent.

It turned out that the little bag had contained cocoa leaves, which are used by the locals to ward off altitude sickness and fatigue. I can only assume that my benevolent bus driver had tried to convey that he had given me enough medicine for the entire race – and probably far more than enough for just one small woman weighing 50kg. I had taken enough cocoa leaves to sedate a large horse for days.

I was immediately given a saline drip. Three hours later, when my blood pressure remained obstinately low, a second drip was administered. Through the mind fog, I realised that my race hung in the balance. Race rules stipulated that racers who receive a saline drip to recover from dehydration will most likely not be allowed to continue the race, and that the decision depended entirely on the race director's discretion. The medical rationale is sound: Chronic dehydration will likely recur as athletes' bodies continue to dehydrate under the cumulative battering of running the equivalent of an ultra-marathon a day for five consecutive days, followed by a further 100km on the Long Day.

I dragged myself out of the hot medical tent and lay down at its shady side, desperate to escape the desert furnace. I had come so far to race in Chile – a long-held and expensive dream. To be sent back at that stage was unthinkable. So many racers had travelled from all corners of the globe, holding high dreams of conquest, of facing hardship and of coming through. My tent averaged the youngest mean age of racers, and youth brought an abundance of exuberance and excitement. It was a beautiful energy.

There was Janelle from the States, a young policewoman with a tattoo curving along the length of her body: "Honesty, fidelity, the futile pursuit of integrity, humility and the truth never pay". It felt to me that she was out there to somehow disprove, mostly to herself, that stark hypothesis of life. Spending time in the desert can heal many things.

And there was Dave O'Brian, a 57-year-old Irish man who had never run much more than the odd half-marathon. He had woken up one morning and decided to run 250km in the Atacama Desert. Driven by a primal desire for challenge, Dave had also signed up for the other three races in RacingThePlanet's gruelling desert series, in the wind-torn Gobi, the scorching Sahara, and the brutally cold Antarctic. I had met him for the first time on the eve of the race. He strode about, smiling under his dashing cowboy hat, his body not athletic but wiry. His eyes were bright with a glint that told me enough about the twin furnaces of his life force and will. There was no doubt in my mind that he was going to succeed in his challenge.

And then there was Samantha, who was super-excited about her first-ever endurance race, and in whom I immediately recognised a hunger to find and stretch beyond her limits. The desert draws on intensity and magnifies it. It is difficult to pin down and articulate why we would go there, but the pull is relentless. After some days of hard running and lying around in our tents, fully immersed in the sand, heat, wide-open spaces and the silence, things begin to make sense in some primal, wordless way. We begin to feel a deep sense of belonging: To each other, to the wilderness, and to the great order of things. One didn't have to proclaim spirituality to feel it.

And this thing draws one, regardless of nationality or gender or age.

There was also Laurie Brophy, a stubborn 78-year-old Welshman, who trudged through the desert, kilometre after kilometre, day after day, coming into camp in the deep hours of night after all of us had eaten and rested for hours. Each night, the finish-line volunteers would beat the drums and rouse us to welcome Laurie home. Each night, we would gather under the jewel-scattered sky and wait in silence with lumps in our throats as Laurie crossed the line, his emaciated limbs blue and white with effort and age. Every night he finished, broken and staggering, but with absolute, unwavering resolve. In his finish was the rawest of testimonies to what lies within each of us, and to our unassailable human will. We all understood that we were participating in something larger than ourselves.

On those nights, I often thought of Laurie's wife who, in their last, precious years of life, had released Laurie to pursue his dream, to spend his life force there in the desert doing what he loved, knowing that the risks to them both were great. I imagined her great warrior heart as large as Laurie's, and I silently paid homage to her love. It is often like that for us desert runners. It is the love back home that propels us forward, strengthening our hearts and minds. Beyond cocoa leaves and saline drips, it is love more than anything else that powers our legs when all of our body strength is gone.

As I watched Laurie cross the line, my heart filled in tribute to Billy and Princess Anastacia, and to the love we had shared, and the love we had lost. I longed with an aching as large as the desert sky for the person with whom I would share my life; for the person who would worry herself sick when I reach 80 years old and am still stubbornly staggering across some dust-blown desert.

The race results for the day were announced: The collapse had cost me dearly as I had fallen to 45th position overall and had not even made the cut to come in among the top 10 women. After the drips, and still lying prostrate in the shrinking shade of the medical tent, I was sinking to my own personal low, waiting for the race directors to decide for or against my enforced withdrawal. The verdict was tenuous.

"What happened, Erica?" I opened my eyes to see Sam's lovely face above me. Sam is RacingThePlanet's Chief of Operations, logistics guru and a deeply kind human being.

I told her my story: The altitude, the nausea, the well-meaning bus driver, the plastic bag and its unknown contents and my unintended overdose.

"How are you feeling now?" she asked.

"Much better. Strong, actually," I lied and made a limp attempt to sit up.

Sam and Mary Gadams decided that I would remain under observation until morning, when the medical team would cast the final vote.

As evening fell, I finally had enough strength to drag myself to my assigned tent. A cheerful chorus arose as I entered.

"Atacama mamma! You're back!" My young tentmates continued to be astounded that a 40-year-old woman could have won the Sahara Desert crossing the year before. In our small tent community, I had pearls of hard-won wisdom to share, and at the start of the race, I had enjoyed the glory bestowed by my eager, young protégés.

But now, I lay fallen from grace and slumped at the door. Sam brought me hot water for my noodles, Diego filled my hydration pack, someone else wet my buff as a cool compress for my neck. Someone else popped a blister for Janelle, and someone else put a bandage across the raw chafing on Sam's boyfriend's back. There is no space for ego or self-centredness out there in the desert. It is the chief leveller that can in one instant topple the leading man or woman from the podium. Camaraderie comes in the smallest and simplest of gestures and can make the difference between someone crossing the finish line or not. We help each other, and help flows freely in return.

Camp life on these multi-day races is a liminal space of possibility; a blueprint of what people and life could be at their best, living together in a close-knit community, motivated by belonging and care. It is the emotional wellbeing that arises from being with each other in this way that makes it hard to go back to life as normal. Often in the later stages of a race, one begins to feel conflicted, wishing for the race to never end, wishing hard and directly against the loud and plaintiff pleading of our raw feet and exhausted bodies.

Day 2 – Conserving energy

42km

At such high altitudes, the temperature plummets overnight. It was a particularly cold night, which greatly aided my recovery. By the time dawn crept across the cool desert floor, I was up with everyone else and eating instant oats around a campfire, all of us swallowing against the nausea of excitement, nerves, and slight over-exertion.

The medics were satisfied. My blood pressure and hydration had reached satisfactory levels and I was given the green light.

I ran conservatively from the outset. In race placing, I had fallen so far behind the leading ladies that there was no use competing. A great relief and sense of ease washed over me. All that was left to do was to run for a finish – a singular goal that depended on no one else but me.

Our course skirted along the high rim of Death Valley. Sharp, purple, undulating folds rippled majestically across the Andean basin below us as far as the eye could see. The vast valley seemed peaceful and strangely lifeless, devoid of animals, birds, insects and sound, and utterly indifferent to our eager lives as we traipsed along its stony collar. There was a peace in it.

The entire stage was a game of preservation and restoration. I drank and ate methodically, restocking on moisture[13] and nutrients, running conservatively and keeping my heart rate low, breathing deeply, especially on the exhale to calm my parasympathetic nervous system. Moment to moment, I emptied my mind of resistance, especially to the full blast of the desert furnace and regrets about the cocoa leaves and my tumble from the podium.

Acceptance is the easiest way through.

The day ended well, and my strategy of ease paid off far more than I had expected: I had crept up 30 places to third place in the ladies' race, and 15th overall. Still weak and nauseous, I lay down as soon as I got to camp and elevated my feet on a camp stool to lymph-drain my swollen feet and ankles. "He or she who recovers fastest, wins," it is said. I was learning the ways of endurance running one mistake at a time.

In the Atacama, the night sky is as thick and black as a river of ink. Our race took place hundreds of miles from the light pollution of any large city. And because it is the driest desert on Earth, there is not a hint of clouding vape in the air. Looking up at night, it felt as if one could reach up and pick one of the billions of glimmering stars by hand.

I sat under the stars on the second night, talking with award-winning film-maker Jennifer Steinman. She had come to the Atacama to listen to and understand what compels ordinary people like us, non-professional athletes and weekend warriors, to pour all of our money and time and every ounce of our life force into what seems an inconsequential reward – crossing the finish line of a relatively obscure race somewhere in the desert, with hardly any spectators, no fame, no prize money or any other extrinsic reward.

Talking together with many of the athletes, our thoughts swirling round and round in that sea of stars, I think Jennifer got a sense of the

13 I subsisted on nuts, raisins, date balls, dried figs, and every 15 minutes, a few sips of water. Many years before, I had given up sugar-laden gels, sports drinks and pre-packaged dehydrated meals, and opted instead for simple, raw food. If I can't pronounce the ingredient, or if I need to google it, I simply don't eat it. This strategy has proven sound in every race I have ever done. The counter is also true: When I stray, I pay.

hidden glory that comes from facing and overcoming oneself, and from doing battle with one's will, and from mastering it. She began to grasp that we are drawn to these liminal places where anything can happen, where the agony, ecstasy and the sheer pressure of the experience is able to shift people from the ordinary into extraordinary versions of themselves.

Jennifer was hooked. A year later, she would return with a film crew.

Day 3 – Getting stronger

42km

On the morning of Day 3, I felt strength surge up in me, like the hydraulics of an 18-wheeler, 36-tonne articulated truck – something like a wild and animal strength.

I reigned myself in, and from the countdown, I committed to racing conservatively – just one foot in front of the other. We were about to cross what would be the toughest stage of the entire race: 42km of wading through salt crud and mud and massive climbs up shifting dunes and steep mountains of slate rock.

The second lady, Diana Hogan-Murphy, who won the Gobi March in China in 2009, was ahead of me by a good half-hour. Newcomer, Briton Jo Zakrzewski, had opened yet another massive gap of more than four hours on Dianne. It would take a small miracle to catch either of them.

For the entire stage, I settled into my own rhythm, aiming to get to the day's end without any further mishaps and, if possible, to finish strong. On the last stretch home, I clambered past Dianne on a giant sand dune and slipped into second place with a modest lead of only three minutes.

At the end of the day, salt-caked and shattered, beaten and torched by the Andean sun, eight more people withdrew from the race.

In my tent, Janelle had such swollen feet that she had to slice her shoes so that her pinkie toes could hang out – like soft, fleshy petals vulnerable to the flame-sharp Atacama salt flats that lay in wait for us on Stage 4.

Next to Janelle and watching the shoe-shredding operation with great interest, lay a beautiful black Labrador, panting in the heat. The dog had appeared out of nowhere at Checkpoint 1, latched on to Janelle, and followed her right into our tent. He would stay by her side for the rest of the race.

A 2012 study suggested that dogs are far more likely to approach crying people than those talking, humming or being quiet.[14] A growing body of research also points to the pet-effect: How spending time with our pets can heal us and alleviate symptoms of anxiety, depression and loneliness. The desert is a magical place.

At 10pm, Laurie came across the line. The camp went berserk, for Laurie had become the unquestionable hero of the race, stirring in us all a hope that one day, when old age comes, we, too, will show up like he did, day after day, and against all odds.

Day 4 – Across the salt flats

52km

On the morning of Stage 4, I woke feeling a flood of clear, clean energy coursing through my veins, burning pure like the hard, blue flame of a Bunsen burner.

It is a strange thing: As the days wear on and my fellow racers grow weary from the cumulative exertion, my physiology and mental state undergoes an unusual transformation in the opposite direction. My body grows leaner and lighter, and my mind clears of noise and chatter, becoming more instinctual and less like my turbulent, over-stimulated, urban, office mind. As the kilometres stack up, I grow stronger. I have often wondered about this phenomenon. Perhaps it is because I sometimes imagine myself to be a little desert gecko scurrying swiftly across the dunes. It is primal. There is a feeling of belonging out there. I draw energy from, in some way, having come home. Positive psychologists tell us that the most restorative spaces for mental rest are found in the wilderness.

Perhaps because I have a small frame, the wear-and-tear on small bodies is simply less than on the big guys, who need more food and water and are prone to overheating. Perhaps it is the wisdom of age and racing conservatively that pays off as the days wear on. Maybe it is because I try as best as possible to focus on my own race and to not waste energy fretting

14 Meyers-Manor, J. E. & Botten, M. L. A shoulder to cry on: Heart rate variability and empathetic behavioral responses to crying and laughing in dogs. *Canadian Journal of Experimental Psychology/Revue Canadienne de Psychologie Expérimentale*, 74(3), 235–243, 2020.

too much about the relative performance of my competitors. In that way, I avoid taxing my body with needless mental stress and excess cortisol. I had no way of knowing then that the better I did, the harder it would become to keep that singular focus.

Perhaps my Kalahari Bushman[15] or African savannah genes remembered how to run down an antelope. In his bestseller, *Born to Run*[16], Chris McDougall makes a strong case that human beings evolved as a hunting pack. Our physical ability to sweat and thus cool ourselves over long distances, and our social ability to collaborate as a group enabled us to outrun and outsmart pretty much every other mammal on Earth, despite their superior physical strength.

McDougall's theory of a long-distance-running hunting pack also explains why women hold their own over longer distances. They had to run with the pack of hunters to benefit from a kill 50 miles from where the hunt started – and often while pregnant and nursing babies. There are many examples of women doing particularly well in long-distance races, especially after childbirth. In 2019, Jasmin Paris, 35, from Edinburgh, made headlines when she smashed both the male and female records of the gruelling 268 mile Montane Spine race along the Pennine Way. She bettered the male course record by a staggering 12 hours while expressing breast milk for her baby at each of the aid stations.

Scientific research is needed to fathom why women fair well over long distances. My hypothesis is that we benefit from a powerful cocktail of hormones and mindsets that imbue the female parent with super-human powers, higher pain thresholds and simply greater endurance. On the longer adventure races, I have often witnessed that, after three days of non-stop racing and severe sleep-deprivation, the women would come out stronger than their male teammates on almost every level. Just watch any mother of a newborn child and how she gets by on little more than a few

15 There is some controversy around using the word "Bushman". In post-apartheid South Africa, the word "San" is used to describe the first-ever inhabitants of the African continent. However, the word "San" means "*vagabond*" and has not been unilaterally welcomed by members of the San. The clan name of the first people who inhabited the Kalahari is */Gwikwe – /Gwi*, meaning "Bush", and *kwe,* meaning "people". My conscience sits well with the word "Bushman". At the very least, it honours their translated clan name.

16 McDougall, C. *Born to Run: A hidden tribe, superathletes, and the greatest race the world has never seen*, Knopf, 5 May 2009.

hours' sleep a night for months on end, and you'll find yourself watching a female endurance racer par excellence. But our modern, city-bound culture rarely recognises this. We cosset our pregnant and new mommies when in fact, they are formidable racing machines. It is, therefore, not a far-fetched hypothesis that we tend to get stronger because we are women, and that the longer the racing distance, the greater our ability to shrink the gender gap.

Perhaps my strength is aided by the pure, clean natural foods I eat, which naturally lead my body into a state of ketosis. Science suggests that as we go into ketosis, our cells behave more efficiently. We make more mitochondria, and the surge in mitochondria improves the way we burn fuel.

Whatever the reason for this bizarre phenomenon, going into Stage 4 of the race with 140km behind us, I felt as strong as a thundering rhino. I had shaken off all of the effects of my Stage 1 overdose disaster. The terrain across the salt flats was treacherous and difficult, and the trick was to move quickly and lightly across the sharp steeples of dried salt which, with one slip, could easily slice one's shins to the bone. For much of the stage, I ran behind Jo, stepping in her footsteps across the otherworldly white blaze, delighting in our quick and easy rhythm together.

By the end of Day 4, I finished a good half-hour ahead of Dianne, and in 10th position overall. I had run myself back into the race for a podium position, but it was far from over. Ahead of us lay the Long Day. By early evening, everyone had eaten and packed for the journey ahead. We lay in our sleeping bags, apprehensively sharing our highly individualised strategies for covering 75km of arduous terrain. Some were going to bust through in one go, some were planning to sleep at Checkpoint 5, and others planned to go hard in daylight and make good time before slowing down during the long night stage.

My main aim was to race conservatively, keep a steady rhythm throughout, jog whenever I could and minimise my time at the checkpoints. There was no margin for error. Diana was strong and continued to chase hard. My lead on her was a thin 19 minutes, but there was a whole 90-minute chasm between Jo and me. In trail running, this is an eternity, but an equal truth is that anything can happen out there: Dehydration, sunstroke, lethal stomach bug-induced diarrhoea and vomiting, a snake bite, a wrong turn that could leave you lost in the dark, desert night. Any of these misfortunes could shift the leader board in an instant.

During the night, a strong wind gathered force outside our tents, whirling up dust and old ghosts that haunted our fitful sleep. My tent companions lay huddled in the cocoons of their sleeping bags, undoubtedly awake and listening to the wind, as I did. Our communal nervous tension hung in the air, dense and electric, and made the hairs on the back of my neck stand up.

Day 5 – A long day past the Atacama Large Millimeter Array
75km

Finally, dawn leaked blood-red across the hazy-blue darkness.

They set us off in batches, from slowest to fastest. Laurie went out first. We watched him disappear into the distance and wished him well, hoping that he would make it before the stage cut-off 24 hours later. Last to leave was Ryan Sandes. He had been running like a desert fiend, supernaturally floating across the desert floor and setting a new course record on each preceding stage. Would he do it again today? He seemed fresh and unstoppable.

The day's course and images merged into one endless montage of white salt flats, impossibly high wind-ravaged dunes, and the roar of the hot, dry wind across that vast open space.

At Checkpoint 1, the momentousness of the challenge had gotten the better of Laurie and he had withdrawn from the race. The day wore on and laid waste to many. Six more people withdrew before evening.

As night fell, the constellations tilted overhead towards the west, revealing their splendour to the 66 wide-eyed telescopes of the Atacama Large Millimeter Array – the largest astronomical facility in the world.

Running there under the stars and across the dark desert, I thought of my mom and the email she had sent to me the previous day, expressing her excitement about our course passing so near the ALMA telescope. My mother sometimes seems to understand things beyond the obvious, as moms often do. She has helped me find sense in what often cannot be seen by the naked eye – the energy of places and of people; the possibilities in the realm of the yet unformed. Because of my mom, I know that our thoughts are powerful and creative.

Science has proven that what we think ultimately shapes our reality – both what eventually transpires and how we experience it. How we think is how we are; and how we are is how our lives become.

And so, when darkness fell, I kept my mind on all of the things for which I was grateful, and thought about the people I loved and about my tent companions and of the fondness that had grown between us. I felt the greatest appreciation for the extraordinary vastness and awe-inspiring beauty of the desert and for all the Earth's wild places.

These thoughts and feelings kept my heart and legs strong to the finish line. I crossed over about 9pm, a mere 40 minutes behind Jo.

I was overcome by an animal hunger and an overpowering need to sleep, but sleep didn't come. Awash with cortisol and adrenaline, I was a night diver who couldn't quite get below the surface. I dipped in and out of consciousness. Sometime in the night, I heard that Diana had arrived. I had built a 90-minute lead on her.

Once the Long Day is done, it is highly unlikely that anything will change in the field placings. We had cemented our respective first, second and third lady podium positions in the top 20 of the overall field of super-strong competitors – a feat for the ladies.

At 8am, I heard the final competitor cross the line. It was apt that the hero's race belonged to a Chilean, Cristian Sieveking. Four days before the start of the Atacama Crossing, Chile had suffered one of the most devastating earthquakes in the country's history. It had claimed the lives of 526 people and laid waste to large sections of the capital, Santiago, destroying half of the international airport. Despite the disaster and the national state of emergency, the Chilean people had rallied and raised $35 million to aid the 20 000 people who had lost their homes. Despite an only semi-functional airport, the Chilean people, with great grace and generosity, had still managed to support RacingThePlanet and had welcomed 156 racers from all over the world to experience their beautiful country.

The one certainty in life is that at some point, we will face difficulty or disaster. The question is not whether it will come, but what we will do when it does, and who we will become as a result of how we respond to it.

Day 6 – Saying our goodbyes
10km

On the final day, we rose with a quirky, emotional cocktail of relief and sadness. It was all over, but for the last 10km dash into the small town of San Pedro. As we trotted in, the leaderboard had remained unchanged.

The race finished in front of a small, white church, beneath banners of red, yellow, green and blue festive flags that wafted in the desert breeze. Every racer was hung with a smart, yellow ribbon medal. We hugged as if we had known each other for years.

I cheered my young tentmates across the finish line and bade them farewell. Janelle came into the finishing strait with the black Labrador trotting beside her. The dog looked up at Janelle for a brief moment, turned on his heels and trotted back in the direction from where we had come. Another desert parting. Profoundly significant, yet over in a moment.

Ryan Sandes had sprinted into town and set a record for the Atacama Crossing. Later that year, he also won the Last Desert in Antarctica, which made him the first person to win all four RacingThePlanet desert races in succession.

Jennifer Steinman went on to make an award-winning documentary, *Desert Runners*[17]. It features distance-hungry Samantha and cowboy-hat Dave O'Brien's inner and outer journeys, as they face the four toughest races on the planet. The documentary opens with Theodore Roosevelt's famous quote, murmured by a runner as he drags himself up a mountain of red sand:

"The credit belongs to the man who is actually in the arena, whose face is marred by dust and sweat and blood... who at best, if he wins, knows the thrills of high achievement, and, if he fails, at least fails daring greatly."

17 Steinman, J. *Desert Runners*, 2 September 2013. Visit www.imdb.com (Accessed: 7 July 2021)

And ultimately it is this that draws us to these races. It is a space where we can dare greatly, where we can reach towards our best selves, where failing is not possible, because the very act of arriving is success. There are no losers on the startline.

I didn't win the race, yet I felt triumphant because I had shown up and given my best. I hadn't quit in the face of adversity, and I had stayed true to my dream of being a desert runner: One foot in front of the other.

I don't know where all of my fellow racers are in the world today, but I know for sure that they continue to live out and infuse the world around them with the same passion that binds us and defines us as desert runners. They are always looking for that edge, always reaching towards the limits of possibility and beyond.

Later in my hotel room, as I binned my salt-flat-shredded shoes, I felt a flicker of excitement about the future. Somewhere out there was another desert and more people of my tribe with whom I would connect. What I didn't know was that fate was already conspiring to take me to the Namib Desert in less than six months from then. There I would meet Linda Doke, the iconic South African trail runner. Our paths would not only cross in friendship, but we would also duel it out for the trophy on the magical dunes of Sossusvlei, where eland and Bushman spirits roam.

"Between stimulus and response, there is a space.
In that space is our power to choose our response. In our
response lies our growth and our freedom."

VICTOR EMIL FRANKL

3

FALLING IN LOVE WITH A BLESBOK AND A BOY, NAMIB DESERT, 2011

"There is life without love. It is not worth a bent penny, or a scuffed shoe. It is not worth the body of a dead dog nine days unburied."

MARY OLIVER

Deserts are not all the same. They are fingerprint-unique, each with their own climate, own animal and plant life and own proprietary desert soul. I didn't find what I was looking for in the Atacama. It wasn't remote enough from civilisation. It wasn't the Sahara; it wasn't hot enough and it didn't feed my heart. So, I started looking for another desert race. I craved wilderness and delirious desert heat.

Not all grief is the same. Losing someone to death is involuntary – and irrevocable. The grief is sharp and clean, and it is free of the gut-twisting what-if doubts and the drawn-out withdrawal pains that sometimes accompany divorce. In death, one loses the person; in divorce, it is love that is lost – love that might inconsiderately pop up on your Facebook feed as a picture of your ex looking alive and happy in the embrace of someone new.

I thought I had come through – that I was done grieving my divorce – but that was not so. I was entering the second year of being divorced, and by then, the euphoria of my newly-acquired freedom had waned. My ex-wife had sent a text: She was getting married. It was a complex feeling. I was glad for her and relieved that she had moved on, but at the same time, I was utterly raw and heartbroken.

I needed to run, like I had in the Sahara, to turn the rawness in my chest into neutral history. To top it all, I was homesick for my parents, my sister, and her adopted son, Bandile, and for sunshine. I longed for Africa where I felt rooted like a baobab. In the UK, I felt as untethered as a tumbleweed blown along by a foreign winter wind.

I entered an African race, the Kinetic Energy Namib Desert Challenge, and at the airport, on impulse, I bought a large Hallmark first-year anniversary card for my future spouse-to-be. I still had hope. It was my only lighthouse and the only way through a feeling of loneliness that had settled in my bones.

The Namib Desert Challenge (NDC) is a 220km, five-day, self-sufficient foot race of superlatives. It crosses the oldest desert on Earth and summits the world's highest dunes. I chose the race because it was scheduled to end in Sossusvlei, the ethereal, white, cracked-dry salt marsh surrounded by sentinels of towering, red dunes. I chose it because the first woman with whom I had ever fallen in love, loved Sossusvlei. She was my roommate at university. Of all the people I had ever met, she had the most profound influence on my life, because she taught me that love is not gendered – the heart loves whom it will.

Sossusvlei. There is romance in the name. Adventure. In Nama, it literally means "dead end". It's the end of the world, a place where one can find rest, because there is nowhere else to go from there. Even the dunes there remain immovable and fixed. They are star dunes, carved by an indecisive wind that blows from all directions – unlike in the Sahara, where the dunes are forever shifting inland ahead of the steady sea winds.

The other ubiquitous feature of Sossusvlei is multiple silhouettes of entranced photographers. They flock there from all over the world to capture the mesmerising desert light. At sunrise, they come for the long night shadows creeping away across the cayenne-pepper-red dunes, and at sunset, for the liquid-gold, orange, pink and purple explosion that lights up the sky. No camera has enough eye to capture it.

And then there are the single-file spindles of people lumbering up the spines of the highest dunes – wheezing, cursing and staggering, yet euphoric. What is it about summits that draw us so? What is the hope that compels us to fight against the loose sand and the burn in our thighs, the profuse sweating and the shortness of breath?

I arrived in the Namib Naukluft National Park on the eve of the race. The evening heat wrapped around me like gift paper. An attractive 30-something racer emerged from the luxury safari tent next to mine. He came to the shared washbasin to fill his hydration pack.

That is how I met Andrew for the first time. I can't remember the content of our conversation, only the sound of the water running and a gentle feeling. There was a kindness about him, and less of the hard testosterone-driven ego one expects to encounter in the men and women who enter these extreme challenges. I went to bed thinking about Billy's fiancée and wondering whether he was like Andrew.

Day 1 – Calibrating the field

42km

Just before 8am, a smattering of 42 runners lined up at the startline. We were a small Babylon of Europeans – the Germans, Italians, French, Irish and the British – and from even further away, the Americans, Canadians and Australians, and a home team of South Africans and Namibians.

While we were chatting and last-minute-fumbling with our packs, it soon became apparent that it was not the size but the calibre of the field that mattered. The startline comprised hard-core adventure racers and trail champions of world-class events, like the Marathon de Sable and the RacingThePlanet series of the Sahara, Gobi, Arctic and Atacama races. Then there was Linda Doke. At the time, she was conceivably the strongest, sponsored female trail runner in South Africa. The winner's trophy was going to be hard-earned.

The front runners set off at a blistering pace, calibrating and pressing each other, watching for each other's strengths and weaknesses. Linda tore off into the distance after Australian adventure-racing demon Damon Goerke, who would dominate the rest of the men's race.

Biding my time, I let them go and did not attempt to chase.

The day was cool, the sun hidden behind a blessing of cloud cover. The first 20km rushed by along a hard-packed Jeep track. Those easy conditions did not play to my strengths. On a flat, wide Jeep track I have the appearance of a honey badger, not really going anywhere fast despite great effort. But give me heat that melts the sky and a sandy riverbed, and I shuffle across it faster than a desert gecko; along a cliff-edged ridge with vertiginous drops, I feel like a mountain deer. Give me dark nights and fast-flowing, technical river crossings, sleep-deprivation and all manner of hardships, and I transform into a fiendishly fast trail beast, more green-eyed puma than badger.

Andrew came trotting by. He was wearing a khaki cricket hat. "How are you getting on? Those front guys are way too fast for me!" he said in a voice as pleasing as a late-night DJ who promises to keep one company into the last, slow hours before morning. We exchanged more pleasantries and then he apologetically trotted off into the distance. There was something striking about his courteous, affable manner. One can spot a good man a mile away – the kind one's mother would delight in.

We ran another 22km across the African savannah, which was far greener than I had imagined. Silky green-and-yellow-tufted Bushman grass covered the Earth as far as the eye could see. We ran among outcrops of buttock-smooth, brown boulders, many of which were rumoured to have been sanctified by Bushman paintings.

When a Bushman painted an eland, the intention was not artistic, it was for her/his life to access the spirit of the twirl-horned, drought-resilient animal. Looking across the vast savannah, I could imagine the Bushman enjoying a thriving life there, healthy and happy for the herds of fat, prancing springbok and the abundance of water.

By the time we came into camp, Linda had opened a strong 22-minute lead over 42km.

"Anything can still happen," she said, generously.

I knew that she would work hard to open the gap further, as any accomplished champion would do. Somehow, it didn't matter. My heart was not fully in the racing.

In the evening, Linda and I lay in our shared tent, which smelled of canvas and dust, chatting about running, life and love. She told me about her adoring husband, who followed her to every race and unfailingly seconded her on her longest challenges, bearing food and water and encouragement and serving up every kind of body, heart and soul sustenance an endurance runner could hope for.

"He will be waiting for me at the finish line," she said into the darkness.

Outside, crickets chirped, and a lone black-backed jackal called into the star-scattered night.

"You are very lucky to have someone like him. One needs a strong heart more than one needs a strong body," I said from my sleeping bag, hiding the painful pressure in my chest – a feeling as if some large animal had come to sit on me, and as hard to ignore.

When I read Linda's race report many months later, I realised that she had not at all understood that the weight on my chest was the size of an elephant. Her blogged worries that I would catch her were quite needless.

In 1939, Professor George Vaillant began to explore the question: "What is needed for a long and happy life?" The study continued for 75 years with a cohort of 268 men from Harvard. It provided astounding evidence about what really matters in the end. Vaillant's main conclusion from the study[18] was that "*the warmth of participants' personal relationships throughout life had the greatest impact on their life satisfaction*".

"Do you have someone you can phone for help at 4am in the morning?" was the question posed to each of the 46-year-old Harvard participants. An affirmative response was the single most predictive indicator of whether that person would still be alive and happy at age 80.

The study showed that longevity and happiness depended more on love than on career success, wealth, regular exercise, keeping a healthy weight and abstaining from smoking and drinking. At a deeply unconscious, biological, and evolutionary level, we have all bought into this truth: Happiness is love. Love of God. Love of self. Love of others – as much as you love yourself. It is no more complicated than that.

I was 40 years old, and I had a large group of friends in the UK, some extremely close to me and dear, but as I slipped towards sleep, I wondered: "Who would I phone at 4am?" Some names came to mind – temporary emergency life rafts. The elephants on my chest multiplied.

---

18 Vaillant, G. E. *Aging Well*, Little Brown, 2003.

Day 2 – Beneath Elim

46km

The second day of the race produced even more easy running along a hard-packed Jeep track, with a few sandy riverbeds thrown in for good measure. Within the first 3km, Linda had disappeared across the horizon.

For the first 26km, I kept a steady pace, keeping well within my comfort zone, until we hit Elim, the longest dune in the world. It had been a season of abundant rain and the Bushman grass stood knee-high, obscuring the treachery of the powdery-red sand beneath. For the final gruelling 20km, the dune sucked at our energy before spitting us out at Camp 2.

Linda had opened another big gap of 28 minutes on me. It would take an inhuman effort to close the cumulative 50-minute gap that lay between us. Linda and I both knew it, and as the competitive pressure eased, a space opened up for a friendship and mutual fondness to grow.

We camped in the shadow of Elim Dune.

Elim had been named after the oasis where the Israelites had camped after fleeing Egypt, *"with twelve wells of water and seventy palm trees."*[19] The Israelites had stayed at Elim for months, gathering their strength for the long trek across the wilderness to the Promised Land.

Like the Israelites, we used the long, hot afternoon to eat, rest and regain our strength for the remaining 180km that lay ahead.

But there were more ways in which I felt like an Israelite – like a desert-tramping fugitive from Egypt. I had been fleeing London for the longest time. I was looking for a way out of the concrete of big-city living and trying to escape office-bound days: The dim boardrooms, fluorescent lighting and many hours tethered to my screen, stuck away in a building, far, far away from the call of the wild.

I was deeply grateful for my career and for the means it afforded me, and I loved the intellectual stimulation of large-scale corporate strategy, but I suffered the indoor incarceration of my job more than anyone I knew. Those desert races were, for me, like Elim – an oasis where I could take in

19 Exodus 15:27, New Kings James Version, Bible.

deep draughts of clean air before I had to descend back into the coalmine of office life.

Sitting at the foot of Elim, I watched the Southern Cross trail slowly across the heavens. I became acutely aware of the radiant wellness in my body and that I was smiling. It was a wellness from being out there, far from the noise, pollution, and pressure, and the constant visual stimulation of a billion advertisements on every escalator wall of the London Underground.

I felt strong, at peace and free. I wanted more of that in my life: A simple, uncomplicated, predominantly outdoor existence. I had no idea how I would get there, but the fact that my life depended on it had slowly become non-negotiable.

Day 3 – Gaining strength from the Earth

42km

At 7am, we set off under a spectacular sky of pink and orange clouds. The weather remained cool and the paths firm across the vast savannah. Again, Linda shot away, chasing Francesco Galanzino, an evenly tanned, small-framed Italian, as perfectly chiselled as Michelangelo's David, and the 2007 winner of the Four Deserts Championship award.

I knew that Linda hadn't completely lost sight of me; and for good reason. Every day, as my heart grew stronger from being in the vast wilderness, fed by the smell of the Earth and by the presence of gemsbok, springbok, geckos, crickets and the breathing savannah, the gaps between us had begun to shrink. I was not quick enough to chase Linda outright – she was far stronger than me and a more experienced trail runner. My only viable strategy was to forget her and to settle into my own rhythm of the long run.

In the Namib Desert Challenge, the daily distances were comparatively shorter than those of other multi-day events. For me to gain ground on my competition, I needed the kind of distances that strike fear in runners' hearts; I needed distances that would allow me to slowly chase down my opponents through unrelenting persistence, the way Bushmen did when they ran down their quarry.

Anthropologists like Louis Liebenberg coined this practice "persistence hunting",[20] when he described in detail the Bushmen hunt he witnessed in 1985. *"The hunt takes place at the hottest time of day ... The kudu takes flight and the bushmen (track) its spoor. The kudu needs to stop and rest ... (They) must get to it before it has recovered. (This) is repeated until the kudu collapses from exhaustion."*

We came into camp after a five-hour burst of 42km. Linda had gained 11 minutes on me. We were camped in an amphitheatre of boulders and vast swathes of savannah grass. Towards evening, the sky, molten-gold and violent-red, rose and purple, swirled so low that it felt like we were inside the sunset. All of the racers fell silent, meandering around in a zen-like state. Some of us tried to capture the moment on film. I tried to take a selfie. I had recognised that a light had come on within me – a vitality, a wild aliveness. I wanted a photo of my eyes, so I could look at them once I was back in London and remember the feeling and re-enter it, like a genie getting back into the lamp.

"Would you like me to take a photo?" Andrew had wandered over to where I stood among the sweet, hip-high grass.

He was soft-spoken and as gentle as ever. A moment passed between us. It was not romantic, but something kindred and more precious, and as ancient as time itself. The colours deepened and the sky bled red into the velvet darkening. I let him take my photo and walked off into the veld, feeling happy and more whole than I had for the longest time – and at least since my divorce more than a year before.

Healing is a long, slow process, and perhaps more than anything else, it is the people with whom we connect who help us along on our way.

During the night, the clouds gathered and rushed ahead of the wind, like a mighty Armada, until they reached our camp and tore open along veined arcs of lightning. Rain thundered down on our tents. We all prayed that the canvas was good for the onslaught.

We didn't have to remain prostrate in prayer for long. Within half an hour, the rain ended abruptly. I stepped outside for the bathroom and

20 Liebenberg, L. Persistence Hunting by Modern Hunter-Gatherers, *Current Anthropology*, Vol. 47, No. 6, December 2006.

found the heavens glittering with newly-washed diamonds. It was a sight as bright as laughter, and it followed me into my sleeping bag, where I had the best night's sleep yet.

Day 4 – Running with a blesbok

56km

Sunrise was as spectacular as sunset on the previous night. The Earth was fresh-soaked, and grass gleamed heavy and fat with moisture, in wave upon wave of fluorescent-green as far as the eye could see.

We set off under a flaming, magenta sky. Ahead of us lay the longest stage of 56km, and at the end of it, the highest dune in the world.

Given the longer distance ahead, we trotted off at a measured pace, running as a pack, in step like a small French Foreign Legion. It felt good to be together like that. It was clear that objectives had shifted. We were no longer racing each other but rather, overcoming the challenges of the course ahead.

The Namib has many snakes. At 8km, we descended into the depths of Sesriem Canyon, a narrow sandstone ravine that had been flooded by the previous night's rainfall. The flooding had flushed all of the snakes from their burrows.

I sloshed through the chin-deep, brown water, barely keeping head above it, carrying my backpack high above my head, all the while on the alert for the swish of a long, cold, slithering body, or the sudden heart-stopping burn of a bite.

Many of the Namib's snakes are highly poisonous. The golden side-winder is a short, thin finger of a snake that buries itself under the porous sand with only the black tip of its tail protruding to attract unsuspecting geckos. There is also the pretty, yellow-patterned, fat puffadder that delivers a painful bite and a cytotoxic poison that causes the affected limb to swell, burst open and rot. But, as I waded, first and foremost in my mind was the fearsome black mamba, measured in fatalities as the most dangerous snake on Earth.

The mamba can grow to a 4m monster that, at a top speed of almost 20km per hour, can outpace most humans. Unlike other snakes, it throws everything into the fight, striking repeatedly and delivering with a single bite enough poison to kill 15 grown men. Even when its victim retreats, the mamba goes after it, continuing to deliver nightmarish strikes until its prey collapses from breathing difficulties.

Despite the mamba's reputation, in truth it is shy, and unless cornered, it will wake from where it is basking in the sun and retreat to safety at the first sign of danger. But then, disturbed by the flood, the snakes would be out in the water, unsettled, nervous, and perhaps even accompanied by their young – newborn, earthworm-sized little mambas, which are just as poisonous as their parents.

I rushed to exit the writhing water and settled back into an easy, long-distance, kudu-hunting trot. The course took us across vast open plains, mile after mile merging into one unbroken spell of steady breathing and rhythmic shuffling under the hot sun.

After about four hours of running, I entered a scattering of stark camel thorn trees. A shadow shifted in the scant shade. The white face of a blesbok peered through the thicket. That little antelope had seen me coming for a while and had stood his ground. His handsome, reddish-brown coat blazed beneath the beating sun.

He was alone. "An old bachelor," I thought.

Blesbok males are fiercely territorial and when they come of age, the young bulls often evict the older males from harems of females and the young. Blesbok bachelors group together and roam the land looking for undefended herds to make their own – pressed forward by a biological urge to mate and belong.

The bull peered at me, his head cocked at a slight angle, the white marking on his face like a dazzling exclamation mark. He stood at ease, with only 50m of desert separating us. As I passed by, he set off on a trot, but kept a parallel course to me.

After 50m, he stopped, turned and watched me close the gap. As I drew near, he again trotted off and stopped a little way ahead.

"Are you waiting for me?" I asked into the heat, my heart welling with joy at the bull's inquisitive attention. Above all, I was glad for his company.

We ran together for at least 10 minutes, until the dunes to the right of him gave way and he turned to follow their wide arc.

It may not seem much, but this stands out as one of the seminal experiences of my life: Trotting alongside a lone blesbok under the scorching African sun, both of us on our own journey through the wilderness, heading towards who knows what.

It wasn't long after the bull had left me that I spotted another shifting shape in the heat-shimmering distance. It was human.

"A runner?" A sharp thrill shot through me. I sniffed the air and felt myself bristling.

I kept my pace and relished the heat that was by then as violently shrill as the cicadas that shredded the silence with their mad midday chirping. I tracked the runner, and with every kilometre, drew a little closer.

It was Linda.

I could see from her gait that she was working hard in the heat. Struggling. I drew closer – as quiet as a tiger. She must have sensed my presence because she darted a nervous look over her shoulder, saw me closing in and picked up her pace. I matched and raised her, and kept shrinking the distance.

Linda glanced over her shoulder every few hundred metres, bent forward and pressed hard towards Dune 45 that loomed red in the distance.

By the time we hit the base of the massive mound of sand, I was on Linda's heels, climbing hard after her on to the S-swirl spine of the magnificent dune. The 5 million-year-old sand, as fine as powder, slid away under our feet. Up and up we scrambled toward the 80m-high summit, where a bright-red New Balance race flag marked the turn-around point.

Linda reached it 30 seconds before me, turned and hurtled down the dune, arms flailing and legs striding out recklessly ahead of her.

I touched the flag and slid after her, crossing the line a minute after her.

It was a good day, a day of gifts: The heat, the long generous distance, the snake-riddled canyon swim, the high dunes and the blesbok blessing. Oh, I felt good.

For the remainder of the afternoon, we all sprawled together in the shade of the communal gazebo, enjoying each other's company, knowing that it would soon all be over and that we would have to return to life as normal – to the mundane, to four walls, and for most of us, to the bustling city. I spent most of my time talking to Linda and Andrew. I noticed that he softened the hard edges in me. I felt gentle around him – not the fierce, wild hunter, but rather, a small-hooved, long-lashed, shy duiker[21].

At some deep level, I had come to understand that my healing from divorce, and from other old hurts, was to be in this direction – towards softness, and in a way, towards surrender. I was slowly moving towards letting go of the reigns, risking vulnerability and, brick by brick, dismantling the walls to let someone in.

In the early evening, as we retired to our two-man tents, Linda said: "You know that Andrew is getting married soon?"

I was surprised at the disappointment that shot through me, embarrassed by the foolishness of it, and that my desert crush had been outed.

"I bat for the other side," I said, trying to make light of it.

Over the previous four days, Linda had built up a 1 hour, 2 minute lead on me, and with only 28km to the finish line, she was almost assured of a win. The size of the gap was a gift because it meant that we could cease racing and simply run for the love of it, fully surrendering to the landscape and to the grand experience.

The splendour of the final kilometres of the Namib Desert Challenge would eclipse every one of the previous near-200km we had run.

Day 5 – Splendour

28km

As we set out on the final morning of the race, Linda hobbled off the startline, complaining of a recurring hamstring injury that had flared up.

We all passed her.

I trotted alongside Andrew for a while before he set off after the front-runners. I was in no hurry to finish the race. I wanted to draw out every last kilometre; I wanted to stay in the fierce desert heat; I wanted to eat the sun and fill my belly with the stars; I wanted to drench every cell of my body with the smell of the sweet grass and the wet-scented cumulonimbus clouds that excited the animals. I wanted to become the white-shinned,

21 A small antelope native to South Africa.

sauntering blesbok and the hardy camel thorns, and so ballast myself against the inevitable gloom of London.

At the 12km mark, our course cut across the white-powdered salt pan of Deadvlei. Blinding light reflected off the white-chapped Earth. The dead, blackened, 700-year-old trees seemed eternally up-stretched and protesting against the sun's endless torching, caught in the netherworld between burning and turning to stone. Everything in Deadvlei remained absurdly preserved. The environment offered too little moisture for the natural processes of decay.

Around the white pan and in the obliterating heat towered the red slopes of the world's highest and oldest dunes, guarding the vlei like sentinels of antiquity, and absorbing every decibel of sound. Even the shrill song of the ever-present cicadas had ceased.

All I could hear was my own footsteps and those of Francesco cracking across the parched earth. When voyaging across such a landscape on foot, delirious from the heat and with only the bare minimum of life's necessities on one's back, it is impossible to remain unaffected. There is a magic in these deserts – a visceral pulse. I have often observed people as they walk there – and without fail, I notice a sense of glee, a gladness in them, because the throb of life is so near and vital and real that it sets even the coldest hearts alight.

There is life in the desert in abundance, but it is hidden.

The dunes in the Namib are extremely porous. The sand is so fine that geckos, beetles, spiders, snakes and scorpions effortlessly breathe and commute in the silky underground. Even the water hides in deep, subterranean water systems and is found only by the patient tap roots of camel thorn trees 60m below. Sometimes water arrives as thunder-lashed flash floods, and at other times, mysteriously and without a sound as ocean fog that drifts across the dunes in the mornings.

The mysteries of the desert reveal themselves only to the most attentive and patient. In the Namib, the dunes are 5 million years old and there, 1 000-year-old welwitschia fossil plants sprawl on the sand like fat, flattened green octopi. There is a feeling in the desert of enough time to calm the heart and mind and to just be.

I think that is why lines of people trudge up the high spines of the dunes.

Francesco and I exited Deadvlei together. Linda caught up with us. She had willed her hamstring injury better, intent on not losing any ground to me, and even more determined to podium in fourth place overall, ahead of Four-Deserts Francesco.

In the far distance, we could make out the giant mass of Big Daddy looming against the deep-blue sky.

The final ascent to the 400m summit of Big Daddy was a private affair for each of us. We took our time to gather that for which we came. To the west, giant, white cumulonimbus clouds billowed up from the hot desert plains. Around us, eternity stretched in every direction. The hot wind trailed long streaks of fine, red sand into the deep-blue sky.

In the climbing, I remembered a Walt Whitman stanza from his long poem, *Song of the Open Road.*[22]

"I inhale great draughts of space,
The east and the west are mine, and the north and the south are mine.
I am larger, better than I thought,
I did not know I held so much goodness.
All seems beautiful to me."

God only knows how deeply I felt Whitman's words.

Standing there on that high peak, the unpeopled desert dropping away on all sides, an understanding far beyond words opened up in me; and I knew beyond doubt that there is something far greater than us that turns the wide gyre of the universe. The ancient dune beneath us sighed powdery-red breaths as we trudged and slid down its sides to the finish line at its feet.

Linda bagged her fourth place, and I finished as second lady and sixth overall, after Andrew in fifth.

We waited together in the shade of a sprawling camel thorn tree for the rest of the field to complete their own hero's journeys.

22 Whitman, W. *Leaves of Grass*, Simon Schuster, 2006.

My heart wanted to stay in that splendid desert forever. I walked off into the heat, the Earth's caress closing like a hot oven around my feet. Andrew had loitered off into the distance, too. Our paths crossed and we congratulated each other. Then he said from beneath his khaki cricket hat: "I am engaged."

I smiled at him and said how lovely it was for him and his fiancée. I never followed their wedding on Facebook, but years later, I had a brief, virtual "Where-are-you-in-the-world?" reconnection with him, as desert racers often do. His Facebook pictures told a story that was exactly as I had imagined: The proud, fine-looking groom and his beautiful bride; then the adoring, love-struck husband and the excited father to be; and then the amazing dad.

Maybe cricket men are like that: Able to stay in one place for the longest time; patient and steady; good fathers and good husbands, who settle like baobabs and the unmoving Elim Dune. Maybe it was my yearning to settle down and make a home that drew me to Andrew and to his calm, velvety voice. I was glad to have fallen in love with a boy and for the gentleness it unrobed in me, and for how it stripped me of the hard shell of grief.

The bus collected us, and as the red swish of the giant Namib dunes receded into the distance, I thought about the one-year-anniversary card I had bought for my spouse to be, and about winter in the UK ahead, and that my heart belonged to Africa. But I also knew that pining for my home country would make a misery of my life in London.

On the flight home, I resolved to fix my attention on everything that was wonderful, beneficial and special about the UK, with the fierce focus of a solo climber fixing on a finger hold. I was going to be fully present in my life and not outsource my happiness to some distant dream of tomorrow. By design, tomorrow never comes.

I set my intention to live, work and race my heart out in the UK. What I didn't know was that I was about to stumble on one of the most vibrant and well-established long-distance racing scenes in the world. The British love to run.

4

FIRST LADY AMONG THE TOUGH NUTS, UNITED KINGDOM, 2013

"A bird may love a fish, but where would they live?"

DREW BARRYMORE

The United Kingdom is a small island, half the size of Japan and also of France. It is 40 times smaller than the United States, yet the UK offers almost as many long-distance running events as the US[23], and more events than all of Europe, Australia, Asia and Africa combined.

The United Kingdom is ultra-Nirvana – not only for its many long-distance races, but also for the opulent calendar of local and more social events that cater for runners and walkers alike. Take for example the Long Distance Walkers Association, which has hosted 15–30 events across all of England, every single weekend, for the past 50 years. Participants have their pick of distances, ranging from 12–150 miles, with locally stocked and manned checkpoint tables that groan under cheese sandwiches, crisps, bananas, jelly babies, and every mouth-watering biscuit and cake you can imagine. The event entry fees cost less than the price of coffee and a muffin.

The UK also boasts some of the best and most prolific long-distance walking trails in the world – and most of them are runnable, like the 630 mile, blue-bell-rimmed South West Coast Path; the 100 mile, green-

23 The entire United States offers 306 races. In comparison, there are 232 high-quality, mostly off-road ultras in the United Kingdom. See www.ultramarathonrunning.com (Accessed: 10 July 2021)

hilled, picture-pretty South Downs Way; the 184 mile, flat, river-hugging Thames Path, the 268 mile, rugged Pennine Way that follows the jagged north-south backbone of England, and the 192 mile coast-to-coast walk from the Irish Sea to Robin Hood's Bay in the North Sea, to mention only a few. The maps of these routes are detailed and accurate, accommodation is plentiful and there are pubs all along the way to satisfy the hungriest runner with a steak and ale pie and a pint of Guinness.

In the months after returning from the Namib, and having decided to fully inhabit my life, I set out to run myself into a long-distance delirium. I entered races almost every weekend. When not racing, I lost myself along the South West Coast path, or some other long-distance trail. I would run all weekend long, carrying only a little tent and a Spartan backpack of necessities, wild-camping my way across England, and taking a train back to London just in time for work on a Monday.

I was so in love with the trails that I wished I had multiple bodies so that I could run and run and participate in every race simultaneously.

Thoughts of Billy waned and eventually disappeared.

Feeling as if I could never grow tired again, I entered my first Ironman[24] from a zero-experience triathlon-virgin cold start. It was a foolhardy bet with a friend that saw me buy a road bike and take some swimming lessons. Within six months, I was lining up for the tough Ironman course in Wales. Within a month, I did another Ironman in Barcelona, and a week after that, I helped a friend across the rain-soaked moors on her first South Downs 160 mile, 48-hour adventure race.

Over the next 40 days, I won the hilly and demanding Pembrokeshire Coast 78.6 miler, ran a personal best at the Greensands Dorking Marathon, and leopard-crawled my way through my first Spartan mud race for a podium position in the elite race, all while sitting my third-year Psychology exams, taking a blitz business trip to South Africa, and starting a small adventure business in Greece.

I felt unstoppable.

---

24 An Ironman triathlon is one of a series of races organised by the World Triathlon Corporation, comprising a 4km swim, immediately followed by a 180km bicycle ride and a 42km run. It is widely considered to be one of the toughest one-day sporting events in the world. Visit www.ironman.com (Accessed: 7 July 2021)

Some of my peers warned me to slow down. Others asked me: "What are you running from?" But such admonishments and questions were poorly aimed arrows in the dark. After healing from my divorce, I was running with gusto towards the exuberance of living life in top gear. Somehow, my life force had plugged into a giant Robo-cop-like Transformer that had hit on a seam of uranium. My energy surged bigger than me, beyond me. The more I took on, the more strength I gained.

I participated in so many races that I can't even remember them all, but some do stand out in the flat landscape of memory. Some races change one forever, because in doing them, one acquires new wisdom – a visceral, physical intelligence that becomes part of one's soul. That happened to me at the inaugural winter Dorking Nuts Challenge of 2013. I learned how far I was willing to go, and that it was further than I had ever imagined.

Dorking Nutter, 2013

Who could possibly imagine that a race by the colloquial name of Dorking Nutter could rank, as measured by the number of withdrawals, as one of the toughest endurance challenges in Europe? The race caught me by complete surprise, as it did 95% of the participants who started but never completed the race course.

The obstacle race craze had hit the UK, with global franchise offerings like Tough Mudder and Spartan races dominating the scene. The Nuts Challenge is a local race held near the small town of Dorking, just outside London. The race website presents vignettes of people of all shapes and sizes: Hen-party groups of ladies with manicured nails and mascara on perfect lashes; shirtless, muscular studs leaping across obstacles, and corporate teams, slightly out of shape and in matching, branded shirts, all laughing and rolling about in muddy trenches. There was not a trace of terror or trauma in those promotional snapshots. To reflect reality, the organisers should have included a few pictures of people being carried off the course on stretchers.

The race came in four offerings: A single lap of 8km, a double lap of 16km, a triple of 24km, and a four-lap 28km monster, advertised as "Tough Nuts". I phoned a doctor friend, a wild-camping, ready-for-anything adventure buddy from South Africa who had moved to the UK years before me. We had known each other for more than 20 years and we made a good team.

"Lizelle, do you want to come spectate? It will be fun." I foolishly promised to finish the 28km course in under three hours.

I should have looked more closely at the race statistics. The world obstacle race champion, Jonathan Albon, holds the Tough Nuts Summer course record of 2 hours, 51 minutes. That is an exceedingly long time for 28km. The reason for this is the brutal nature of the course. Of a single-lap circuit, only 10% is runnable, with the remaining 90% comprising leopard-crawling, vertical wall-climbing, bog-swimming, mud-wading and kilometre upon kilometre of icy river-forging.

The winter course is a different beast altogether. There is nothing, but nothing I fear more than being cold. While the desert turns my body into a veritable running machine, cold reduces me to a mournful ball of misery. It so happened that 2013 was the coldest winter recorded by the MET office in the history of England. By late February, the Earth had lost all memory of heat. The days were short and the sun, a meek, blue-yellow haze in the unrelenting, grey iciness.

On the morning of the Nuts Challenge, the mercury had barely risen to 3°C and was forecast to drop even further during the day.

I have great difficulty running in long sleeves, or wearing much clothing in general. I prefer to be as naked as the ambient temperature and social context allow. Minutes before the race start, I discarded my thick fleece trousers, multiple upper layers, gloves, beanie and scarf and stood shivering at the startline wearing only small running shorts and a vest. There were about 300 of us braving the cold. I was surrounded by fierce-looking, square-chinned men.

"Where are the fun-loving office teams?" I wondered, feeling a little anxious.

The gun fired.

We ran out hard, leaped clear over the first farm gate, and immediately ducked low under a roof of barbed wire to crawl for 100m across the gritty, icy mud, sheering off every bit of skin on our elbows and knees. I was already shivering and trying to calm myself, imagining that real soldiers also had to contend with the enemy firing at them.

Muddy from head to toe, we scrambled and slipped across a 5m-high mound of rubber tyres, up into high, vertical shoulder-width pipes, scratching and trampling each other as we climbed up and up into the dark. On the other side, we tumbled down a giant cargo net, trying to not break an arm or leg. The obstacles followed one after another so fast that they became a blur of disbelief.

"This is a fun race?" I grumbled to the guy beside me as we clambered into the sky, up a web of tyres, from where we leaped into an icy pool of brown mud far below, and sunk so deep that we never found the bottom.

I moved steadily forward among the horde of groaning and grunting, zombie-like, mud-covered creatures who crawled out of muddy pools and swung across wide trenches on monkey ropes. Some swung too short and landed with sickening thuds on the gritty edges, before sliding back into the mud pools with walls too sheer to climb. People flopped about like hapless fish, grasping and crawling, somehow making their way up a 5m-high vertical wall, only to be faced at the summit with a set of two fireman's type sliding poles, rudely positioned a whole metre away from the platform.

Incredulous people crowded at the top, somehow resisting the clear fact that one had to leap at the pole in an act of sheer hope. The man next to me leaped, missed and landed two storeys below with a nauseating crack. The medics rushed in. Then there were more cargo nets and more lakes of mud. Some mud pools were latticed with wooden beams set half a metre apart and a few inches above the mud, forcing one to take a deep breath and go under to forge forward blindly in the thick, cold sludge and come out the other side gasping, just to go under again and again for a good 100m. That seemed to be the most popular point for spectators. As we surfaced, blind and half-drowned, we were met by the cheers and incredulous laughter of supporters who had by then, like us racers, begun to doubt the sanity of the race organisers.

The next section had us racing through a makeshift Vietnam jungle-village that was obscured by suffocating teargas.

"God? Seriously?" I thought and noticed that by then all laughter among the racers had subsided.

At the 5km mark, the course dropped right into a quick-flowing river, sacrificing us into its waist-deep icy embrace for more than a kilometre.

Racers cursed and stumbled forward, twisting their ankles on the loose river stones, only to exit the river and face a blue-cold swim across a wide lake. Then there were more cargo nets and another long stretch of leopard-crawling – that time with fine buckshot being fired at just more than half a metre above us, to ensure that we stayed low. That was followed by a 10m-long, coccyx-cracking, soap-covered slide into a deep mud pool. We crawled out the other end, bent beneath heavy truck tyres, as we dragged ourselves up and down three steep army barrack hills to the final 500m, heart-stopping lake crossing, across a set of floating lilos, and then onwards to the finish line of the first 8km circuit.

I was frozen to the bone and shell-shocked by the extremity of the course. It seemed unfathomable that I still had another three laps to go. Lizelle held a banana aloft for me to grab as I entered the second loop. She had a look of equal parts hilarity and worry on her face. Who could have possibly taken those mud-smeared athletes seriously? It was also clear that the day was taking a distressing turn. The medics were already attending to several cases of hypothermia. I shoved the mud-smeared banana into my mouth and set out hard and fast for the 8km hell of freezing mud and ball-busting obstacles that lay beyond.

Along the route, medics were attending to the fallen. At every turn I passed shivering, human mud-heaps wrapped in silver emergency blankets. By the time I came out of the second loop, the temperature had plummeted to 0°C.

"Are you okay, Bokkie?" Lizelle asked as I came through. She was one tough lady, having completed her medical training at Baragwanath Hospital, where doctors learn to toughen up and face the most traumatic medical emergencies with poise.

"People are being airlifted out of here," she offered as a way out, in case I was thinking about withdrawing. A chopper took off for the nearest military hospital.

I crammed another banana into my mouth, blue-lipped, shivering, and desperate. "God I would give anything for coffee. Can you get me something for the next round?"

But there was no coffee, only the inevitability of the third loop and my greatest fear of dying from the cold. I am African, Antipodean, and inescapably sun-powered. I suffer from severe Raynaud's Syndrome, which means that at the slightest sign of cold, when, for example, I take a tomato from the fridge, I lose all blood and feeling in my hands and suffer excruciating pain and corpse-pale fingers.

At the start of the third lap of Tough Nuts, my hands had become angry-black-and-blue and swollen, as if frostbitten. I had the clearest admonition from my body: "You are failing. This is dangerous. Do something." I cast a glance around, found a discarded emergency blanket and wrapped it around my stomach.

"I must keep my organs warm. I must just keep moving," I thought, and pushed on through the cold mud.

At half-way into the third round, I realised that apart from the shivering marshals, I was almost alone on the course. Where were the 300 warriors who had started out with me?

At the start of the fourth lap, I found Lizelle, statuesque but shivering, at the food station. She was fighting her own battle.

"Go, Bokkie!" she cheered through chattering teeth.

It seemed impossible. Another loop loomed.

In the distance, I saw one stoic racer digging deep and heading out on the final lap. Emergency blankets littered the deserted, mud-gouged course. It was like a scene from Armageddon. Racers had abandoned their food stashes. I grabbed a protein bar, a packet of jelly babies and two unclaimed bananas from the table. My body was on the brink of plummeting into hypothermia. Unashamedly, I wrapped a silver foil blanket around my head. Pieces of torn emergency blanket protruded from my mud-covered shorts and shirt. It was macabre. I set out on the fourth lap, a brown-and-silver-shimmering creature, crawling my way over and under obstacle after obstacle, along a completely deserted course, propelled forward by nothing but the brute will to persevere.

By the time I finished the race, the temperature had dropped to –5°C. The commentator welcomed me into the deserted finish strait: "First lady ever to finish the inaugural Winter Tough Nuts!"

Lizelle and the last remaining medic cheered. It was bizarre.

Of the 160 people who had started on the three- and four-lap challenges, only 13 finished. I was the only lady among the Tough Nuts, and I staggered across the frozen finish line in fifth place overall.

That obscure, local, fun mud race forever changed my perception of myself as an endurance racer. I now understand that my will is stronger than my fear of pain, and that I have the power to stay the course if my heart is in it. This single insight has made me brave in life. It has given me the courage to start, whether a race, a business, a relationship, or a dream, despite the fear that is always present in beginnings. But there was an even deeper insight: I understood how powerful it is to set oneself a goal, and how the goal pulls one forward across the jagged edge of endurance. I understood that as human beings, we are as naturally drawn to goals as birds are to the air. We are autotelic in spirit – we need pursuit to experience our lives as worth living.

I also understood that there is a self-fulfilling potentiality in setting a clear intention, in committing to a goal, and that once one sets out on a clear path, unforeseen things happen to support one's journey.

Scottish mountaineer William Hutchinson Murray understood this all too well. Inspired by thousands of hours of mountain experience and by author Wolfgang Goethe, he wrote:

"Until one is committed, there is hesitancy, the chance to draw back, always ineffectiveness ... There is one elementary truth: that the moment one definitely commits oneself, then Providence moves too... Whatever you can do or dream you can, begin it. Boldness has genius, power and magic in it."[25]

Over the years I have experienced over and over again that the real goal, and the deepest work, is to lift our energetic state into congruence, into love, bestowing blessing, awe, forgiveness, hope, faith, discipline, commitment and deep belief. When we do, we are like giant magnets that attract and direct the energies of the universe to flow into the clear formations of our hopes and dreams.

At the end of 2013, the electromagnetic superstorm of my life was inexorably drawing a French girl towards me. Recently single, she responded to my message on Guardian Soulmates, one of the UK's more discerning dating sites. Her name was Sabelle.

---

25 Murray, W.H. *The Scottish Himalayan Expedition*, Dent, London, 1951.

Ma belle, Sabelle

I met Sabelle on the evening of a work Christmas function for a quick drink at a bar near our offices. Her lips were full, and her hair fell in soft, dark waves around high cheekbones and perfect complexion. She was as near a classic French beauty as one would ever find. Our eyes wandered each other. Her cheeks became flushed with wine. One glass became two as we shared our stories. She was a mom to a beautiful 10-year-old boy, an archer, a purveyor of excellence, avoider of discomfort, servant to pleasure, and wholly aimed at the Epicurean life. She was my opposite.

Wanting to stretch the little sliver of time we had together, we shared a taxi to my Christmas function. Sabelle cheek-kissed me goodbye. I leaned in and kissed her on the mouth, gently and just briefly. There was a jolt – the fissures in the Earth opened. Her lower lip – I tasted its cracks, its softness, full and dry from red wine. The neon signs on every building flickered and surged. That evening, I floated all the way to my seat at the CEO's table, high on the most powerful drug on Earth.

Sabelle, the urban navigator of navigators, left for home and got hopelessly lost on the street. Once on the Tube, she missed her station. She reported via text message that such a thing had never happened to her. Sabelle and I had stepped into the boat of our highest hopes, and we rowed hard towards love. We were a pretty bird and a dolphin, entranced by each other and as in love as we were fatefully incompatible.

Our romance unfolded in the lavender-and-thyme-scented fields of Provence, under the cypress trees and blue skies of Van Gogh's paintings. During long afternoon siestas in her parents' stone-walled villa, we rested together behind blue, wooden shutters. Outside, heat-roused cicadas shrilled beneath the harsh sun and fat, purple figs burst open from their own sweetness.

In the early evenings we would wash and dress for aperitifs with her family: Summer dresses, dainty sandals, mascara and perfume. Sabelle brushed her curls in a way I could never forget. Every evening we emerged from our quarters; Ma belle, Sabelle, grand on my arm. Even her conservative parents smiled at seeing their daughter in the full blush of love, and entirely ceased mourning Sabelle's divorce from a wealthy and loving ex-husband.

How I loved her son. Christian and I bonded early on. In Provence, we would sometimes take his grandad's BB-gun into the fields to hunt. We never shot anything – nor really intended to. He was the sweetest child, and the three of us lived happily in the early days of our love cocoon.

I ran less and less, and I didn't care. Not at first.

West Wind #2

"There is life without love. It is not worth a bent penny, or a scuffed shoe. It is not worth the body of a dead dog nine days unburied."

MARY OLIVER[26]

26 Oliver, M. 'West Wind #2', *West Wind*, Mariner Books, 1998.

5

CALL OF THE WILD, 1989 - PRESENT

"He loved to run in the dim twilight of the summer midnights, listening to ... the sleepy murmurs of the forest, reading signs and sounds as a man may read a book, seeking the mysterious something that called ... waking or sleeping... for him to come."

JACK LONDON, *THE CALL OF THE WILD*[27]

My life in the UK involved more than running and love – there were also the matters of earning a living and paying off a mortgage. I worked in finance, in the chrome-and-steel belly of London's banking industry.

I had arrived there by the most unlikely career path imaginable.

Trading the outdoors for the office

I did well at school and earned a bursary to study Engineering. It seemed a safe career choice – it offered jobs and the prospect of earning a good living. However, I soon realised that I had chosen a career that would, for me, become a downward spiral of unhappiness.

My first vacation job incarcerated me in the small town of Sasolburg, with its industrial plants in a hellhole of concrete and chemical smoke. My second vacation job was even worse. I was the only female intern. My boss, who wore crotch-tight, shiny trousers that hitched up over his hairy

27 London, J. *The Call of the Wild*, Arcturus Publishing Limited, 1903.

ankles, and shirts unbuttoned to his pecks, had a centrefold of a naked woman pinned behind his office door, as if it were the most normal thing in the world. He wouldn't allow me to perform the same tasks as the young male interns. "Too dangerous for a woman," he would say, perhaps out of genuine concern.

Unable to stomach either the patriarchal sexism or the chemical fumes, I ran away, far, far away from Stellenbosch. The very name of that university town conjures up heartbreak. To my shock and disbelief, I had fallen hopelessly in love with my roommate – a girl – a blue-blood straight who was earmarked to bear blue-blood children for her eminent family line.

She was my first love – and I knew right from the start that I could never tell her what I felt. When she fell in love with a beautiful boy, with long, blonde sun-kissed curls and an even surfer's tan – and brought him over for the night – I knew I had to leave before my silence shattered, along with my heart.

I had a loyal friend. His name was Kent and he never denied me any wish. Kent and I scraped together a total travel budget of R700[28] and struck out north, heading into Africa without a map or a plan.

We zig-zagged our way across the southern African interior, mostly hitching rides with fleets of transport trucks. In return for passage and sometimes a meal, we guarded the trucks against marauding thieves at night. Kent was a large, burly man, good for defending spare wheels, and I was good for sleeping tucked beneath the vulnerable engine belly.

I told my mom that we were headed for Malawi, but once we got there, we just kept going. I had no idea how far I would have to travel to outrun my heartache and confusion. I didn't think I would ever go back home, and Kent faithfully followed me deeper into the hinterland.

Eventually, we had hitchhiked all the way from Cape Town to Lamu, a strange, otherworldly island on the Kenya-Somalia border. We had travelled 8 000km while sleeping rough and living on scraps, without a single thought of how we would get home.

---

28 In 1992, R700 was the cost of renting a small single, unfurnished room for a month in Stellenbosch.

In Lamu, we came to rest for New Year's Eve. Kent and I danced to *No woman, no cry.* His heart was as broken as mine. We had also spent the last of our money. Perhaps we would have found jobs and stayed, or perhaps I would have married Kent, but fate rolled a different dice. In December 1992, there was a botched general election and large-scale unrest in Kenya. Foreigners were advised to evacuate. Our return journey was a blur of diesel trucks, hunger and the random kindness of people along the way, who kept us fed and safe from harm through Kenya, Tanzania, Zambia, Zimbabwe and finally home to South Africa.

I never returned to the anguish of silently living alongside my roommate, or to the industrial job environment that I had fled. Providence moved, and on our way back home, a land surveyor gave us our final lift into Cape Town.

He described his career as: "The most wonderful job you can imagine! You are outdoors all day, often in remote places that you can only get to by 4x4, or on foot. The work is mostly taking measurements and doing calculations – lots of physics and math and physical challenge. Not many women do it." I was instantly hooked.

Being a cadastral surveyor was the most romantic job imaginable. A surveyor, at any moment in time and space, is able to triangulate themself to the last millimetre exactly where they find themselves in this great, big universe. A surveyor is a theodolite-armed magician who can, with the help of old, musty maps and elegant trigonometry, point to the earth and say: "Dig there," to uncover property boundary markers that have been buried centuries before by people long dead.

I so loved the outdoor nature of that intellectually stimulating, quixotic and physically demanding discipline that two years later, I graduated with Honours.

In my subsequent compulsory internship year, I worked at a small, family-owned surveying firm in Stellenbosch. The fact that they had hired a female intern was progressive, but in daily practice, my old-school bosses struggled to send out a young woman all alone into the veld with a 4x4 and a team of workmen. I spent many frustrating days at the office, relegated to admin and menial tasks.

On the occasions I did get to go surveying, I loved my job and my life, because my days were spent outdoors. But those elated opportunities were too few and far between. Financially, I was bent double beneath multiple student loans while scraping by on less-than-minimum wage, without any clear pathway for my situation to change in the near future.

My mom, who saw into the beyond with the astuteness of a clairvoyant, sent me a job post that she had found in a newspaper. "They are looking for 'something different, someone eclectic'," she said, knowing that I needed and would almost certainly get that job.

I competed the application forms somewhat reluctantly – a day too late, even – not knowing the firm, and not realising that I was about to be granted the opportunity of a lifetime. That seemingly small event held within it an energy that unexpectedly twisted my lifepath in a bizarre fashion towards an entirely new destination – and gradually further and further away from the outdoors.

A letter of invitation arrived – for an interview – and before long I was drawn into a battery of sessions for a position with Bain & Company, one of the top three strategy consulting houses in the world.

On the day of my interview, I arrived at the posh glass-and-chrome Cape Town office, fresh from an off-site job where we had surveyed all day, still dressed in steel-tip boots and khaki shorts. My peers were smartly collared and suited, and my interviewer was dressed in Armani, three-piece elegance.

From veld to city

Despite the unlikeliness of the fit, I was offered the job – in Johannesburg and far away from the life-giving ocean of Cape Town. In 1996, I swapped my steel-tip boots for heels and traded the great outdoors for 16-hour days in the office.

I found myself among a peer group of ambitious high-performers from the top universities in the world, and I was suddenly sucked up into the glitz and glamour of big-business strategy consulting and everything that went with it. The learning curve was stellar, and the opportunities for growth and career exposure were beyond anything I could ever have imagined. Within two months, I had been catapulted from the veld to the executive boardrooms of South Africa's most powerful banks, presenting strategic proposals to their CEOs and their executive teams. It was surreal.

Suddenly I was travelling regularly – internationally – to the posh playgrounds of Chelsea in London and Martha's Vineyard in the United States for training, and to Mauritius and Paris as vacation rewards for work well done. My salary increased 10-fold.

But despite appearances, it was not the life I had imagined. Unbeknown to anyone, I suffered what felt like indoor panic attacks, every day crushing myself into a suit, and under the fluorescent glare, like an anxious rat in an experiment, comfort-eating at my desk while pining for sunlight. I experienced the soul-obliterating stress of being a square peg in a round hole, and suffered such extreme exhaustion that once a day I would lock myself in the ladies' toilets and pass out on the cold, tile floor.

I became clinically depressed. My health deteriorated, and every few months I came down with a bad cold or the flu. The truth was that my body and soul were pining for the outdoors and for clean living – for less of everything: Less glitz, less performance pressure and less killer stress.

The year I started working for Bain, Princess Anastacia winged into my life like a God-sent angel. She held me steady as I sailed too close to the winds of a nervous breakdown.

The official burn-out tenure for top-tier consulting is pegged at 2.3 years; but recognising the once-in-a-lifetime opportunity to boost my career on to an elevated trajectory, I stuck it out for as long as I could. Finally, after three-and-a-half years, I stepped off the gangplank.

In 1999, with Princess Anastacia by my side, we relocated back to the salt-and-kelp smell of Cape Town so that I could complete my MBA beneath the green-and-granite hem of Table Mountain. I lived with Princess Anastacia in a one-room bachelor flat overlooking the shimmering Atlantic. It was a happy year full of learning and physical wellness – a year of reprieve from the concreted life we had lived in Johannesburg.

Right outside our door sprawled 20km of the most spectacular coastal promenade in the world. It was impossible to resist the urge to roam along that glittering coastline. Two or three times a week, I managed a 5km jog. It was the beginning.

I could have stayed there forever, as a student living on the bare minimum and at the foot of the salty sea with my princess. Yet, even if it seemed that we had all we needed, at the end of my studies, driven by the momentum of success, we moved back to Johannesburg where an abundance of attractive career opportunities beckoned.

I made the most of my first opportunity in corporate: I was hired by a former client, one of South Africa's big four banks. I worked hard, and early on in my appointment, I was set on a fast-track talent development path for new leaders. I was 29 years old and the future looked promising.

A nature boost

But something was missing: I was longing for the great outdoors-and-running-induced vitality that I had experienced in Cape Town. It was therefore no surprise that during that time I fell headlong into the full-body nature immersion of adventure racing. It helped to counter the long hours at the bank.

And it brought me Billy.

Together, Billy and I swapped restaurants for mountains, and gradually lost all interest in wine and late nights out. My life cleaned up spectacularly, and five years later, in 2006, I reached the pinnacle of adventure racing when I competed in the World Championships in New Zealand.[29]

Both work and sport were powerful anvils that changed me over time – and for the better. I learned the emancipating truth that we are not fixed, that our DNA and backgrounds are not our destiny; that we can change, and that, with hard work, we are capable of remaking and rewiring ourselves, almost any which way.

I was happy in life, sport and work and had no desire to leave South Africa, yet there was an alluring invitation: A few years abroad was a blank slate on which both Billy and I could remould and remake our lives. There was the promise of the unknown, the liminal where anything could happen. We took the bet.

---

29 The Adventure Racing World Championships covered 500km of wilderness terrain, which participants had to navigate on foot, by bicycle and by kayak, over five days and five nights with almost no sleep.

I resigned from my adventure racing team and we both quit our jobs. We sold all we had until there were only a few crates of sentimentalities, two suitcases of clothing in storage, and two bicycles remaining, the latter which we stripped down to their barest, simplest parts for a six-month journey through South East Asia. We bought a pair of hair clippers and shaved our long, wavy auburn and blonde locks right to the skull – for ease of travel.

For six, extravagant months, we were as free as two tumbleweeds. We lived on $2 a day and spent 8 to 12 hours in the saddle, day after day – and all of it in the great, glorious outdoors, under the tropical sky and swaying palms, and freer than either of us had ever been in our lives. Eat – ride – sleep – repeat.

Yet, to our great surprise, towards the end of six months, the unbridled freedom turned into a feeling of irrelevance. We were perpetual observers, watching others live their lives. We both craved jobs, community, somewhere to belong, routine, and even a mortgage.

So, in 2007, after our cycling journey, Billy and I were ready to settle and work and we moved to London to build our wedded life there – and failed. Our relationship ended because we simply didn't try hard enough. We were too young and foolish to recognise what we had, and so gave up too quickly when we encountered the disagreements and steep conflicts any relationship inevitably has to scale.

Three years later, when everything was lost, we went our separate ways to find solace. Billy became a British middle-distance triathlon champion, and I began a life-long love affair with long-distance trail running.

Perhaps our paths had to fork in that way, because after Billy, my running and my career took off like never before. My racing vigour fed my work, and vice versa. Success in one gave momentum to the other.

Snowy Davos

In London, I worked alongside extraordinary and powerful people – with CEOs and top executives, and the chairmen and board of a gigantic and global FTSE100 organisation. Those leaders shaped and inspired me to think big, to step forward, and to lead with conviction. They made me bold.

Halfway through my 10-year UK career, and at about the time I met Sabelle, I knocked on my CEO's door late one afternoon. He listened attentively, looking out across the sprawl of the Thames River, as I outlined my thoughts on building deep corporate consciousness and sustainability-thinking into our core strategy. It was a progressive move for business at that time, and doing so would make us a leader in our industry.

A few weeks later, I was appointed Head of Sustainability Strategy for our global group of businesses. The job was exhilarating. It gave me a deep sense of purpose and presented me with opportunities beyond my wildest dreams.

In 2015, I accompanied our group CEO and chairman to the World Economic Forum[30] in magical, snowy-white Davos. It was an extraordinary experience to share the space of that small, Alpine village with about 2 500 of some of the most influential people in the world.

Sabelle was beyond herself with pride, and at every opportunity mentioned that I was away in Davos.

Canary in a cage

I was inspired, committed to, and on fire for my London job, but there was one fatal problem: I still had to brace myself every day to survive the 8-10 hours of artificial indoor lighting and the concreted separation from Nature.

To survive the indoor panic of the London office, I commuted mostly by bike and, whenever I could, I stood barefoot at my desk, even long before standing desks or barefoot shoes became a thing. I also took frequent natural-light breaks away from the deadening fluorescent glare, where my desk sat at the centre of an open-plan nightmare.

Throughout my office-bound career, I had thought that I was alone in my intense body-need to be out in Nature, but I was wrong. I was

30 The World Economic Forum is the international organisation for public-private co-operation. The Forum engages the foremost political, business, cultural and other leaders of society to shape global, regional and industry agendas.

simply the canary in the cage[31] – perhaps with a fraction greater indoor-sensitivity than my peers. We all need time in Nature[32] to settle our hearts and overworked adrenals into a more peaceful rhythm.

And even more so, the children.

In his book, *Last Child in the Woods,*[33] Richard Louv diagnoses our children with nature-deficit disorder, and shows how 21st century children's rapidly increasing obesity, attention deficit disorder and depression are linked directly to spending less and less time outdoors. The tragedy of our time is that the path back to the wilds is rapidly fading for our children. Without this, how could they ever be well or whole, or be proficient guardians of our blue planet?

Over time, I experienced that running out in Nature not only supported my physical and mental wellbeing, but it also gave me a remarkable mental advantage. The more I ran, the better I did at work. Every big, creative and transformative idea I ever had in 20 years of work came to me not at my desk, but out there somewhere under the wide, open sky, and with some trail, or the blessing of the riverside Thames Path, beneath my feet.

That is what I discovered through running – that there is an intelligence in the body that has a logic and a source-truth of its own; that in the hotbed of action, and often just fresh from the arena, when we are still panting and sweating, we are directly connected into a primal place of knowing that is more potent than ideas or words.

This is not a new idea. Rumi, the revered Sufi mystic, wrote: *"More intelligent than intellect, and more spiritual than spirit... the throbbing vein will take you further than any thinking."*[34]

In my final year with Billy, I had enrolled for a degree in Psychology, which I then completed in 2014. However, I found it wanting. It did not provide the answers I was seeking. The science concerned itself with

31 Miners would carry a canary in a cage down with them into the mines. If dangerous gases were present, the canary would die long before the miners and alert them to exit the mine.

32 Nature therapy is now prescribed as a treatment for stress. In Japan, businessmen regularly go on facilitated 'forest-bathing' retreats to regain their edge.

33 Louv, R. *Last Child in the Woods: Saving our children from nature-deficit disorder,* Algonquin Books, 2008.

34 Body Intelligence, *The Essential Rum,* Coleman Barks, p 151, HarperCollins 1995.

curing mental illness rather than improving mental wellness. It didn't pilot a way for how to move from 0–10 on the scale of life. When the student is ready, the teacher appears. In mid-2014, a month after completing my Psychology degree, I enrolled for a two-year Masters degree in Applied Positive Psychology at the University of East London in the UK.

Sabelle clasped her hands to her head and said: "Ah no, *Mon Coeur*! Not another thing!".

I did the best I could with the scarce hours between work, commuting, training and studying, but both of us felt the pinch of too little time, and it became a contested resource in our relationship. If only we had shared the thirst for running, or if only I had been able to stay still long enough to become an archer. If only. Beyond the sweet kisses and family holidays in Provence, there was no seam of overlap in our lives.

In the midnight hours that were left, I read voraciously, and throughout it all began to sense what Einstein meant when he said: "The greatest gift is to get lost in the mysteries of existence." Einstein believed in God. "I believe in Spinoza's God, who reveals himself in the orderly harmony of what exists," he said.

And it was in Nature, especially in the vast, awe-inspiring wilderness, where this orderly harmony spoke to me most clearly. The outdoors drew me like the moon draws the tides.

Towards a vocation – call of the wild

Somewhere in the quantum field of energetic possibility, a vocation began to mould around my own struggle and seeking. My indoor discomfort shaped into the keenest yearning to call people back to the wild – to someplace where one can smell the wild grass, be with the wind in the trees, and bask beneath the life-giving sun; to a place without highways and high-rises, where one can still see far and hear only the heart-soothing sounds of Nature. My yearning was especially strong for children – to call them back to their birthright of a relationship with the forests and the veld. In 2012, two years after Billy, and after I had begun trail running, and a year before I met Sabelle, I had planted the first seedlings of a small, new business – not in the UK, but on the magical, olive-tree-covered, silver-shimmering island of Lesvos, Greece.

Alongside my full-time London job, Teach a Girl to Fish was born as my part-time work of love and passion. Its purpose? To help people rekindle their connection to Nature.

"Your work is to discover your work and then with all your heart to give yourself to it."

BUDDHA

6

TEACH A GIRL TO FISH, GREECE, 2014

"Everybody needs beauty as well as bread, places to play in and pray in, where nature may heal and give strength to body and soul."

JOHN MUIR

Greece. There is something about it. One can't quite put a finger on it. It could be the brilliant, bright quality of the light, or the endless, blue-glittering Aegean Sea. It could be the silver iridescence of the endless olive groves, or the Greek songs and dance filling the village squares with an ancient and nameless longing. Perhaps it is in the ouzo, the fresh fish and the dense sheep's milk feta that smells of wild herbs, and the feasts of good food late into the night. Perhaps it is the olive-skinned Greek women and their beautiful men. Whatever it is, Greece has a quality, a soul, that steadily and imperceptibly steals one's heart.

Greece moves one to poetry. It stirs the wild, free life within. Her music propels the late-night Greek dancers on and on into the early hours of morning, enabling great feats of endurance, fed by a great fires of love, passion and patriotism.

In the same manner, the love of Greece quickened the feet of Greece's Yiannis Kouros, the greatest ultra-runner of all time. In 1983, he ran the fearsome 246km Spartathlon from Athens to Sparta and set a world record in just under 21 hours.

Spartathlon: The race of races, inspired by the epic run of Pheidippides, a Greek messenger who ran from Athens to Sparta in 2000BC, to beg the

Spartan's help in war. It is the stuff dreams are made of: A garish nightmare of a non-stop race of six marathons back-to-back, run in September when the temperature in Athens reach upward of 30°C. It has an inhuman cut-off time of 36 hours, with all 3 000m of elevation gain occurring after the 100km mark, crushing even the most valiant racers with a monster 1 000m climb at the 150km mark. To qualify for entry, one must complete a 100km race in less than 10.5 hours. Only 400 entrants are allowed, and of these, more than 70% will not finish. It is without doubt the toughest race in the world. It killed Pheidippides.

Yiannis ran it three times after his record, thus recording the four fastest Spartathlon times ever logged. His world record of 20 hours, 25 minutes still stands almost 40 years after he set it. It is nearly two hours faster than that of world champion ultra-running phenomenon Scott Jurek.

In addition, Yiannis holds a staggering number of ultra-distance world records. He is the fastest man alive over 100 miles, 1 000km and 1 000 miles. He holds the world record for the furthest distances run in 12 hours, 24 hours, 48 hours and six-day events.

Sport scientists have studied his training approach, diet and race strategy, but have found nothing out of the ordinary. He is vegan, as is Scott Jurek. He sleeps only four to six hours a night, rarely runs more than 12 miles at a time, sometimes twice a day, and no more than 80 miles a week.

Perhaps the scientists were looking in the wrong place. When asked about his phenomenal performances Yiannis said: "It is simple. When I get tired, I tell my body that it is not tired and then it just keeps going."

Yiannis appears to have found the trapdoor to ultimate endurance and endless resources of energy in his love of running. He revels in the long distances – the longer the better. He does not wish for it to end and he does not fight the miles. He has found a way to love the pain.

The fire that motivates his superhuman performances is of a poetic nature. The way he rises to the inhuman demands of super-long distances is by completely disregarding his competition, and by disassociating from the pain by composing music and poetry as he runs. Every race is as much an artistic feat as it is a physical one.

If one watches race footage, one will see Yiannis running alongside a support vehicle, the car's speakers blaring passionate Hellenic songs of valour and bravery. Yiannis runs tall and broad-chested, propelled by a force far greater than the will to succeed. He is driven by a raw and fierce love for Greece, and for beauty. In his inner eye, he is Pheidippides running to Sparta. He is the timeless hero running to save his motherland.

I understand Yiannis Kouros and the love and music that fuels his running. I have two songs that fill my heart that way – the deep rhythm-and-drum of Africa, and the sweet bouzouki songs played at night in the village square of Lesvos, the other heartland of my soul – the island where I run Teach a Girl to Fish kayaking trips.

The island of Lesvos is an unsung darling of Greece. She is a secret beauty, a gleaming green-and-silver jewel tucked into the protective crook of Turkey's north-west coast. The Greeks say that once you have been to Lesvos, you will always return to her shores. She will call you back with sweet memories of simple, inexplicable joy. Every year, Panayiotis collects me from the airport. Every year, he reminds me how Lesvos compares to the other Greek islands: "Santorini, Mykonos – they are like a beautiful woman who spends many hours getting ready in front of the mirror. Men want to be with her; and they have to pay – a lot! But when you get close to her, you see she has nothing. *Tipota!* Lesvos is the girl who puts her hair in a ponytail, pulls on sneakers and tracksuit pants; you don't notice her. Oh, but when you get close, then you notice. She has everything!"

Lesvos is the third biggest island in Greece. It shimmers beneath a covering of silver olive groves and has the highest density of olive trees per square metre in the world. It is the birthplace of great poets and writers, laureate-nominated and Nobel prize-winners like Stratis Myrivilis and Odysseus Elytis, the latter who said of Lesvos: *"Nowhere, in no other spot on Earth, do the Sun and the Moon reign so harmoniously, do they share their powers so justly, as on this piece of Earth … I speak of the island which, when later peopled, was called Lesvos."*

Her beauty stirs the soul and moves the pen. Eden of the east, all of Lesvos is a secret that she reveals only to those who draw near – not as tourists, but as seekers and pilgrims.

On my first visit to the island, I arrived at the tiny, beach-rimmed airport with a dream of escape in my heart. My soul needed wide horizons, and above all, it needed sun and light. I set off by bicycle to circumvent Lesvos, not knowing that I was about to discover my Elim, an interim oasis – somewhere I could flee to escape the clamour of London; its concrete, and loud, secular grasping, and the unremitting entertainment unto death.

It was the beginning of a life-long love affair.

On my bicycle trip, I met Nektarios Paraskevedis, my Greek soulmate – a fellow adventurer and the brother I never had. He lent me a kayak, drew me a map on a napkin, and sent me off on a five-day journey to recce the north coast of Lesvos. I felt like Columbus stepping on to the shores of the New World. I had discovered a soul's paradise and a dream journey for future kayaking trips. With his help, I started Teach a Girl to Fish, a small adventure company that has, for many, served as a means of escape to health and sanity.

Kayaking along the north coast of Lesvos has given me the doorway through which to lead others to the same profound Nature connection that I experienced in long-distance running, but with much less effort and lower hurdles of athleticism. When we embark on a Teach a Girl to Fish trip, we go in small groups of no more than six people, so that we can hear and feel more clearly that which we experience along the way. There is something in the air on that north Coast of Lesvos that inspires reverie and awe. After a day or two on the kayaks, one feels it welling up from deep inside. On the second evening of the trip, standing on the high terrace of Golden Beach Taverna and looking out towards Turkey as the golden-red orb of the sun sinks into the sea, one gets a sense of eternity. My kayaking-companions often fall silent as the first shimmer of lights come on in Turkey – just there, across the thin strip of sea. The Greeks look out with great longing. "*Arnandevo,*" they say, remembering a time when their fellow countrymen were incarcerated in a foreign land by the indifferent machinery of big politics.[35]

Just sitting there fills one's heart with a longing so large that my company of newly-met kayakers are moved from initial shyness to declaring the deepest love and fondness for each other across tables laden with the feasts

35 In the Greek-Turkish conflict of 1919–1923, large numbers of prisoners of war were incarcerated by both countries.

of the sea and the harvest: Firm sardines from Plomari, Greek salads – the tomatoes and cucumbers fresh from Nikos's home garden; olive oil from the local press; homemade feta cheese; courgette flowers stuffed with cheese; beetroot; green beans; grilled aubergine, and local cheese crumbed and deep fried. And ouzo.

"Do you have spinach?"

"No, it is not yet in season says Yannis, the waiter, from beneath his bush of Freddy Mercury hair. Nothing is imported. Every morsel is organic, without effort or pretentiousness.

The ouzo clouds over the ice. The night is young. My kayaking companions have not felt this free, this alive and this new for years. It is what happens after three days of kayaking on the open sea, visiting uninhabited islands, swimming and playing all day, rediscovering our inner children, absent of all self-consciousness.

On these trips, we don't see mirrors for five days at a time. It is a blissful absence; it is a freeing forgetting of the self and of appearances. The sea washes us clean. The salt and the sun brine us. All that remains in the end is the spirit inside, and our connection to each other and the natural world around us.

With each moment, the connection deepens. We are renewed by the shimmering of the sea and the care-free journey; toughened by immersing ourselves in Nature and all of its moods: The high waves and the sometimes howling wind, but mostly we drift peacefully on the mirror-still sea.

The Greeks say: *"Nero san tho ladi."* Water like oil.

Occasionally, we spot dolphins, their smooth backs slipping in and out the crystal-clear water. God is there, in the light and the crystal-patterned reflection of the sun on the white-sand sea bottom.

All along the coast we visit small, Greek churches no bigger than a child's room. They are the places of worship for the fishermen and the herders who visit daily, still praying for protection and good fortune, and for a safe voyage. They are places where the poetry of thanksgiving and awe can spill into a welcoming receptacle. My cup overflows, after being tossed on the Aegean Sea for five days in the company of fellow pilgrims.

After the journey, my kayaking companions all seem to walk 6ft tall. It is a new confidence born in the crucible of action – an affirmed knowing that they can trust themselves. Many gain clarity about problems back home and, over the course of our voyage, gather the necessary courage and momentum to do something about it. Many of my clients have gone home to simplify and unclutter their lives: Some to quit dead-end, soul-crushing jobs, others to move cities, get divorced and get married, and still others to adopt new training regimens or spiritual practices, or at the very least, to ensure that they get out into Nature far more often.

Being out in Nature in this way burns away the accumulated junk of life and strips everything bare until only the essentials remain.

One of my friends said the trip made her realise that her body was not just an aesthetic ornament. "I realised that I could do stuff. My body is strong and able."

Returning home to London, she packed away her handbags, and for six months, strutted the streets of London in flip-flops and cut-off jeans – not because she rejected dressing well and looking grand, but because she felt liberated from the edicts that govern women's appearances.

"I have never felt stronger or freer in my whole life," she said. When winter came, she swapped out for sneakers.

There on the water, everything is stripped down to basics; each of us carrying no more than two shoeboxes-full of belongings. By the end of the five days, even that seem too much, as we stare incredulously at the trolley suitcases we have left at base camp. As the days go by, despite the absence of a clean set of clothing, make-up, brushes or dancing shoes of any form, people become exquisitely beautiful; washed clean of worry, released from the constant wrestling with the self-imposed trance of our appearances never being quite good enough.

"Sea cowgirls!" That's how the local Greeks welcome us as we paddle into the ports of small villages to get supplies or dine at the tavernas. The moment is enough. We all remain in the now without trying to do so. We hope for nothing, we fear nothing. We are free.

I have had the extraordinary privilege of taking people on this life-cleansing journey for 10 years thus far. Many people, like my friend, Aurelia, have been back four or five times. Aurelia says the trips nourish her body and soul.

After one trip, Aurelia said: "I felt empowered because I could actually deal with Nature. I also understood that I don't have to be okay with the status quo – in anything. I can make changes. I'm not stuck in anything – not ever. I am free to do anything I choose. I can live the life I want to live."

In all of my years of working, I had never experienced greater job satisfaction. I held the space. Nature and the people themselves did the work. The Greeks held us safe.

Every year, I fall more deeply in love with Greece, and I feel the Greeks to have become my closest family. Every year I stand at Eftalou Hot Springs, after dipping in and out of the ancient, white-domed, mineral-rich water and into the cold sea, every cell in my body exhilarated and my mitochondria dividing at a million cells a second, realising yet again how much Nature rejuvenates. It is my privilege to take people back there, to reacquaint with Nature in the gentlest way, and to make us fall in love with her all over again. In the process, we heal ourselves.

Every year, after taking the spa, and after a healing massage from Niki or her mom Elefteria, I sit with Elefteria's husband, Phillipe. We sit together, looking out at Turkey, now and again reaching across the English-Greek language barrier. He plays with his komboloi worry beads, the spice of mirth in his eyes. He is a sailor, a man who loves the sea as much as he loves his family. He would give the shirt off his back to anyone who asked. He is proud, beautiful, grey haired, muscular, evenly tanned, and his eyes are bluer than the sea. He calls me "Captain", and the year my father died, he saved me from drowning and held me for the longest time until my tears had run dry. The Greeks are like that. They have not yet forgotten what is important.

In 2014, while running a kayaking trip, I got a text message from my mom: "Please phone home. It's urgent." A cold chill shot though me. My mom never texted like that. I knew in that moment that I had lost either my father or my sister.

Two days earlier, my father had felt so desperately ill that he had packed a small suitcase and driven 150km to the hospital in Mosselbay. I had seen my father three months before on an impromptu business trip to South Africa. We had spent three days together, my dad seconding me while I ran 55km along farm roads. He was always terrified that some harm would come to me, and he chaperoned me on every run, driving 5km and then waiting under some tree, or whatever other shelter he could find, until he could see me. Then he would drive off again and repeat the process for as long and as far as I needed to go. We had great adventures together. He was so proud of me. I never knew what a bastion of support I had in him until it was too late.

The last time I saw him, he looked ancient – suddenly grey and frail, almost translucent. His skin hung on his bones like that of an emaciated old elephant. He complained of painful headaches and a pain in his neck. He said it was probably nothing serious. How did I not see it? Was I blind? How had the doctors misdiagnosed him for what seemed like years? He had full-blown leukaemia. The disease had ravaged his bone marrow and the soft tissue in his bones. When he admitted himself to Mosselbay Hospital, the doctor there diagnosed him and gave him three months to live.

"We are fetching you first thing in the morning. You are coming to stay with us in Cape Town," my mom had said. Together with my sister, she had set plans in motion to drive the 400km to Mosselbay. My mom and dad had been divorced for 20 years, but neither had remarried and their friendship was more beautiful than their marriage had ever been. My father, as reckless and as wild as he was in his youth, became as gentle and as kind with age.

That night, my dad made a last phone call – to tell my mom and sister that he was tired. I think he was telling them that he was leaving. I never got to speak to him. He died in the early hours of the morning. He took his leave like a gentleman, with grace and without becoming the burden that he so feared he would be.

The funeral service was scheduled for five days hence. There was no reason to rush home. My father was gone. I sat overlooking the shimmering Aegean Sea. The shock and grief were so overwhelming and complete that they blotted out every sensation of living. Every thought.

They say that the greatest life stressor is losing someone dear to you to death. There on the Aegean, despite the shock and grief, something else took over. I think it was life.

I continued to lead the kayaking trip for the rest of the week, and the five women on the journey formed a circle of love and care around me.

We kayaked along that serene, olive-tree-covered coast; we swam; we made fire, and we camped and lay out at night, looking at the stars. I wept into the endless, accepting sea, and its salt washed my sorrow.

At the end of the trip, I drove to Skala Eressos in the south of Lesvos. There I climbed a mountain at dusk, up to a small, shepherd's church, and planted a wooden cross for my father. As far as the eye could see, the magnificent Aegean Sea had turned pink and purple. I stayed at his cross until nightfall, remembering, grieving and giving thanks. The Greek stars bore witness. I walked back down the mountain by starlight. There, surrounded by that vast ocean, standing in the full ebb and flow of life, I could not have wished for a better way for my father to take leave of me. I can't imagine anywhere else in the world that could have held me or his memory more tenderly.

The first months after my dad's passing were shrouded in shock, but with time, the reality of his absence solidified and became a body of grief. My GP suggested antidepressants to help me cope. Why would one flatline one's grief? I took the pills for a week, quit, and cried for as long as my heart needed to process that one of the two main ramparts of my life had forever been demolished, that no one would light my father's pipe again or ask about Princess Anastacia and Billy and their whereabouts in the particular way he did. He never met Sabelle, but I know he would have approved. He had an eye for beauty.

Lesvos

Here
on these wide waters
my mind clear of all thought
and in my heart a long song
from which the words have all gone

All that remains
Is the rhythmic refrain
of the ebb and the flow,
the sun's golden glow,
and God's grace as far and as wide as the sea.

7

PUSHING INTO THE RED, UNITED KINGDOM, 2015

"If your dreams don't scare you, they are not big enough."

ELLEN JOHNSON SIRLEAF

Amidst leading kayaking trips in Greece, doing my sustainability work, for which I had a deep passion, loving Sabelle, and my frequent business trips to South Africa, which I relished afresh because of the opportunity to spend time with my mom, I still managed to keep to a decent training schedule.

On weekdays, I did high-intensity strength training at the gym. At lunchtime, I did 30 minutes of all-out bootcamp: Blow-ups of burpees, push-ups and clean-and-presses. In the evenings, I repeated this, before jumping on my bicycle to ride 10km home. Some weekdays, I added a short, slow lunchtime, cobweb-clearing run. On weekends, I packed in two back-to-back long runs of 3.5-5 hours on Saturdays and Sundays – and sometimes six glorious hours of trudging through the driving rain, sleet and icy winter sludge.

Following a relatively low-mileage schedule meant that I was seldom overtrained or injured, and that my love of running remained as fierce as Yiannis Kouros's love of Greece.

I had run many multi-day races, but never more than 100km in one go. I wanted to step across the threshold into the unknown, and the UK calendar offered a prolific choice of races to match my desires. I was inescapably drawn to the beastly distances because they made me giddy with curiosity. I wanted to step into that liminal space to see who I would become when pushing into the red, and then beyond.

ONER is a race that strikes fear into the hearts of the UK's toughest ultra-runners. The event is run by Brutal Events, and is a suffer-fest of three challenging back to back trail marathons along the jagged Jurassic Coast of England, covering 136km and ascending 11 000 ft. That is the equivalent of climbing up two-thirds of the mighty Mont Blanc, with the most challenging climbs and technical terrain only being met in the second part of the race and in the dead of night. The race has a noose-tight cut-off time of 24 hours and a withdrawal rate of more than 50%.

ONER is a real chiseller that mercilessly carves away at the things that deter us from our best performance. I ran the race four times. Each of those times, I truly suffered, and every time the suffering paid off. I got better and faster.

On the eve of my second ONER, Sabelle sent a barrage of text messages and kisses: *"Run well, Mon Coeur. I am with you every step of the way."*

The pride she took in my running carried me far. She didn't have the faintest grasp of the physical challenge, but she did understand the competitive stakes and that I often won; and ma belle, Sabelle, she really did love a winner.

We started ONER 2015 at midday from sun-glittering Charmouth Bay, a charming English village on the UNESCO world heritage Jurassic Coast, an ancient coastline of fossils and dramatic cliffs.

The race tore straight up the first 45-degree, green-grassed Dorset hill. The leaders set a lung-shattering pace. We were all pushing against the clock, knowing that the best strategy for ONER was to race as hard as possible in the first half, to put miles in the bank before the inevitable cobra-strike of the final hours of the race came in the dead of night.

We chased hard up and down the undulating hills. A batch of five muscular and lean women raced neck-to-neck with me, each making it clear that they were aiming for a win. I didn't engage and instead focused hard on every next step.

At 10km, we hit the first checkpoint at West Bay car park, and without stopping, rushed out again on to the ankle-twisting surface of Chesil Beach, a surreal near-30km-long, 150m-wide spindle of pebbles reaching all the way to Portland.

The wind streaked across the brown-white-and-blue churned sea. I felt wild and free, strong and whole, right down to the insides of my mitochondria.

For 10km, our route cut inland, on and on through endless waves of green-shimmering wheat, and then cut back to the ocean at almost 30km into the race. All the world smelt of salt and the lime-frothed sea.

Close to Checkpoint 3, I caught up with Christopher Warner. He was a military man, like my father in his youth. I immediately warmed to his company, and he welcomed mine. Christopher was running with the precision of someone out on a martial operation. He had pre-empted every ascent where the gradient would warrant hiking poles, and had a clear sense of his anticipated time splits for every one of the 13 stages. His wife was stationed at strategic sections along the way with the most appropriate food for each stage. He said his toughest training in the preceding months had involved learning how to devour an entire pizza while running and, more poignantly, how to continue running on a splitting-full stomach. He had prepared for the race in every way possible and aimed for an 18-hour finish. My best time for Oner was 20 hours, 36 minutes.

Having caught him in the first 30km, I figured I could stay with him, and hooked on to his quick heels. God alone knows that strategy is almost always a fatal mistake.

Around 50km, and as the sun began to dip towards the horizon, we pushed the pace on to the tear-drop island of Portland. An eerie wind flapped at us as we rounded the disused, white stone quarries that had first been carved out by convicts in the mid-1800s. In the deepening dusk, we ran past beautiful sculptures of women, owls, fish and angels – all legacies of the rough quarrymen's artistic expression, and their longing so stirred by the inviting, skin-smooth, white stone. Further afield, the stone inspired the majestic St Paul's Cathedral in London, and later the United Nations Headquarters in New York.

The night before the race, I had read about Portland's pagan history of sexual freedom and gender equality, when women had been treated as equals and had the right to vote, and when everyone had been free to participate in sex outside of marriage until pregnancy occurred. That then obliged both parties to take nuptial vows. It seemed to be a good system – no babies out of wedlock, no women branded as bad, and a population of mostly satisfied and mollified men.

Right at the teardrop end of Portland, we reached the red-and-white, candy-striped Portland Bill Lighthouse. It had an end-of-the-world feeling to it. We had been running for more than seven hours without stopping. Something of eerie Portland blew right into the pores of my exhausted body, as if I could sense a long-forgotten song of the quarrymen and the long-gone pagan ceremonies under a full moon. Perhaps I was just getting tired and feeling the trickery of a long night of running ahead.

At 60km, and as the last light of dusk disappeared, Christopher and I rushed into the halfway checkpoint, which doubled as the 40km checkpoint. It had been transformed into a scene of great suffering: Exhausted athletes who had reached the 40km mark lay prostrate everywhere, and speechless people sat hunched over steaming bowls of pasta. The air reeked of sour sweat and boiled Vienna sausages.

Christopher and I gobbled down bowls of pasta and soup as fast as we could. Ten minutes later, we ran off into the night, in fourth and fifth places, respectively. Christopher followed his game plan, and I followed his. Mine was never a clever plan.

Night fell and soon the Jurassic Coast began to bare its biggest teeth. We fought our way up and down the muddy paths of Osmington Mills and towards the horseshoe beach of peaceful Lulworth Cove. There was not a soul about. Stars spilled across the water, and I said thanks, remembering the horizontal rain and sub-zero temperatures of the 2012 race in which I had got lost and hypothermic.

By midnight, we reached Kimmeridge Bay. Ancient Kimmeridge. The village was set on a cliff of shale and clay, above the straight lines of limestone ridges running off into the sea as far as the eye could see. God's geometry. And oil. We ran past the nodding donkey of an oil drill that was tirelessly pumping up and down to drink from the fossil-filled Earth, and off into the night.

I was getting tired, and the climbs were getting steeper and steeper. Ahead of the climbs towards Durdle Door, Christopher hauled out his hiking poles. Four-legged, he sped off up the hills. I hung on for dear life, but at the 100km mark, I felt the failing in my limbs. I felt like I had suddenly been unplugged, and hit the wall so hard that I felt dizzy.

I unhooked and released Christopher into the night.

Alone at the bottom of the infamous Stairway to Heaven, I glanced up the endless staircase climbing up into the stars, and passed out stone-cold.

I don't know for how long I lay collapsed and unconscious on those wooden stairs, under the shimmering stars. When I came to, the Earth around me felt warm and comforting. The night was still. I dug out a nut bar and ate it, unhurried. The dark peaks and troughs of the Jurassic Coast stretched away for miles and miles to the west. I drank some water.

Finally, I stood, steadied myself from the headrush and took the first step, and then the next up the stairs, at my own sweet pace, to the windswept checkpoint at St Aldems Head, the naval look-out point facing south to the ink-black English Channel.

At the checkpoint, I filled up on orange Jaffa cakes and banana bread, waved goodbye to the stoic checkpoint marshals, and followed the pre-dawn coast through the Stonehenge stacks of Winspit Quarry. I felt light-headed and disoriented, still paying the high energy tax for allowing myself to be beguiled into Christopher's quick pace.

A few kilometres further, I saw lights on the path above the one on which I was running.

"God, please, I don't have the energy to get lost," I thought and quickly clambered up the hill to where I thought I had seen the headlights. A thicket of English gorse blocked my way.

"I can bundu-bash this," I thought, eager to get on to the correct path, and forged forward.

After a few minutes, it became apparent in the blackness that the thicket was, in fact, an impenetrable, dense, thick-thorned bramble hedge.

Every time I tried to lift my leg, the sharp thorns grabbed and gouged at my flesh. I tried to free my legs, but the thorns ripped into my hands.

"God! Stuck!" I thought, slightly panicked, my heart thumping hard. I stood there in the darkness, alone in the world, not a headlight in sight, completely entangled in a waist-high bramble thicket, warm blood streaming down my legs and soaking my socks.

It was a beautiful moment. And funny. I laughed out loud. It seemed to help – to also break the panic and the light-headedness. I put on my leather running gloves and picked myself free, one bramble thorn at a time. It took 23 minutes to free myself.

Disregarding the disorientating phantom lights, I turned back down to the path and ran hard along the flat sea shelves of Dancing Ledge and on towards Anvil Point Lighthouse, where the first streak of red coloured the dark sky, then on and on into the dawn and on to the manicured paths of Swanage. I pushed on across the early-morning deserted beaches and out of town again, along the long, dead-leg loop out and back to Old Harry's Rocks, which is soul destroying after 125km of non-stop effort.

There were only 8km left to go when I saw her on the return leg from Old Harry's Rocks. She was bent over, running hard, eyeing me with a thin-lipped fierceness that I knew so well. She must have been chasing me for hours – a bloodhound on my tail.

I felt my body and mind answer her chase with a wilder call still. I picked up the pace. My body stretched taller; my legs strode out, and there, pushing the needle into the red, I found the powerful rhythm of an impi warrior woman. That is who I become at the outer limit. Africa's pulse drummed hard in my veins.

It was exhilarating. We both worked hard along the silver sand of Studland Bay, sprinting the last 5km along the high-tide mark. Raw energy powered my bloodied legs around the sharp turn into Shell Bay, where yachts' sails billowed brightly in the morning sun. I crossed the line in 19 hours, 36 minutes, with a wild grimace of pain and delight on my blood-and-mud smeared face. A whole hour faster than the year before, I was the first lady home, and in 9th place overall.

Britain's Maryann Devally finished 3 minutes after me. She looked disappointed – it was not the outcome she had expected. Christopher had run the perfect race. After leaving me at the bottom of Stairway to Heaven, he had reeled in the two racers ahead of him to finish second overall.

Once I was on the Weymouth train back to London, I sent Sabelle a picture of my torn, shredded and blood-smeared legs. She gasped and tut-tutted and immediately made her way to a romantic little bar in St John's Road, Clapham. There we cuddled and caroused until we had finished two bottles of Prosecco to celebrate my win and every great thing about our life together.

Yet, there was a shadow of discomfort creeping into our shared London life. Despite having achieved several racing victories, my routine with

Sabelle began to imperceptibly veer away from the disciplined Spartan routines of an endurance runner. When I was not studying or working, my training and races were being forfeited for wonderful late nights feasting and toasting life in London's entertainment and gastro-opulence. Sabelle loved nothing better than Michelin stars, and I wanted to please her.

At a deep level, our life was incongruent with what I needed, and the dissonance caused a subterranean unhappiness and frustration. It was no-one's fault. The bird and the dolphin were struggling to find somewhere suitable to live.

A year later, in 2016, greatly inspired by Christopher's excellence, I ran my best ONER ever. I trained methodically, stuck to my own game plan and tackled it with a military precision that Christopher would have saluted. In the process, I shaved another 20 minutes off my finishing time and improved my placing to sixth overall.

It was a great performance, but I was only the third woman home.

Anna-Marie Watson won the race in an astounding 17 hours, 35 minutes – a mere 5 seconds behind the winning male. Determined Maryann Devally had finished as second woman and, staggeringly, third overall in just under 18 hours. That placed us three women in the top six of arguably one of Britain's toughest trail races. Women really are getting faster and claiming their place in endurance sports.

Humans are getting faster and faster. In 2019, the 2-hour marathon barrier was breached by Eliud Kipchoge. I have no doubt that, as a species, we will push against this new boundary. We are wired for it. Nobel Prize-winning biologist Albert Szent-Györgyi describes the phenomenon as "syntropy', the innate drive in living matter to perfect itself. Often, running is the stage on which we are able to do this work; a place of focused effort where we can carve away at what must go, and then build on that which makes us better human beings. The price of superhuman performance is extraordinarily high, and few are willing to pay it to become the next Eliud. What is certain, though, is that we can all become better.

In his book, *Talent is Overrated*[36], Geoff Colvin makes an evidence-based case that it is not raw talent that creates superheroes, but rather

36 Colvin, G. *Talent is Overrated*, Portfolio, 2008.

intentional practice, a deep intrinsic motivation towards excellence, and starting young.

Perhaps the boat of youth has sailed for many of us, but what is certain is that greater performance is available to every one of us – if we love the thing we do and if we are willing to invest in deliberate, intentional training – in other words, spending time outside of our comfort zone and getting better at the things we are not yet good at.

A friend of mine tells of arriving at 5am to work in her father's butchery. He would greet her gleefully: "Christina, good morning! Do you feel like working this morning? No? Well, let's do it anyway!"

Who of us really love hill repeats? Whose performance would not benefit from them? Who feels like intermittent fasting or saying no to a second slice of cake – or God forbid, even the first one? No one. We just grit our teeth and do it anyway.

"Do it badly; do it slowly; do it fearfully; do it any way you have to but do it."

STEVE CHANDLER

8

OVER TIME, THE GRIT IN THE SHELL BECOMES THE PEARL, 1978

"Pain nourishes courage. You can't be brave if you've only had wonderful things happen to you."

MARY TYLER MOORE

When people hear of my ultra-distance exploits and stories of perseverance and struggle; of pain and thirst and exhaustion; of shredded legs and running alone through the dark night; and of the sacrifices of intentional living; and even more intentional training, the incredulous question is invariably asked: "Why? Why do you do it?"

The immediate response in my belly is a chuckle – a warm and gleeful mirth, laced with a darkish Monty-Python-like edge, "I don't know why – because it's fun?"

But that is far from the truth – it is very often not pleasurable at all. The answer to "Why?" is far more layered and infinitely richer.

I run long distances because I can; because I am addicted to the euphoria of it; because of that place of great awe one so often arrives at; because of the camaraderie and the deep friendships along the way; because there is a deep, inner joy that comes from a life of discipline; because of the feeling that one is becoming uber-resilient and unbreakable.

Perhaps, above all, I run long distances because of the thrill of mastering myself despite myself, and the abiding sense of self-respect and grounded self-confidence that one derives from it – a deep trust in myself that: "If I can get through this, I can accomplish anything. The world is my oyster."

There is for me also a starker flipside: "If I can get through this, I can survive anything. Even the worst."

There were moments in my life that made a mess of me, but there is also a story of how my pain and stuff-gone-wrong made a better and stronger person of me, and how it prepared me to be of greater use in the world. Human nature seems to be rigged like that – towards active empathy, in that we wish to release others from the stocks and chains and the signature pain that once held us down. Our mess often becomes our message.

When I was 10 years old, my father contracted Guillain-Barre syndrome. He went to hospital for almost a year, three months of which he was kept alive only by the suck and gasp of a heart-lung simulator and my mother's constant presence at his bedside.

During that time, a new girl arrived at our school. We became friends from the word go. Her family was from Johannesburg, and her stepfather had come to look for work on the gold mines. Occasionally, after school, I played at my friend's house, which was just across the way from the bus stop. She had three sisters, the oldest a tall, lanky beauty. Whenever her stepfather was home, he'd call the oldest sister away on some random errand, all the while sucking at his long, rat-like teeth.

There was a sickness in that house: A smell of leaked urine and hopelessness. I watched the deadness in their mother's eyes, the despair without fight as she bore witness to her oldest daughter being routinely molested. I saw her stony surrender so that her children would have a roof over their heads.

From the earliest age I witnessed how women were often forcibly bent to the will of the men in their lives by a wholesale financial dependence. The truth of why I left my perfect surveying job for a career in financial services, against the very grain of my sun-hungry body, and against the direction of my soul, is that I never wanted to share that fate of this terrifying entrapment.

According to Dr Nthabiseng Moleko of the University of Stellenbosch, the rate of femicide in South Africa is five times that of the world average.[37]

---

37 https://africacheck.org/fact-checks/reports/femicide-south-africa-3-numbers-about-murdering-women-investigated (Accessed: 8 July 2021)

Five times! It rings true for all that I saw growing up on a far-flung farm in South Africa.

I knew another Nthabiseng, too. She was my best friend on the farm for as long as I could remember. She was beautiful, bright and had a life force as strong as that of her mother, who was an eccentric and dramatic woman. Nthabiseng lost her virginity to a friend of her father when she was not even 10 years old. It was only the beginning of a life of abuse. Nthabiseng was a fighter and she had high hopes for her life. She wanted to go to university, perhaps to become someone important, like Dr Moleko. She died of Aids at age 25.

And I saw far worse things.

I sat on the high wheel cover of the red Massey Ferguson tractor whenever my dad drove around the farm to check the integrity of all of the wire fences; that all of the windmills were in working order, and that the animal cribs had water. He was a fastidious man – and complex.

Once every month, we took a tractor trip to the pigsties on the furthest wing of our farm. A neighbour had rented two hectares of land on which to raise pigs. He had employed a man to live there part-time and to care for the livestock. The pigsties stank of sourness, rotting fruit and panic. There was always a dishevelled little girl there, not older than five or six, her hair a coarse, caked mess, and her dress a dirty cloth of rags. Thumb-in-mouth, she trailed after her uncle like a lost lamb.

The story was that when she was orphaned, her uncle took her in. When Nthabiseng's mom alerted my dad: "That pig-man is not doing right by that little girl," my dad called the Child Welfare Services to the farm. A doctor's examination revealed the heart-rending brutality of that little child's short life. She had severe vaginal tearing, syphilis, gonorrhoea, Aids and mental stunting. Who knows what became of her? The pig-man was fired, that's all.

When I was six or seven years old, a migrant farm worker came to help with the winter harvest, and he befriended me. He had a bright smile. I remember his white teeth – the flash of a cunning predator. One afternoon while we were playing at the chicken coop, which was out of earshot of the farmhouse, he lay me down on the rank manure and scattered feathers, and did the unthinkable.

I hurt for days afterwards. I didn't tell a soul – perhaps because I felt it was my fault, that I had somehow made it happen.

Perhaps I didn't tell because I didn't want to get myself or my rapist into trouble, because I knew that my parents would want to kill the bastard. Maybe my silence had even more to do with the fact that I wanted to save my parents the pain of knowing, and of not being able to undo the terrible thing that had happened.

Throughout my childhood, I had told my mom the graphic details of everything, and still do today, as a middle-aged adult. But of that, I couldn't speak. Despite all of my retrospective explanations, I still have no idea why.

I had an infection afterwards. My mom treated me for parasites, which we thought I had picked up while swimming in the winter-stagnant Palmiet River. That was good because I think I had those, too.

The telling of these awful stories is important because they break the silence. South Africa has been labelled the rape capital of the world.[38] The latest statistics reveal that one in three women in South Africa will be raped in her lifetime, and that one in four men has raped someone. Forty-five percent of all rapes reported to the South African Police Services are of children. Children!

Eighty-five percent of these cases are by perpetrators known to them – by their own family, flesh and blood, or by close friends of the family. In the end, only 4% of perpetrators are convicted.

The worst, perhaps, is that most cases of child abuse go unreported.

These are statistics – they are cold and mute. They don't convey the shame that victims feel or the lifetime of struggle to ever again trust in the goodness of people. Rape is not just a physical act of violence in a moment of time, it reverberates through an entire lifetime and forever shatters one's sense of safety in the world. I want to help break the silence and shatter the taboo so that we will talk about it everywhere and so that victims, especially children, will feel freer to call out for help.

---

38 *World Population Review*, Rape statistics by country, 2020; https://worldpopulationreview.com/country-rankings/rape-statistics-by-country (Accessed 9 July 2021)

But I also tell my story to offer hope – the hope that no matter what happens to us, it is possible to get through it; that we are able to heal and flourish, despite our pasts and our pain.

It is a bizarre paradox, but often the thing that hurts us most is the very thing that calls us forth to service. By facing our greatest fears and challenges, we grow stronger. The stronger we become, the more we have the capacity to step into the ring for others who are suffering the same headwinds. We are not what happened to us. We are who we choose to become because of it. We have agency.

I can't remember what I made of it all in my young mind then, but what I do know is that somewhere deep inside of me there was a decision as firm as a rod that I was never going to be at the mercy of anyone ever again. I decided to grow so tough and so strong that no one would ever harm me again. I decided that I would one day join the army and became a little warrior, a wild, bush-child Amazon, and a tomboy unlike anyone had seen before, with my BB-gun, my pet lamb, and a will of titanium.

As I grew up and ventured into the world to make a life for myself, I chose the same – never helplessness, never fear, and never to feel myself the hapless victim of circumstance. I chose instead to hold myself accountable and to become the ultimate architect of my life. This deliberate choice has served me greatly. It has helped me to run very, very far.

"The only person you are destined to become
is the person you decide to be."

RALPH WALDO EMERSON

9

RUNNING WITH RUMI AND THE MASTIFFS, LYCIAN WAY, TURKEY, 2015

"Sell your cleverness and purchase bewilderment."

RUMI

After ONER 2015, I was motivated to race harder and to become more disciplined in my life. I yearned for less wining and dining and more Christopher-like focus.

I had just come back from leading kayaking trips in Greece. My body pined for the outdoors and for sunshine, for the blue-jewel coast of the Aegean Sea and the simplicity of life on the kayaks. The moment I returned to my fluorescent-lit office desk in London, I signed up for the Uzunetap Lycian Ultra, along the south-west coast of Turkey, where I knew the sun would still be bright well into October.

The race would follow a section of the Lycian Way, a 2500-year-old footpath. It was a standard format – a self-sufficient foot race of 260km, run over six days, building in a tough, Long Day of 102km across challenging terrain on the fifth day.

I stumbled upon a superb website that compares trail races across the globe using a five-star rating system.[39] It awards the Lycian Ultra the

39 www.runultra.co.uk rates the Comrades Ultra in South Africa as a 2-star intermediate race. The internationally renowned 100km mountain beast, the Ultra Trail Cape Town (UTCT), which has a finishing ratio of 45%, and the Kalahari Extreme Marathon get 3 stars, respectively.

highest, brutal, full five-star rating. I hoped it would satisfy my desire to push against my new boundaries.

In the aftermath of the race, I strongly propose a sixth star for accuracy.

In October 2015, I flew to Turkey and arrived at the otherworldly Uzunetap race village near Fethiye. We gathered for the race briefing under a large, low marquee, where we were seated on gold-trimmed scatter cushions on a lush Turkish carpet. It was like a set from a movie, complete with little, round foot-high tables, small cups of sweet tea, ornate spouted kettles and beautiful women.

Most of the racers were Turkish, and uncharacteristically of these races, at least half were female athletes. During the briefing, I watched the women with great curiosity, for I had understood that Turkey's gender repression was nowhere near abating.[40] The women had taken great care with their appearances and were dressed in well-fitted, colour-coded outfits. Most were cover-girl beautiful, with large, expressive eyes, long, flowing hair, beautiful olive skin, and mascara on their long lashes. They exuded a natural, evocative vivacity; a palpable life energy. Drawing near them, I sensed on top of that an irreverence – as if the experience of physical strength in their bodies gave them a taste of something forbidden – something they were never meant to know.

There was an air of illicit freedom in the race village, and the seductive Turkish music and revelry continued until way after midnight. No one seemed to care about race performance and early nights.

Day 1 – Hasan

36km

Morning came quickly on the heels of the late-night party. It promised to be a tough first day, just short of 36km but with a hefty ascent of 1 800m.

All around me, under the start banner, exuberant racers jostled and hugged and shouted. At the end of a hurried countdown in Turkish, they

40 According to the World Economic Forum, Turkey ranks 130th out of 144 countries on the Gender Gap Index (2018). Only 34% of Turkish women were incorporated into the workforce, half that of the average across Europe. 2019 statistics show that 40% of women in Turkey still suffer regular domestic abuse. Visit www.weforum.org/ (Accessed: 8 July 2021)

sprinted off at high speed, leaving me far behind. I felt slow and heavy, exhausted from too many intercontinental trips for work, too many nights eating hotel food, and too many elaborate reunion dinners with friends and Sabelle.

Ma belle, Sabelle. My enduring picture of her is in a Ritz-fancy bathing suit with matching jewellery, her pretty face in the shadow of a broad, white Sophia-Loren hat. She is lolling about in the aquamarine shallow end of her parents' swimming pool at their villa in Provence. She slowly strolls the width of it. Then turns. And strolls the other way. She does this all day long with great grace and patience, as lonely as a cloud, waiting for me to return from long training runs in the surrounding Alpille wilderness.

By the end of our second year together, Sabelle had, by no fault of either of us, become a running widow. She had never run a mile in her life and had never promised that she would, and I was fast developing an allergy to the sulphites in wine. She was always going to be lonely at my side. I wish it weren't so, but we fell in love from two opposite corners of the universe, and sometimes all of the love and compromise in the world is not enough to bridge the gap between how two people choose to inhabit their lives. The writing was on the wall.

The path tilted steeply upwards, and the sun lashed down. I reached for my hat, and with a sinking feeling, I realised that I had left it on a table in the turmoil at the startline.

"Six days! I am going to get as withered as a raisin."

At 10km, I was still labouring beneath my 7kg backpack and the wallow of dark ruminations – about my hat, my life, and my failing relationship. I struggled on like that until the distinct moment I noticed the downward spiral of my thoughts and its great tax.

I worked to shift it with the same urgency as a drowning person thrashing towards a lifeboat. As my dark thoughts were displaced by easier thoughts of appreciation for the privilege of being there and for the time to just run and run, and as I stopped beating myself up for not training hard enough, a wave of physical ease and calm washed through my body. My legs loosened and my feet lightened. My thoughts ordered themselves into a mantra: "Relax. Let go. Just breathe. Nothing else to do." I gave myself permission: "Just enjoy!"

We become what we think, and our bodies faithfully follow where our minds lead. I started overtaking people. Then the faster guys, and within 30km, I had worked my way right into the leading pack.

On the final approach to the finish line of the day, I spotted the treasure of a discarded hat. It lay in tatters on the verge of the gravel road. It must have been driven over a thousand times. Only half a visor and some of the headband remained. The entire head covering was gone. Ecstatic, I swooped it up. It was a small thing, but that providence from the universe bolstered my spirit. I sprinted into the finishing strait, the first lady of the day and sixth overall, feeling much more rested and rejuvenated than at the onerous start of the stage.

The man who finished just ahead of me was a wiry electrician from Istanbul. From what people told me, he was one of Turkey's best distance runners. He must have been in his late 40s. When he moved, the muscles in his arms and legs rippled beneath his thin, zero-fat, sun-leathered skin. I shared a tent with him and seven others. I was the only woman and the only foreigner.

When I entered the tent, he looked surprised that I had arrived so close on his heels, but quickly drew his hooded eyelids over his expression and introduced himself as "Hasan". He came in a pair with his lifelong friend, Ferda, who had a good command of English.

The three of us sat together all of that afternoon, Ferda translating, and me stitching and patching my cap, using the cotton strings from my teabags as thread. It was a most pleasing project of resurrection.

There was a glint in Hasan's eyes. It was an intimidating mix of fierce determination, a dark sense of humour, and a flash-quick temper. He didn't say much, not even in Turkish, but when he did, there was a depth of feeling that showed from beneath his cover as a no-nonsense, practical electrician. Hasan felt deeply familiar to me. He reminded me of my father – the everyman poet who practises beauty in secret and is quick to anger.

In the absence of words, and with animal acuity, we directly sensed each other's essence. By the time I had fashioned a fine peak for myself, and without a single, direct word spoken, a mutual fondness had grown between us. For the remainder of the race, I ran alongside Hasan – until the Long Day, when the sheer battle of surviving the ordeal would turn us against each other.

In the evening, the matriarch of Turkish trail running beckoned me over to where she was sitting beneath the pines, holding court with a crowd of admirers. Bakyie Duran was chisel-jawed, muscular and tanned, a world-class adventure racer and a woman well ahead of her time. She was recognised in Turkey as a celebrity speaker and a pioneer of Turkish endurance running.

She looked at my hands and crooned: "Married? No? Children? No?" Her eyes narrowed disapprovingly. She didn't say it out loud, and neither did I, but we both knew that it was plainly understood.

"Yes, I'm gay," I thought defensively, and suddenly wondered, like a fish out of water, what the Turks made of bisexuality or even, Heaven forbid, homosexuality. Bakyie offered me a Turkish biscuit from the large pack through which she had been crunching, her eyes locked on me.

"No thank you," I declined the sweetness, salivating, but suddenly feeling conspicuous and uncertain in a foreign place and sensing the undercurrent of unwritten rules for which I didn't have the script.

The written race rules for the Lycia Ultra were extremely strict. Any Ultra-racer caught receiving food from anyone in the village or on the route would immediately be disqualified. The rules had to be draconian as we shared a race village with 150 fully supported racers. That meant that while the self-sufficient six-day Ultra-warriors were held in a sort of quarantine, subsisting on a meagre diet of freeze-dried food, all of which we had to carry for the six days, our fully supported race companions dined on barbequed burgers, grilled kebabs, and salads so fresh that one could smell the lettuce from 50m away. It was a form of slow torture, the kind that motivated us ravenous Ultra-runners to search the deserted campgrounds in the dead of night for the luck of a fallen morsel. Not even the rubbish bins were out of bounds. Anyone who has known hunger knows that it is a roaring beast that rips right through the thin veneer of dignity and social norms. It will be fed.

Day 2 – Adopted by Bakyie Duran

46km

On the second day, we again sprinted off as if the Devil himself were after us. That time, I kept up with the gooseflesh-inducing pace.

The first leg of the 46km stage shot up a long, thigh-shattering hill, then plummeted into a sheer canyon so steep that sections of it had to be roped for safety. We teetered along the narrow ledges with zen-like concentration. I devoured the section, dangling and leaping and slipping down towards the sea, comfortably holding my own among the top 10 male challengers.

As soon as we entered a section of farmland, four enormous dogs came thundering towards us across the flats. They were Turkish mastiffs, originally bred to fight off wolves and bears. Their massive heads were as big as my torso. Not even 10m from us, they screeched to a halt in a swirl of dust, fangs, saliva and wild killer instinct, barking as if possessed.

"Whatever you do, don't run," whispered Ferda, his eyes stiff in their sockets. I smelled his acerbic fear. We stood there for some minutes, enduring the dogs' alarming mock lurches. Then suddenly, as one, they turned and trotted back to their farmyard.

As we ran off, I glanced back at the retreating pack and thought of the Long Day and long night ahead, parts of which I knew I would run alone. My scalp tightened in terror.

"They could literally bite me in half," I thought woefully.

There are very few things I fear, but of being eaten alive, especially by wolves, I have a full-blown phobia. Who knows what ancestral machinery is at work behind our deepest fears? It was as irrational as it was inexplicable. I grew up in Africa and had never encountered a wolf in my life.

Terror of the long night began to gnaw at me.

Leaving the dogs, farmland and Ferda behind, Hasan and I ran out on to Patara, the third longest beach in the world. We ran hard, shoulder to shoulder and in complete rhythmic sync, our feet splashing through the shallow water where the sand was hardest underfoot. The sea glistened for miles ahead. Neither of us said a word, because we felt it – the primal beat, the blood in our veins, the euphoria of being able to see and run so far, and the bond that continued to be forged in the rhythm of our swift feet.

Hasan and I ran across the second day's finish line in fourth and fifth places, respectively. No betting man would imagine that changing for the rest of the race, but any endurance runner would tell you differently. Endurance racing is capricious, and it was only the second day of a long race.

We camped in a small bay on the emerald hem of the sea near Kas. The Turkish racers sang romantic ballads late into the night. Bakyie's hoarse voice rasped into the darkness: "This is about a reunion with family. If people want to sleep early and run fast, they must go road racing."

About 80% of the field was Turkish. The rest of us, mostly Europeans and a few Americans, seemed somewhat stiff-kneed and awkward among the sultry rhythms that filled the night and the ease with which the Turkish men broke into loose-hipped dance.

Mahmut Yavuz, a driven and serious-faced young racer from the Turkish Army Special Forces, stepped forward, with an ecstatic smile, his arms squared and aloft, his fingers clicking, hips gyrating, and feet pivoting to the cymbal beat. Normally reserved, in the dance he was even more flamboyantly expressive than the beautiful Turkish women.

Bakyie strutted over to where I sat slurping instant noodles. I had forgotten my spoon in London and was improvising with a twig.

"KAEM?" Bakyie asked, pointing at me, and then pointing at herself. "Me KAEM", and she held up five fingers and put them to her heart.

It transpired that Bakyie's favourite international event was the South African seven-day Kalahari Augrabies Extreme Marathon, which is the second-oldest multi-day race in the world, after Marathon de Sable. Bakyie had returned to do it five times, having found in the South African event owners, Nadia and Estienne Arndt, a family of kindred spirits.

I nodded enthusiastically, and with much gesturing, communicated that I had won the very first KAEM race ever held.

Bakyie threw her arms in the air, chuckled like a sailor and drew me into a hug, squeezing hard. And just like that, gay or whatever, I was adopted into the inner circle of the Turkish racing family. Before she left, she handed me her spoon, gesturing that I couldn't possibly eat my noodles in such an uncouth manner.

Day 3 – Carob pods

35km

The third day of the race covered 35km and 1 300m of ascent over challenging, technical, single-track and large sections of grass-covered and treacherous scree.

We ran at full throttle across the stony ground, high on concentration and the bliss of swift, sure-footed forward motion. We ran through field upon field scattered with ancient sarcophagi, as large and high as Turkoman horses. The tombs stood in the high grass as constant testimony to the devoutly spiritual Lycians who invested in the afterlife as much as in life itself by burying their possessions together with the deceased for later use.

The Lycians were the Swedes of their time – a sophisticated, educated, and wealthy people; a politically neutral nation; a matriarchal society in which women presided over the senate as often as men, and a fiercely proud nation that preferred mass suicide to being captured by their Roman and Persian invaders.

As we crossed through the remaining ruins of eerie Aperlae, there was no wind, only oppressive, humid heat and a thick silence. Most of the city lay sunken beneath the shallow, emerald water of the sea, but one could still sense the city's powerful presence. There was a feeling of fight in the air, as if the energy of old battles still lingered there, and blood still steeped the soil and grass.

For me, it felt like a place of ghosts, but for the Turkish runners alongside me, it was a place of profound belonging, where they felt viscerally reconnected to their ancestral roots.

"Bury me here. I am happy,." sang one of the racers, his expression radiant with reverie. There is simply nothing dull about the Turkish spirit.

From Aperlae, we descended into a large scattering of carob trees. I smelt the carob pods even before I saw them: Sweet, like warm molasses.

Carob pods are brown, as long as a middle finger, flat and as thick as a peapod. They contain a delicious, chewy fudge-like flesh that packs 1 600 kilojoules of nutrition per 100g, along with a whopping load of vitamin C, calcium, magnesium, iron and potassium. It is also called

St John's bread, after John the Baptist, who purportedly subsisted on carob pods during his God-inspired time in the Middle East.

I felt a rush of excitement. Hasan was only a short distance behind me. I had time. As far as I was aware, there was no official race rule against eating from Nature's pantry, but I didn't want to test the organisers' strictness. The carob pods were fresh and thickly scattered beneath the old, gnarled trees. It was a gift of gifts! I was hungry beyond care and hurriedly stuffed about half a kilo of the sweet, carob meat into my backpack and skipped off.

I was still munching at the pods as we entered the finish line 15km further, me in fourth, and Hasan in fifth position by only a few seconds. By the end of the third stage, the second lady was a cumulative near-6 hours behind me, making it safe for me to shift my aim towards moving up the male ranking. Doing so meant that I had to start opening a gap on my friend, Hasan.

During the afternoon, all of the racers rested together in the deep shade of a large marquee. One of the volunteers came around offering a tray of ice-cold fruit juices – strictly for the supported racers.

Hasan asked something in Turkish. The volunteer answered animatedly, and Hasan took a juice. I reached out for one.

"Don't!" urged Mehmet, one of the female racers from the supported category and a kindred spirit with whom I had felt an immediate connection. "You could get disqualified."

Uncertain again of the unspoken rules that governed our small community, I declined the juice, noticing that my tongue had stuck to the roof of my mouth with sheer desire for something cold and sweet.

It would turn out to be a wise decision.

Day 4 – Manti

11km

The fourth day was an 11km sprint from Kas to the race village at Finike. The three-day event's racers joined us from there, introducing new blood and fresh excitement. It encouraged us to run even harder. I flew down the technical, rocky single track together with Ferda and Hasan – three mountain goats at full tilt and completely unstoppable.

Within a few hundred metres, we started overtaking the new racers who, unlike us, ran without backpacks. Within 5km, we tore right past the leading female, who marvelled after us in shock and surprise.

Oh, to feel so young and so alive!

It was such a short and quick stage that race seedings remained unchanged: Hasan in fourth and me a few seconds behind in fifth place.

In the late afternoon, Tolga, the race director, announced that there was a surprise treat for the emaciated ultra-marathoners. We were invited to a fully catered traditional Turkish meal of manti, which are small little ravioli-like dumplings of deliciousness stuffed with lamb and served with yoghurt and an array of spices, and, lo and behold, bread rolls! As many as one could eat!

I had two man-size servings of dumplings and five rolls.

I lay down for a carbohydrate-induced afternoon sleep, and as I drifted off, I sensed instead of contentment a slight feeling of regret. It was interesting that in the moment of the feast the pleasure was great, but having satisfied the hunger, something was lost. In these endurance races, there is something of an optimal physical and mental state that we access through extreme physical exertion and Spartan-like eating. Through the feast, the golden thread was cut. Blunted.

Perhaps, this is why endurance sport is increasing in popularity. We crave a means to get back to a healthier way, particularly in western societies, where we rarely get a break from an unnatural norm of ubiquitous abundance. The idea that long-distance running offers a pathway to health was gaining ground like a veld fire across Turkey. One of the Turkish racers on the supported course ran for the Association of Physical Activity, to raise awareness in a largely sedentary Turkish society of the health benefits of exercise. Whenever he was interviewed on camera, he exclaimed: "Moving is medicine! Run for your life!"

One of my seven tentmates, Gürkan Açikgöz is a full-blown Type 1 diabetic. If his blood sugar gets out of control, he can die. In these endurance races, one's blood sugar is a crazed bull, bucking all over the place, unless tethered with the utmost discipline of pacing and nutrition.

Gürkan has defied the limitations of diabetics and the cautions of modern medicine. He has experimented for years and has devised ingenious ways to regulate, check and control his blood-sugar – especially at the point when it begins to drop off a cliff. He now runs to create awareness that having diabetes does not mean you have to stop living. He is evangelical about exercise. "What is the way to change diabetes? It is to move!" he says.

Following our manti indulgence, while we were lying about like lazy lizards in the afternoon heat, Tolga appeared at the tent and called Hasan and a few other racers to step out.

We could hear Tolga explaining something in his deep, stern, Turkish voice. A fierce commotion broke out, and the racers shouted and argued. I peered out of the tent. There was much arm-flinging, stomping and head-shaking going on. It appeared that Hasan and six other fruit juice-drinkers had been given an hour penalty for their transgression.

By evening, when the race results were made public, I had jumped to third place overall, and because of Hasan's penalty, I was now an hour ahead of him on the cumulative placings leader board.

Day 5 – Much further than we expected

127km

By morning, the affected racers had decided to boycott the race by withdrawing – and there was more calamity in store. By mid-morning, we received news that the three-day racers had suffered a bus accident. There were no serious casualties, but it did mean that the start of the 102km stage would be delayed – indefinitely.

We mulled around restlessly for the rest of the day, not sure when to sleep, eat or drink. All of our race strategies had been blown out of the water. The hiatus gave the six penalised racers an opportunity to rethink matters.

Finally, by 6pm we were called for an impromptu race briefing. It was brief, mostly in Turkish, and wholly inadequate to prepare us for what lay ahead.

Because of the time lost, the organisers had combined the long day and the final day into a monster route of 127km, with a total ascent of more than 4 300m, the latter of which we were not prewarned.

We were scheduled to start racing at midnight.

"*Mashalla, Mashalla!* God willing!", exclaimed my excited tent companions as they packed their bags and taped their feet.

For reasons that I can't now fathom, perhaps owing to our proximity to the sea, I assumed a relatively flat course. I estimated the calories I would need for the last stage and, to save on weight, left most of my remaining food behind. That turned out to be one of the worst rookie errors I would ever make in a race.

An hour before we set off, I awoke to an unexpected, wholly out-of-cycle aching in my lower back and a familiar tearing pain in my ovaries. My worst fears were confirmed. But what was there to do but run?

At midnight, we set off in a peloton of six, running hard. Hasan ran by my side, wholly unaware that I was fighting back a feeling of my insides ripping right out of my body.

Drill sergeant Ahmet, the leading male, set a military-style pace, with Carlos The Jackal, his challenger, right on his heels. The rest of us were right on theirs, following their rhythmic pace. We ran as one, with the extreme efficiency and the deep, archetypal thrill of being part of a quick-moving impi; a six-strong squadron on the advance. I easily settled into the exhilarating cadence.

Dogs barked from the darkness.

Four hours later, sweat pouring off us and the sky still dark, I desperately needed a bathroom stop, but what to say to my swift squadron?

I dropped off the back and did what I needed to, accepting the fact that I would lose them and run alone.

I thought I saw something large lurching towards me out of the black night. I didn't quite see what it was, and with my running shorts still half around my knees, I sprinted hard after my pack as if my life depended on it. By the grace of God, I caught them and stayed with them until the 50km checkpoint, where, for safety reasons, we had an enforced stop until dawn.

"Safety from what?" I wondered, as I fell into my sleeping bag and shivered myself to sleep.

An hour later, we set off as the sky began to lighten towards the east. My legs were swollen, fat from the monthly oedema women know all too well. "It's going to be okay. Only 80km left. Paracetamol at sunrise," I soothed myself and trotted heavy-legged after Hasan.

As the sun lifted above the golden horizon, we had caught the Turkish racers on the shorter distances. Alongside them, we clambered up the steep, hot, pine slopes of Gelidonya Lighthouse, up and up, and away from the emerald sea.

A Turk pointed ecstatically to the soil beneath our feet: "Oh, the beauty! Mythology is underneath here. History is underneath here!".

Another exclaimed: "Lycia – where nature and history got married. We come here to understand our roots, our deepest roots!".

It was the most extraordinary treat to be among a group of people who all sounded like Rumi, who had as much reverent dance in them as the Sufi mystics, and for whom running was more spiritual than physical. That resonated deeply with me.

The thing about distance running is that we get to the edge. Over time, running exceptionally long distances had become an act of self-transcendence for me, and it is that for many other runners, too. It gives us a quiet and private place to be with that which we sense but cannot see.

Perhaps I could go as far as to say that running had become a spiritual occupation for me, a place where I could go outside myself – and often out of necessity. It is easier to surrender when my body and breath fails. It is easier to call for help when hobbling on sore feet or when brought to my knees. It is in those moments, when my own strength has run out, that I am forced to surrender and call to that greater presence that holds all of the universe together. It is there that I find my greatest peace.

The other thing about distance running is that it almost always immerses us in Nature. It is hard to remain unbelieving in the face of such abundant evidence.

Walk out into Nature and *"abandon your cleverness"* says Rumi *"and buy bewilderment"*.

We all need a receptacle for our praise and wonder; something to receive our overflowing joy. We all need something or someone to whom we can say: "Thank you," a place and space in our life to say grace. We all need something to believe in.

The Turkish people know this in their very bodies and souls. Perhaps that is why, when the Turkish runners came across the finish line, no-one seemed to be exhausted. Like Yiannis Kouros in Greece, they were carried forward by something much more powerful than the sheer force of their bodies, and by something much deeper than the motivation of sports performance. They were hard-wired to worship.

Beyond Gelidonya Lighthouse, Hasan and I ran together for another 30km, until the 100km mark.

All of the energy and will had bled from my body. Among the tall pines, Hasan witnessed my fall from grace as I transformed from fiery-eyed Amazon to a slow-waddling, ill-tempered hippopotamus. At first, he slowed to stay with me, but he grew impatient and took off, muttering under his breath in disbelief.

He left me in the wilderness, and I knew that when night came, I would be alone and smelling of blood, at the mercy of the terrifying packs of mastiffs.

Spurred on by that thought, I ran hard and caught Hasan at the second-last checkpoint. He glanced up and looked unpleasantly surprised. For the first time, I realised that he was afraid of being "chicked" – the term we use for a man being beaten by a woman. Hasan limped off into the darkness. He had sprained his ankle.

I rushed through the checkpoint, set after Hasan and a few kilometres later, paced past him. By my calculation, we had only 20km left of relatively flat terrain and mostly easy Jeep track, which should have taken no longer than 2.5 hours to complete. I ate my last three dried apricots. The carob pods were gone.

A few kilometres later, the path tilted unexpectedly and hideously into the mountains. Not good. After two hours of relentless climbing, I had not even covered 8km. The route continued up and up into thin air. I had completely misjudged the course.

A crushing sugar low gripped my legs. Over the course of the past six days I had burned through all of my reserves, and then, running on the thin red line of starvation, I realised that I would have to find food, or literally cease, stopped in my tracks like a car without gas.

Perhaps it was the desperate tenor of my hope that produced the miracle, but not 500m from where I hit the empty gauge, I emerged around a bend in the road and stumbled upon two Swiss hikers. It was the most unlikely of occurrences out there in the Turkish wilderness. They were the first non-racers I had seen in six whole days. They were sitting on their packs – dejected and seemingly lost.

I staggered over and begged: "Anything really. I will eat tea leaves at this moment."

The woman didn't hesitate and stuffed a 100g bag of almonds into my hands. "Go! Quickly!" she said, scanning the road behind me, following my furtive glances back along to where Hasan would appear at any moment.

I stuffed a handful of almonds into my mouth and within minutes, I felt a surge of energy in my depleted muscles. Another handful. The sugar-low panic receded. It was the most extraordinary linear energy conversion I had ever experienced in my body. For the remainder of my racing years, it attuned me deeply to the magnificent machinery of our bodies; of how food becomes energy, becomes our performance, becomes our achievements and our destiny.

Hasan limped into sight, frowning hard. He upped his pace and overtook me, smelling of sour sweat and cortisol. I pushed to stay with him, my brow furrowed. What a pair we were, mortally engaged in our fierce battle out there in the middle of nowhere with not a soul to witness it.

I counted the remaining almonds. There were 45 nuts, which gave me 15 for every 3km to the finish line, which I estimated to be 10km further, and with who knows how much climbing still ahead.

Night came and a deep darkness settled in the woods. I fought, sweating profusely, exhausted and determined. I thought of Turkish wolves and the giant wolf-eating dogs, and laughed out loud. There was not another sound but my chuckling and footfall padding across the pine needles.

Laughter is strong medicine. In the darkness among those towering pines, miles from any human settlement or help, the fear of being hunted shifted out of me. I loped through the shadowed pine forest feeling feral and as strong as an animal. I ran into the finishing strait five minutes after Hasan. He was euphoric and sang a Turkish song. He had not been chicked, even though in the official rankings, because of the juice penalty,

I had beaten him. We had survived the race and developed a beautiful friendship. The night was young, and we each had a beer in hand. What more could one ask for?

That night, Tolga came past our tent, "I bought you something at the market," he said and handed me the lightest, hand-carved wooden spoon. "For your next race," he said, and left.

There is video footage on YouTube of Ahmet, the special forces hero, and his friend, Carlos The Jackal, finishing together at dusk, two hours before Hasan and me. Carlos does a traditional Turkish dance and everybody around him is twirling, singing, crying and laughing. Their life force burns as brightly as the stars.

Running in Turkey felt pure and in-the-moment. I felt deeply at home there. As I left the finish line of The Lycian Way with the women's trophy under my arm, I had already decided to return, to reunite with the family of Turkish runners into which I had been so unconditionally adopted.

As soon as I returned home, I signed up for Runfire Cappadocia, a race in which we would run through arguably the oldest and biggest, 250km-long churchyard in the world. It would turn out to be one of the best races of my life.

NOTE: A few years later, I looked for the 2015 results and found that they had, for some reason been removed from the internet. I was pleased. Officially, I placed third overall, but given the 100g of almonds, I think a fourth place behind Hasan was just about fair, and the correct record of events.

"I am in love with every church and mosque and temple and any kind of shrine because I know it is there that people say the different names of the One God."

HAFIZ

10

IT'S A MAN'S WORLD, RUNFIRE CAPPADOCIA, TURKEY, 2016

"We've begun to raise daughters more like sons ... but few have the courage to raise our sons more like our daughters."

GLORIA STEINEM

Runfire Cappadocia in Turkey is recognised as one of the 25 most difficult races in the world. Like the Lycian Way, it gets a full 'brutal' ranking on the barometer for toughness.[41]

The race's difficulty is matched only by its otherworldly beauty. It takes place across the volcanic landscape of the vast Anatolian planes and weaves its way through an eruption of twisted and gnarled rock pinnacles and vined, tree-lined river valleys, where hundreds of 2 000-year-old cave-churches were cut into the soft, volcanic tuft by the very first Christians.

In my mind's eye, Cappadocia was one, big, natural, rock-hewn, pomegranate-and-apricot-dripping place of worship. I knew that my whole being would feel at home from the very moment I set foot there, but I had no way of knowing just how significant that race would be, both in my own life and for the Turkish women who would be watching at the finish line and from afar.

2016 was a year of gargantuan upheaval. Donald Trump was elected US President, the Brits voted in favour of Brexit, and hundreds of thousands

41 www.ultrarunning.co.uk (Accessed: 7 July 2021)

of Syrian refugees fled across the Aegean Sea, via Lesvos, to seek refuge in Europe.

The global upheaval also seemed to find resonance in my own life. Teach a Girl to Fish suspended kayaking trips as a result of the Syrian refugee crisis, and the company for which I had worked for 10 years announced its delisting from the London Stock Exchange, the closure of its London head office and the blanket retrenchment of all of its staff. Sabelle and I had also given up trying to build a discomforting life together.

Even now, many years later, I can still feel her fingers in the wild curls of my hair and the adoration and puzzlement in her wide-eyed gaze. She was ma belle, Sabelle, my magnificent gold-and-green-and-malachite-blue sunbird – always hovering near, and seeming a little surprised at finding me there with her. She knew I was from somewhere else and that eventually I would have to return. She was of the air, and I was born of water.

The only consolation in our shared heartache was the knowing that in the long run, we were each both better off without the other. The bird and the dolphin gave up a life in mid-air so that we could fully and happily inhabit our own lives.

2016 was the beginning of a monumental transition in my life – in work, love, sport, and in where and how I lived. I discovered in the ashes of things past, reason to look forward to the future; to building a life that more closely aligned to what my soul needed most. It is often like that: When the fire has raged across the land, it creates the space for new growth to push up through the blackened roots.

I had reason to believe that I was heading for the Promised Land, that everything I had hoped, dreamed and worked towards for 10 long years was finally shaping into reality, and that I would finally find my way back home, back to South Africa.

Turkey was facing its own transitions. On 15 July 2016, there was a violent, but failed, military coup to overthrow the dictatorship of the uber-patriarchal President Recep Tayyip Erdoğan.

The coup happened six days before I was to fly to Cappadocia, which is in the geographic centre of Turkey. The British Tourist Advisory counselled against travel to Turkey, British Airways cancelled all of their flights, and my travel insurance company withdrew its cover. Naturally concerned, I emailed the race organisers an elaborate list of safety-related questions.

Only two days before my scheduled departure, I received a warm-hearted, one-line email back from race organiser Ozgur, whom I had met on the Lycian race: "*Come Erica. All will be well. We are waiting for you. Safe travels.*"

It tasted of my first desert run in Egypt – liminal and edgy. The excitement lit me. By the time I arrived in Cappadocia on a near-empty flight, 90% of the international race contingent had withdrawn.

In stark contrast, the Turkish racers were making merry at the race registration. They were joyous and excited, laughing and celebrating their multiple reunions as if they did not have a care in the world. I asked about the coup and was generally met with a shrug of the shoulders and: "S*orun yok.*" There is no problem.

Perhaps more inclined to insurance than the Turks, I sealed my passport and two photocopies of it in a waterproof Ziplock and stowed them away at the bottom of my backpack. Just in case.

The race started from Uçhisar, a small town carved into the soft, volcanic rock of Cappadocia. Beneath it lay a labyrinth of ancient underground cities.

On the morning of the race, I woke to the Muslim call to prayer ringing from Uçhisar's mosque minarets. An air of mystery hung over the slowly waking town. As the sun climbed above the horizon, a sparser than usual scattering of brilliantly-coloured red, purple, golden, yellow and blue hot-air balloons filled with enthralled tourists lifted above the white, caramel and ochre spires.

I had a feeling about the race – an even-keeled excitement that something was going to happen. I felt confident, quietly fierce, and in excellent physical shape – perhaps the best form I had ever been in – fit, lean, muscular, rested, and at peace that Sabelle and I had parted ways. I was also high on hope for the future.

I was ready to go all out, because I could, and because my body felt good in the Turkish heat. My feet felt welcome on those pilgrim's dust paths, and my soul felt at home in a landscape ringing with prayer.

Day 1 – Easing in gently

31km

I gathered at the race startline alongside a small and determined field of six-day ultra-marathoners.

The race started gently, with a moderate 31km course along open Jeep track and easy trails, with a manageable ascent of just over 1 000m. It gave us a fair chance to acclimatise to the heat and the daily rhythm of run-eat-sleep.

I ran well within my comfort zone, taking the time to exfoliate away the crust of city living, and allowing the sweating and pounding to cleanse my body and mind.

At the end of the first day, I already felt great relief as a new vigour had flushed out all of the post-flight heaviness from my body, along with the remaining sadness about separating from Sabelle.

I came across the line in fifth position overall, and was beaten by three of my tentmates. I shared a tent with eight men: Four from Turkey, one of them my good friend, the diabetic warrior-hero Gürkan; two men from Kuwait; one retired 68-year-old British Army captain, and of course me, the only girl. I wondered whether my small running shorts posed a cultural challenge to anyone.

I am friendly, but not the most talkative of people, and during these desert races I revel in the opportunity to talk even less. The guys mostly chatted among themselves. Beyond the difficulties of language and culture barriers, what would they say to me anyway? I enjoyed the verbal reprieve.

The exception was sweetest Harry, the retired army captain and an accomplished multi-stage desert racer. He chatted non-stop and made every effort to include me in his troop, not sparing me any of the lewd jokes that poured from him with staggering frequency and increasing uncouthness. I attempted, with as much grace as possible, to navigate my way through a barrage of prostitute and pregnant-woman yarns. My feminist friends would have started a riot. But there was another way to look at it: I understood that Harry had been moulded by 45 years of army barrack-culture. His humour was in no way meant to offend or exclude me – and I would argue that he meant quite the opposite.

The short distance and easy terrain had played to the strengths of my fast, and mostly younger, male tentmates. The first day's results had cast a new hierarchy in the tent, and I sensed in their relaxed attitude that the boys had written me off. It was in the air: "This girl poses no threat."

That perspective changed very quickly.

Day 2 – Grandma climbs the rankings

54km

The second day was a long, hard 54km slog along high-altitude farm roads flanked by dew-wet crops of pumpkin and maize. The longer distance afforded me enough time to work my way up the rankings. I finished in fourth place, and suddenly the gentlemen in my tent noticed – especially young Ozcan who had slipped into fifth position, a good 20 minutes behind me.

From the outset of the race, Ozcan had nicknamed me "Grandma". Now Grandma was ahead of him.

I didn't feel the need to take up the gender gauntlet. Not yet, anyway. For most of my life I had lived in a predominantly male environment: On our maize and cattle farm in South Africa, the gender ratio had been four men to one woman; at the University of Stellenbosch, where I studied Engineering, I was one of only six women in a class of 350 freshmen, and in adventure racing, women made up less than 25% of the field.[42]

I didn't feel intimidated by the covert and subtle sexism in our tent – perhaps, alarmingly, because I was used to it, and more positively, because I saw it for what it was – a toothless tiger, unable to detract from my experience that women are just as smart, strong, able and successful as men – when given the opportunity.

The way my parents raised me was instrumental in my belief. My father, a conservative man, treated me as if I were every bit as capable as a boy, taking me along at 3am in the morning to plough, or plant, or whatever needed doing on the farm, for the entire day. My mother had taught me to

42 These contextual inequalities were as much gender- as race-based. The global endurance racing field showed up the same gender and racial profile imbalances that I had encountered in South Africa.

drive our little Datsun pick-up truck by the time I was seven, and the large farm tractors, before I turned 10.

On church Sundays, instead of forcing me into frilly frocks and driving me away from God forever, my mom allowed me to wear my favourite denim dungarees. I was raised without gender discrimination or proscription, free to follow my own path, without any compulsion to prove my gender's worth either way.

My parents allowed me to roam free on the farm, my airgun slung over my shoulder, and my pet lamb and mongrel dog, Snuffels, in tow. I climbed the highest windmill and stayed out late among the flock of sheep to watch the sun setting and the stars filling the sky – Huckleberry Finn of the Free State. Who knows how I managed to bury my childhood trauma, but I don't remember ever being afraid, even after what had happened. I just remember the feeling of climbing up the windmill at dusk and the sense that all the world was full of magic. Forty years later, I would learn words like "dissociation", and terms like "PTSD". It made no difference. I still had that windmill-climbing feeling.

When I was a child, I watched my mom working shoulder to shoulder with the men on the farm, and bore witness to her Amazonian physical strength, but even more so the fire of her life force and spiritual belief. My mom was titanium – a woman of profound emotional and mental strength, who rose above life's challenges with grace and equanimity. Whatever society's doubts concerning the comparative ability of women, my mom erased them from my mind forever.

It was the blessing of having such a strong role model, as much as it was an act of deliberate will that I grew up never experiencing myself as inferior to men, or allowing myself to feel treated in any derogatory or secondary way – not in sport, not in the boardroom, and not in love.

My distance running confirmed this equality, and its physical wisdom spilled over into the rest of my life.

When I was 15 years old, I attended a two-week adventure camp[43], along with six dozen other young women.

43 Outdoor adventure experiences were designed to build resilience and character.

A remorseless drill sergeant pushed us along on military-style runs every morning before sunrise until we were sick. Afterwards we were commanded to swim far out into the dark water of Swartvlei, and then to go round and round an army-calibre obstacle course for hours on end until some of the girls wept with exhaustion.

We were sent on a 48-hour-long, non-stop march – our peloton of eight teenaged girls armed with a map, out on night manoeuvres in the wilderness. It was beyond exhilarating. In the final trial, we were each dropped off in the backwoods on our own for night of solitude in the quiet forest, with no food, penknife, torchlight, sleeping bag, pen, or even a warm jacket. I built myself a shelter of fallen branches and smeared myself with the leaves of a Cape sour fig to keep the mosquitoes at bay. It was one of the most exquisite experiences of my young life.

At the end of the two weeks, my motley crew won the Best Team award, and for my part in it, I was awarded the Leadership and Good Fellowship cup.

Looking back, it was clear how that experience carved in me a large moat of an appetite for endurance sport. I never joined the army, but the inevitable path to distance running seemed to have been cut early on, and without a racetrack in sight.

During RunFire Cappadocia, when the jokes and the sexist banter became too much, I found welcome distraction in the company of Brice, a journalist from France. Brice had the heart of a poet and would, to my great delight, recite reams from one of my favourite authors: Adventurer and aviator Antoine de Saint-Exupéry.

On the evening of the second stage, we stole into the orchards near camp and ransacked the trees for stray end-of-season apricots, which were tart, sweet and juicy on the tongue.

"What makes the desert beautiful is that somewhere it hides a well," quoted Brice from Exupéry's *The Little Prince*, his cheeks bulging with the unexpected find of still sun-warm apricots.

I laughed, feeling such a pleasure of kinship. Like Brice and Exupéry, and all of the guys in our tent, and multi-day endurance runners everywhere, we understood deeply that less is sometimes more, and that abundance is often not found in plenty but instead in the house of scarcity. I have yet to taste better apricots than those illicit Turkish ones.

Day 3 – Size is not everything

29km

Day 3 was tough. Distances can be very misleading. The 29km course started from the rim of the volcanic crater of Lake Nar, the Lake of the Pomegranates.

The route exacted a steep ascent of 1 800m in ambient temperatures well above 32°C. The conditions suited me, and by then well in my stride and having entered the high-performance, fat-burning state of ketosis, I outsprinted most of my tent companions and shifted into third position.

By doing so, I unseated formidable Turkish racer Özgür Tetik. He was a bush-bearded giant and a likeable man with a big smile. In six days, he had said barely 10 words.

I had also reluctantly passed Gürkan early on among the pumpkin fields. He was in the grip of a full-blown glycaemic episode and waved me on. I stayed with him a while, witnessing as he heroically clawed his blood sugar back from the edge through a series of strategies that included injecting insulin, feeding and then sitting down for as long as it took his body to recover.

The day's performance brought me close on the heels of Faisal from Kuwait. He was light and slight, built for distance. He had about him the air of an academic. He was the polar opposite of Yussuf, his fellow countryman, who was broad and tall, dark-veined and muscular, with calves the size of my head. He looked like a bodybuilder. Faisal and Yussuf's friendship ran deep, having been forged over thousands of miles of endurance running.

At the end of the third day's racing, Yussuf came limping into the tent, his feet a mess of blisters. Faisal helped him wash his feet and consoled him gently, all the while piercing and dressing Yussuf's painful, blood-blotched sores.

Gürkan crossed the line, and by evening he had fully recovered, having regained the beautiful smile that made him the well-loved poster-boy for beating diabetes. It is hard to fully appreciate how great and heroic a feat it is to run extreme distances with a debilitating condition like that. Gürkan has shown through his example of great perseverance and diligent consistency, how one can completely rewire both body and mind, one neuronal connection at a time. He has inspired people all over the world to reclaim their lives and participate in sport, despite diabetes.

Day 5 – A river valley of churches

25km

Day 4 of the race covered only 25km, to provide respite before the big 100km day.

There was great excitement in the camp, as an intake of three dozen Discovery 4-G competitors had joined in for the remaining four days of the race. Unable to contain their excitement at the startline, some racers broke into vigorous Turkish dance. We all felt it – that raw throb of feeling wildly alive.

Our route followed the flow of the Melendiz River through ancient groves of shimmering poplars and orchards of pistachio, plum and apricot trees in the enchanted river valley of Ihlara. It was a mesmerising paradise of dappled shade, cool, rippling water and blue doves cooing in the morning heat.

More than 100 spectacularly frescoed cave-churches carved into the sheer canyon walls magnified the magical quality of the valley. It was easy to run quick and light, carried along by the gentle energies that surrounded us.

By the end of the day, I had maintained my third position and closed in a little more on Faisal. The Kuwaittees' attitude towards me had shifted markedly to one of consideration and demonstrative respect.

Less generous was young Ozcan, for the greater the gap I opened on him, the sharper his jokes and "Grandma" jibes became.

Day 6 – For the girls

102km

Early the next morning, we were transferred by bus to the startline of the Long Day – undoubtedly the highlight and trademark of Uzunetap-organised races. We were to cover 102km across the mercilessly hot and vast Lake Tuz, one of the largest hypersaline lakes in the world. The entrants for the one-day, 100km event joined us in camp. Among them was my friend, esteemed distance racer Bakyie Duran.

The bus ride to the race start was long and hot. We bumped along, watching the endless, white salt-lake trail pass the bus windows for what seemed like hours.

Harry kept us entertained with a volley of jokes, and when he ran out, Ozcan stepped in, no doubt trying to be funny. "Grandma, you know this," he said, pointing to the vast salt lake outside. "This ultra-running thing is a man's world."

Everyone laughed.

"Give me your phone. I will play you a song," he offered.

James Brown's classic song filled the bus with its warm, mellow drawl: "*It's a man's world*." The second verse conceded that women are necessary to make it whole – sort of as a supporting act.

Ozcan eyed me to see whether his joke had hit its mark. I gave him a broad smile, said nothing and took my phone back, all the while feeling a hotness rising from my belly, filling my body, and my spine being stacked tall and girded, as if with iron plating. I felt a clear and physical inner forging, of sorts, taking place. I was eager to get running. More eager than I had ever been in my life.

I set off on a steady, gentle pace, breathing and easing into the heat so intense and complete that it folded us into a cocoon of delirium. As we entered the vast, flatter-than-flat endlessness of Lake Tuz, we stepped into a surreal world in which all geographic references disappeared.

In the far distance, the hard-white glare of the horizon and the blue sky melted indistinguishably into each other. To the east and west, and north and south, there was nothing but a blinding whiteness. Eternity stretched away in every direction.

As one enters the salt flats, one is filled with a sudden, primitive euphoria. I saw it in the others, too. Despite the heat, everyone ran with their arms uplifted, their chests thrust forward, and their heads thrown back in ecstatic glee – like prisoners suddenly released. I can only think that we were all overcome by the elation of experiencing infinity. Perhaps that is what Heaven is: Coming free from the physical and the bounded, consciousness finally liberated from the mortal shackles of the body.

Running across that white desert, we came close to such bodyless euphoria. Soaring across the white flats, I experienced the most profound reverie and a deep appreciation for my life, for the people I loved, for my career, the great fortune of personal freedom, and for sufficient savings and health to be running as free as an Anatolian lynx across those vast planes of Cappadocia.

"Forty-five years old, and who would have thought?" I mused as I remembered the incinerating words of my first teenage boyfriend: "You are going to be a good housewife one day; perhaps a little plump, but you'll make me happy enough." I ran a little quicker, overcome with joy that I had escaped a life with him and his droll prophecy.

In the far distance I picked out the elongated, stick-like figures of the fastest runners. Steadily I reeled them in, one by one, effortlessly borne along on the steady rhythm of my breath.

At the 50km mark, only young Ozcan and formidable runner Utkuer Yasar remained ahead of me. Utkuer had won every stage of the race thus far. Steadily, the gap between us continued to shrink, and at 60km, I caught up with them. Ozcan had the weak, staggering gait of a horse with sleeping sickness. Utkuer kept a sturdy pace, but even he looked limp and weak-kneed from the crushing heat. Glad for company, I slowed to stay with them for a while.

We exited the salt flats and made our way across an arid, grassy plateau. A fierce whirlwind manifested as suddenly as a genie and carried two lone tumbleweeds upwards in its dervish whirl. Up and up the tumbleweeds climbed on the wild wind. It was a sight of extraordinary beauty. My heart lifted along with the tumbleweeds, up and up into the clear, blue sky.

The rapture of it nudged my body forward. I needed to run and run and run, like dogs do after a whole day of being cooped up at home. I bade Ozcan and Utkuer farewell and sped away for the final 42km to our camp.

Utkuer gave chase, leaving Ozcan wilting in his wake. Utkuer caught up with me as we entered another section of white-sheened salt flats. We ran alongside each other without much talk, after thanking each other briefly for the shared understanding that it is the great silence of the salt flats for which we went there in the first place.

Utkuer reminded me of Jacques Mayol in the *Big Blue*. He was slight and quiet, and appeared far more at home in the vast desert than I could ever imagine him being in the harsh loudness of a big city. His presence was soothing. At the 75km checkpoint, Utkuer sat down. "I have to eat. Sit with me," he implored.

The young racers in Turkey have a different race strategy from me. They run hard and fast, almost with a reckless innocence, until they crash. They take longer breaks at checkpoints, sometimes even cooking a meal to recover and refuel.

"I can't sit in checkpoints, Utkuer. My way is to keep running. Please forgive me, my friend." I felt bad for leaving him – like I was not acting quite within the unique spirit of the Turkish races. And yet, at the same time, I knew he had the capacity to run me in from behind. And I knew that if he could, he would.

There were 2.5 hours of daylight left, and doing a rough calculation, I realised that I had to keep a pace of 10km per hour across technical terrain to finish before nightfall. The image of a pack of killer mastiffs tearing through the darkness flashed across my mind. I picked up my pace and felt a current of strength surge through my body.

I repeated my mantra: "Quick, light feet," over and over again, like a dream. The more I said it, the more my cadence increased, and the lighter my feet felt across the Earth.

Twenty kilometres on, and in the last 5km of the race, I ran at 12km per hour, flying across the shrub-covered plain as a sickle moon formed in the lavender and pink evening sky. One small, bright star appeared. In the distance I saw the Uzunetap finishing banner and Brice running towards me.

"Look!" I said, when he was near enough, and pointed at the star.

Brice laughed and shouted: "Yes, *mon amie*, just like the star of the *Little Prince*."

It was a perfect moment. I felt whole and powerful, fierce and gentle, euphoric and calm, big-hearted and invincible all at once. I felt myself indistinguishably part of the universe and everything and everyone in it. It was a simple, profound, and an unforgettable high point in my life.

By the time I had entered the final 100m, the entire race village had gathered, yelling, ululating and beating drums. As I broke through the ribbon, the Turkish women went berserk. It was a war cry, a moment of victory over things unspoken, over invisible limitations and impossibilities. Ozgar and Ozge held me tight, and several people picked me up and carried me around, like a prize. Everyone hugged me, some wanted pictures taken together, and others asked for autographs.

The Turks' welcome made me feel like an Olympic champion. In the greater scheme of sport, it was a small, obscure race, and an event that would barely make it beyond the local news tabloids. But for us there, on that star-spangled finish line, it was a significant moment. It was the first time ever that a woman had outright won the Long Day of any Uzunetap race. It was a new blueprint of the possible – if we dared to imagine it.

Utkuer came in an hour after me, and Ozcan more than four hours later.

The men in my tent grumbled felicitations. Utkuer was generous enough to convey his wife's message: "Thanks for doing it for the girls," she said. Ozcan didn't say anything. Not even a single jab or joke.

At 9am Bakyie Duran, an icon of female strength, arrived at the finish line. The whole village gathered to give her a hero's welcome. Bakyie flung her arms around me as if we had known each other for a lifetime. The way she greeted everyone made me understand that she was all heart and no ego. A true champion.

Day 6 – May the river bring you back to us

18km

The final day's course could be likened to sprinting through an 18km, tree-lush, white-and-rose-coloured garden. I raced alongside young Ozcan and men's champion Utkuer, climbing up through Rose Valley, Dove Valley and finally, Love Valley, to the end. The two men ran on either side of me, like an escort, and held my arms aloft as we crossed the finish line.

Since I was heading directly to the airport, the Turks put me on a makeshift podium and awarded my prize: A handpainted vase patterned in the tradition of their most ancient Hittite ancestry. It was no ordinary winner's cup, for I understood that they had gifted me something as sacred as their proud history and heritage. I held it high with pride. The Turks cupped their hands towards the trophy and shouted and danced.

There, in the shadow of Uçhisar Castle, at the highest point in Cappadocia, I looked out across the magical fairy chimneys and at my Turkish friends dancing to a music in their hearts, and my heart filled. It was full of what I had experienced in that many-layered, mystical country: Acceptance as family, despite my religious and cultural differences, and of all of us coming through safely, despite the coup. I wished for them to be free from the conservative dictatorship that bridled their vibrant spirits.

Ozgur, Tolga and Ozge walked me to the taxi. Ozge poured water after the car. "May your life be easy and flow like water, and may you flow back to us." she said.

My eyes welled up and I waved as they receded into the distance. I knew it would be unlikely that the rivers of life would take me back there. There were too many other races in the world that piqued my interest. I was getting older and had to be discerning in my choices of where to invest my finite physical and financial resources.

Taking off from Istanbul for London, I sensed within myself a hint of impatience. I was ready to go home to South Africa; to be rooted again in my country and among my people in the way that the Turks were strengthened by being among their own. I was eager to belong again, to build a new life, and to do work that felt to me like a calling.

But the time had not yet come, and my mind was set on making the very most of the UK's race opulence. I arrived back in London in top gear – ready to race.

"In the spirit of intl women's day
i want to apologize to all the women
i have called pretty.
before i've called them intelligent or brave.
from now on i will (also) say things like, ***you are resilient***
or, you are extraordinary.*"*

RUPI KAUR[44]

44 Kaur, R. *In the spirit of intl women's day* by Rupi Kaur, *Milk and Honey.* (@rupikaur_), Createspace, 4 November 2014.

11

BEYOND TOO FAR IS FURTHER, UNITED KINGDOM, 2016

"Only those who risk going too far find out how far they can go."

T.S. ELIOT

London to Brighton, 2016

The United Kingdom has the sixth highest levels of per-person charity donations out of 195 countries in the world. In 2018, it raised £10.1 billion[45] through charitable giving, and predominantly through sporting events, like the London Marathon, which is the largest annual fundraising event on the planet. In 2018, its 40 000 runners raised a whopping £66 million.

Perhaps this is one of the reasons why the United Kingdom's long-distance racing scene is so vibrant. It offers people an opportunity to get fitter and healthier while making a real difference to the lives of others through fundraising.

Every year, 2 500 runners and walkers line up for the 100km London to Brighton Charity Challenge to do just that. People arrive to walk, crawl or stagger the race – the 'how' doesn't matter. What matters is the 'why'. Runners are there to raise funds for cancer, Alzheimer's and dementia-related charities, because they have, or had, loved ones whom they lost or were afflicted by the diseases.

45 Charities Aid Foundation, www.cafonline.org (Accessed: 9 July 2021)

The spirit of the race is collegial rather than competitive; the food stations are a delight and a temptation beyond description. One year, at Checkpoint 2, there was a complete, campervan-sized pick-and-mix stand! The course gets prettier and prettier with every mile, as runners slip away from London and draw closer to the coast.

In 2016, I set off with the walkers, rather than the runners, preferring the company of the pilgrims over that of the nervous racing snakes. Right from the outset, I ran at ease, all along the tree-lined Thames path, along the glistening river, past the ducks and the swans and the moored canal boats. It was a sunny, balmy spring morning and yellow daffodils swayed in the light breeze. Life felt easy and full of promise.

Our path cut across the green hills of the North Downs and past one feast of a water station after the other. I passed large groups of walkers and joggers of all shapes, sizes and ages. Everyone was animated; some wore hiking boots and bore giant backpacks and walking sticks, while others were in light trail shoes, carrying only small hydration packs. Everyone greeted me as I went past.

At about the 60km mark, I steamed past the leading female who exclaimed to her male companion: "Where did she come from? She can't possibly still be running at that pace!" The truth was that with every mile, my pace gathered a little more speed – the gratifying reward of starting slowly.

At 70km, feeling as strong as a beast, I effortlessly overtook a platoon of fit British military runners. At 88km, as we started heading up and up the steep, green flanks of the South Downs, I felt as fresh as at the start of the race, sensing within myself a bottomless reserve of energy. I muttered under my breath in amazement: "This is bloody unbelievable!"

Still in disbelieving euphoria, I entered Checkpoint 8 at 90km, when someone distinctly called my name. As I turned, I saw, like a mirage, Billy sitting with her two young children on a picnic blanket, there on the green lawns of Plumpton College. I had not seen my ex-wife in more than four years. Having just stuffed several Jaffa cakes into my mouth, I stood there for a moment, frozen in time, trying to find my bearings. Her toddler crawled across her lap. It felt like no time had passed, and yet like a million years had fallen between us.

I walked over, gulping at the dry cakes, and bent to kiss her on the cheek. She smelled the same: Athletic and clean. Billy. Perhaps with an added whiff of baby powder. There was no expectation of words. The moment passed in the flash of reciprocated smiles.

I dashed out of the checkpoint feeling a bittersweet pain, and yet strangely free. I ran my fastest splits in the final 12km over the high spine of the South Downs and tore across the finish line at the Freshfield Brighton Racecourse in 10 hours, 23 minutes. I was the first lady home and claimed the title for the second year in a row.

The first year I won, my darling Sabelle had cheered wildly from the stands. I remember her so vividly – flushed cheeks and rouged lips, all exuberant and proud. She made the winner's cup taste effervescent, like all of life was alongside Sabelle.

That second year, the spectator stand was vacant. The bareness of it, and the anticlimax of my win, was underscored by a tender yet measured text message of congratulations from her. She no longer addressed me as: "*Mon Coeur*".

I wanted to text back and send her a picture of the trophy and invite her to a celebratory glass of prosecco. I was dying to tell her that I had, on royal invitation, dined with Princess Anne at St James Palace the week before; that there was a small intimate gathering – just four representatives from Opportunity International[46], an NGO of which the princess was an ardent benefactor, and my boss and me, for our company's notable support of the NGO. I knew Sabelle would have enthusiastically quizzed me on every detail – about every course at dinner… and the wine… and the princess's frock. I wanted to tell her I missed her and Christian, and that I had never taken our love for granted.

Instead, I texted an appropriately brief and tactful: "Thank you," knowing that Sabelle would prefer the decorum of me keeping my feelings to myself. There was no use telling her how I felt. Our paths had already

46 Opportunity International is a global non-profit organisation that provides innovative financial services solutions to help break the cycle of generational poverty. Visit: https://opportunity.org/ (Accessed: 7 July 2021)

irrevocably diverged and my time in the UK was fast coming to an end. In the wake of the delisting of my company from the London Stock Exchange, we had been given a year to finalise the transition of the head office back to South Africa, where the company would relist in Johannesburg. I was finally going home, back to my roots. Africa.

Mizuno Endure24, 2016

Thanks to a wonderful and active office culture, we often participated in sporting events together. It just seemed fitting that we would end our company's 15-year stint in the UK by participating in a race of equal ceremonial proportion. We signed up for the Mizuno Endure24.[47]

We entered two corporate relay teams, each team comprising five athletes, who would take turns to run the 8km circuit and bag as many laps as possible in 24 hours.

I was the only girl among them, and had entered the solo category, which meant that I would run for 24 hours without passing the baton to anyone else.

The plan

I was deeply curious. How far could I go? Where were my limits? It was an unknown race format to me, so I had no ambitions of winning, and no ideal target – I was free from that weight. However, I did have a meticulous plan and had made myself a schedule of what to eat, when to eat, when night would fall and when my heart could look forward to sunrise.
According to my calculations, and according to the arithmetic of high hope, it would be possible to run 208km if I never stopped once during the 24 hours. It was a rough estimate, yet somewhere in my subconscious, it settled as a target. I wrote it down and let it go.

47 In 2019, the Mizuno Edure24 event won the award for Best Ultramarathon in the UK. It has become so popular that there is a two-year-long waiting list for solo entries. Remarkably different from similar races, the Mizuno challenge also has a rare 50/50 gender split. Visit https://endure24.co.uk/ (Accessed: 6 July 2021)

The plan became more creative than I could ever have imagined. The "208km" in print set a scaffolding of possibility, and on the day, it created a centre of gravity towards which the energy of the universe would flow and become a reality.

Race day

That race day in June 2016, the weather played in our favour. The green fields of Wasing Park exuded a lush mid-summer humidity. I had arrived by train, armed with a mixed bag of curiosity and equanimity, and a small cardboard box of sandwiches, fruit and nut bars, bananas, painkillers, rehydration salts, fruit juice and a spare pair of shoes – just in case.

Sabelle had texted her good wishes. It was a strong talisman for the long hours ahead.

My colleagues had set up a team tent on the opposite side of the field from the solo entrants. They were bantering about, knowing that each of them faced anywhere between four to five laps, and a maximum distance of 40km over the 24 hours. They had stacked up crates of beer for the long night ahead.

The solo warriors had our own section, away from the excitement of the relay teams. Around me serious-faced, furrow-browed soloists prepared their unmanned aid stations. Each of us brought to the battle years of experience, our favourite power snacks, energy drinks and several changes of clothing, for all kinds of weather.

At midday, the start-gun fired. The top team sprinters set off at an incredible 17km per hour. I shuffled after them at a modest 10km per hour.

The first three laps were the hardest. My body was in pain – perhaps in anticipation of what was to come. At first, I fought the discomfort, which only intensified the spasm in my lower back. Then I let it be and willed myself out of ruminating, and out of the gooseflesh terror and worry as the team-relayers rushed past me. I took my mind off the pain in my body and dialled in my focus on the tree-lined path, the oak trees rustling in the wind, and the long trek up Heartbreak Hill.

I imagined myself at 50km, and then at 100km, and then at nightfall and at 150km, and on up to 200km. That brought my mind right back to my breath, and to the next step, and then the next, deliberately creating long-distance thinking in my mind. I was rewiring my neurons for the distance. During my years of running, I had learned that our minds are faithful to where we set the horizon. It is all relative. If one runs a 10km race, fatigue comes at 8km; in a marathon of 42.2km, it sets in at 36km, and when one runs a 200km race, fatigue doesn't come for the longest time. There was no point rushing.

At 24km, the end of the third lap, my body began to ease into the run. At about the 50km mark, the pain in my left hip and lower back returned sharply. It vanished again on the seventh lap.

A delicious peace enveloped me. I settled into a calm, meditative state as I ran round and round Wasing Park at an average pace of 9.5km per hour, keeping my mind clear and my thoughts light. Easy. Steady.

Lap 8, lap 9, lap 10 … grab a sandwich and eat it on the run … Lap 11, lap 12 …

Dusk and the cold of the approaching night settled across the steady shuffle of runners. Even the sprinters had eased into a more manageable clip. Headlights bobbed along the dark path.

For all of lap 12, I fought my headlight. Something had gone wrong with the wiring, and for most of the lap I ran blind, intermittently closing my eyes to adjust to the deepening darkness. A watchful spectator noticed my predicament and produced a spare torch. Warmed right through by his gracious help, and armed with a beam as bright as a train light, I set off into the night.

Lap 13 – halfway! I felt euphoric.

The headtorch cut a tunnel of light into the darkness. On lap 14, my average speed had crept up to 10.5km per hour.

Lap 15 … lap 16 … midnight.

Coming around to the start of lap 17, I noticed my colleagues' company-branded tent, all lit up and warm and cosy. Someone stood silhouetted in the doorway, drinking a beer. I thought of the guys taking turns to snooze and run and wondered which one of them was on the course with me, doing battle with the night. It was immensely comforting to know that I was not alone.

At the end of lap 17, I had crossed into unknown territory – 136km – further than Oner, further than I had ever run in one stretch in my life. The camping village had gone dark and quiet. Everyone was asleep but for the stoic runners sleepwalking along the path.

The pain in my back, and then both hips, had returned with great persistence. I took another paracetamol and started out on lap 18. For all of the long hours after midnight, my eyes strained longingly toward the east for a sign of dawn. The miles felt endless.

At the start of lap 19, around 3:45am, the blackness lifted. It was a feeling like salvation.

I started lap 21 under a soft, dawn-pink sky, noticing that at 168km, I was still right on track, as per my hand-scribbled schedule. I observed this fact through a mist of sleepiness and pain, not knowing or caring who was ahead or behind me. Pain had seeped into every cell of my body, yet there was a sweetness to the aching; a strange gentleness: A peaceful surrender like drowning.

The sun rose and warmed our battle-numbed bodies. The smell of coffee hung thick and delicious in the air. The village bustle resumed, and around and around we went.

By lap 23, it felt like I was walking on red-hot coals. I pulled into the transition area, and for the first time in 21 hours, I sat down to change my shoes, in the hope that would bring relief. A colleague brought me a gift of steaming hot, milky tea.

It was so good to sit. The tea was a warm and sweet and the soft fingers of comfort had already begun to lure my muscles into cooling down. Transitions are indeed treacherous places in a race. Realising that I had already spent nine minutes there instead of the planned five, I struggled to my aching feet. The race clock under the startline banner showed 3 hours, 10 minutes remaining.

"If I run well, I can still make five laps," I thought and hobbled out of transition for lap 24, amazingly rested by the brief stop.

At the start of my 25th lap, my colleagues whistled and cheered as I came across the line: "You have won the ladies' race! You can stop running now," they laughed, jogging alongside me for the final lap, proud and beaming. They held my hands high as we came across the finish line.

I glanced up at the clock and noticed that there was still a good hour left before the 24-hour cut-off. I felt strong and the pain had gone.

"Guys, I am going to bag a last lap," I said and sped out of the finishing strait. The crowd went wild.

I did my fastest lap of the race, and 42 minutes later, I stormed across the finish line, having run 208km over 26 laps. I was the first lady home by five laps, and second overall, only one lap behind the winning male, Paul Beechey. I had set a new ladies' course record. Three years later, in 2019, the record still stood. The closest challenger fell 24km short of the 208km feat.

The abiding sensation as I came across the finish line was one of wanting to carry on running. I had come to find my boundary and discovered that it was somewhere beyond 208km. Who knows how far beyond? In the instant I left Wasing Park, I forgot the pain. All that remained was a curiosity as strong as addiction to know how far I could go.

In June 2016, I was about to turn 46, and I was by no means done with seeking the outer limits of my boundaries. I was curious about what I may find there, beyond the beyond. Perhaps my soul already knew that I was running towards happiness and a sense of peace.

Leaving the United Kingdom, 2017

It took a year to tie up all of the loose ends at work and to effectively transition the company's London Stock Exchange listing and associated head-office operations to a new continent. By September 2017, my part of the transition work was done. A 10-year phase of my life was coming to an end, and in its wake came a lifetime opportunity to realign my life with my heart's deepest desires.

I wanted to work outdoors; I wanted to write and to teach. I wanted to give people a way to access the wholeness and wellbeing that arises directly from spending time in Nature. It was a strong calling, as hot and as urgent as desire. With time, it grew.

I had worked side by side with wealthy and powerful people, and I had considered the science of what really makes us happy. Over time, I had seen behind the veil. I knew a valuable truth: Having more stuff, more money, status, power, fame, adventures, or even more miles on your STRAVA profile, or more followers on Instagram, does not satisfy. They in themselves are empty pursuits. Happiness is a direct and inner work and is more causally linked to the quality of our thoughts about our circumstances than our circumstances themselves. I burned to share that emancipation from the 'getting' and the 'having' – especially with kids.

Over the previous 10 years in the United Kingdom, I had built for myself a handsome life of work, sport and lifelong friends. My life had been good, and I was on the brink of bidding it all farewell, with all the commensurate fear, uncertainty and vertigo that comes with stepping off the precipice into the unknown.

I could not unhear the calling – I had to plant my seed. I took the plunge, left my corporate career and turned my intention and attention south to a new home and towards a fledgling business. Thrive Guru was already registered, the website had been built and the dream of it billowed in my heart with the hope of making a meaningful difference to many people on my path. The 'how' was not yet clear to me, but I knew that it would all come out in the wash.

I had a final farewell autumn ramble through Richmond Deer Park with a bright battalion of 30 of my best friends. I then emptied my cupboards of 10 years' worth of books and writing, rented out my house, left my job and bade Billy farewell over a heartrending family supper at Nandos in Wimbledon. It felt like last rights, with all of the commensurate tenderness and regrets, all under the tender gazes of my ex-mother-in-law and two ex-sisters-in-law. Then I met with Sabelle for one last glass of wine at our favourite pub.

I think both Billy and Sabelle were perplexed by my tears. I wept because none of the love had gone away.

And it is so for every person I have ever loved. Love doesn't die. It just changes shape as life carries us off on the river of time. It is like energy – its existence at a point in time can't be denied or destroyed; it can only transmute into something other than what it was, and mulch us over and over again until we can become better soil than we were before. And wiser.

I wept also because I knew that once I left the UK, nothing would be the same again.[48] Sabelle, true to her stately nature, never messaged me again.

I also understood that once I lived in South Africa again, I would not be able to jet as freely all over the world to race, nor would I have the means to support it. And so, while I could still afford it, I decided to make use of the convenient global jump-off point of Heathrow to take on one last major international racing challenge. My heart pointed west, to the great American deserts of Arizona and Utah. I found the perfect race: The great Grand to Grand Ultra in Utah.

The Grand to Grand is a world-class, 275km, tough-as-nails course that zig-zags across Utah from the northern rim of the Grand Canyon to the Grand Staircase-Escalante in Dixie Forest National Park. The elevation profile of the race looks like a dragon's back – all sharp spires of undulations, starting at 1 600m and climbing to an altitude of 2 600m. It has a cumulative ascent of 6 000m, which is higher than climbing Mount Kilimanjaro – except that we'd be running it and carrying everything we needed for six days.

I noticed that the race weighed in with a hefty 5-star difficulty rating[49]. I pushed away my concerns and entered anyway. Had I known what I was signing up for, and had I taken a moment to acknowledge the cumulative fatigue of relocating my life, I may perhaps have skipped the adventure and booked a direct flight back to Africa, to where my new life beckoned.

"You can never cross the ocean until you have the courage to lose sight of the shore."

CHRISTOPHER COLUMBUS

---

48 Christian and I remain in touch. He has become a beautiful and kind young man. Sometimes, he passes on news about his mom. Billy and I continue to message each other for birthdays and Christmas, and I hope we will continue to do so until we are no more.

49 www.runultra.co.uk (Accessed: 7 July 2021)

12

WOMEN WHO RUN WITH WOLVES, GRAND CANYON, UTAH, 2017

"Go out into the woods, go out. If you don't go out into the woods, nothing will ever happen, and your life will never begin."

CLARISSA PINKOLA ESTÉS

By the time I landed in Las Vegas, I had not slept for 48 hours. Behind me lay 10 years of living in the UK. My life was neatly crated, occupying little more than a 10th of a shipping container and somewhere on the ocean on route to Cape Town. Ahead of me lay a three-hour drive to Zion National Park in Utah. I ignored the red-eyed jetlag and my body-clock's demands that it was 1am in the morning in London and time to sleep.

I pressed hard on the gas to escape the 5pm Las Vegas traffic, which heaved and spewed carbon monoxide. I wanted to flee the oppressive and slightly morose atmosphere of a city built for a gamble and good time, and ultimately rigged to disappoint.

Interstate 15 swept me out into the no-man's land of the Arizona strip, one of the most sparsely populated areas in the United States. Apart from my little rental car, there were only reverent Joshua Trees, their prickly arms held aloft in praise or beseechment, and the endless blue strip of road. God's country. Here and there, truck stops dotted the barren flatlands of rock and scrag, dispensing obscenely large coffees with cream and corn syrup in every conceivable flavour. I worked my way through the sugary options and, exhaustion-wired to the hilt, I arrived in Springfield at the foot of the Zion National Park somewhere long after dark.

Like the rest of the racers, I should have gone straight to race registration in Kanab and rested there, but Zion was a grand-scale natural marvel, and it was so near Kanab that I could not resist. At first light, and after a broken and jetlagged sleep in a small Springfield motel, I packed a daypack and escaped the long queues of tourists waiting for shuttle buses into Zion by running the 8km into the park.

By the time I got home that evening, I had covered 45km of running and clambering up to the spectacular heights of Angel's Landing; up the crazy-steep switchback trail to Observation Point; and swimming and canyoneering up and up to the head of the Narrows Slot canyon, being watchful for flash floods. In one single day, I had covered the entire park on foot and visited every sight that had been marked on the brochure as worth seeing. The one-day adventure was as spectacular as it was exhausting – and not smart on the eve of a 275km race. I instinctively knew that sitting around in Kanab would have made me feel even worse. I had to keep my momentum or risk stalling completely.

The next morning, on my way to race registration, I stopped somewhere in the middle of nowhere for a final slow and gentle 10km jog to help kickstart my running engine. My body felt flat and drained from the past three months of life, and trampled by the altitude, which would only increase over the next 10 days.

On the run along that deserted, straight, blue line of Route 89, I had the clearest of visceral premonitions that the race was going to rake and scoop me out and then toss me to the vultures. For the first time in my racing life, I genuinely felt afraid. I knew that I didn't have the necessary reserves for what lay ahead.

Back at the car, a rough, rhymeless poem fell from my pen. It was a reminder of the rites of long-distance running, of the wisdoms beneath the flesh, of the reservoirs of energy that become available when one stops fighting what is. The poem was a message from some nether place to prepare my spirit for the moment of stepping into the fire that was sure to come.

Remember

Remember that long distance running is a long dream
surfacing through the body.
And that when the dream turns flesh and bone and breath,
it understands with a phenomenal frizz of delight
that great discomfort is an avenue
not to be avoided,
but to be entered,
with curiosity and a certain immeasurable pleasure –
as of having found new water in a dried-up well,
even one drop enough
to shock us back to the pulse of our life.

Remember, remember,
That beyond great discomfort,
and beyond its twin euphoria,
lies the great big river of acceptance –
which is the vastest reservoir of energy,
and of ease –
a pathway as sparse of thinking as the desert is of trees.
Enter.
Now we are effortlessly floating,
having shed our heavy selves and our worrying,
and having left all burdensome thought and fight behind.

I tore the page from my notebook and stuffed it in my race pack, as a reminder to look for the doorway through the difficulty.

Registration

I screeched into the Wild West town of Kanab just in time for the end of race registration.

A sharp, high-altitude wind cut into my bones. In my mind's eye, a tumbleweed rolled across the deserted road. At registration, I kept feeling like I should be tipping my Stetson hat and saying: "Howdy!"

That sentiment was quickly squashed as I walked up to the table where a terse and military-like marshal awaited to check my race equipment. The atmosphere at check-in was the polar opposite of what I had previously experienced in laidback Turkey. We were given strict instructions to mark every piece of equipment with our initials and race number – even down to every last item of food.

"For every item you drop in the desert, whether intentionally or by accident, we will award a one-hour penalty. There will be no exceptions," read the race regulations. The organisers were unwavering on this rule, which ensured that we would leave no footprint on the pristine environment.

"No, no, no. This won't do!", said the lean, square-chinned young race marshal and tossed my headlamp aside.

"Needs to be 300 lumens, not 240," he commanded, frowning with displeasure. I was about to argue that I had done more races with that headlamp than I could remember, when he picked up my signalling mirror.

"No!" he exclaimed almost plaintively. "This has to be at least three inches long – minimum!"

Given his serious countenance and the increasing pitch of his voice, I nodded apologetically. But when it came to my food rations being deemed inadequate, I vehemently argued my case with facts of this and that race and "20 years' experience".

He would have none of it, "No! You need at least 10 000 calories more. This race is at altitude, and you need more food for the chill factor."

My race bib was withheld until I produced proof of the required equipment and additional calories. Stocking up on significantly more food than my body would need not only robbed me of my usual competitive advantage of a super-light pack, but also deprived me of the opportunity to race near the thin, red line of optimal fuelling, which I have found is just on the lee side of being hungry. I have come to understand that our inbuilt, evolutionary fear of deprivation often make us pack and eat far more than we need on these races.

My provisions weighed in at just under 8kg wet. That was 2kg more than my optimal pack weight, and it weighed on my heart like an elephant, adding to the breathless oppression I was already experiencing at altitude.

The great Grand Canyon

By then, those who had been holed up in Kanab for several days had worked themselves into a froth of anxiety. The buses ferrying us to the startline were full. It was a blessing, because it meant I could drive with race director Colin Geddes, and so avoid the nervous crescendo during the three-hour transport.

Our journey took us deeper and deeper into the wilderness. Ahead of us stretched 200 million years of geology in layers of multi-coloured cliffs, creating the sensation of driving through a giant bucket of Neapolitan ice cream. Vermilion and chocolate cliffs gave way to coral-pink sand dunes, and further north, to spectacular white and grey cliffs, and finally the pink cliffs of the Grand Staircase-Escalante at the finish line.

As we drove, I quizzed Colin about the availability of water; edible plants; what animals roamed out there; the changing nature of the terrain from south to north; the temperature variations between day and night; which the toughest days were, and whether participants knew how to use compasses and signalling mirrors.[50]

"I have never met anyone who asks as many questions as you," Colin exclaimed an hour into the drive. I took that as a subtle request to cap my curiosity.

Since arriving in Utah, I had been testing the air, trying to understand the landscape, to get to know the spirit of the place. No matter how much information I acquired, the landscape continued to feel otherworldly and foreign. The whisper of the wind in the sparse junipers sounded different from the wind's sweet and dusty breath in Africa. There in Utah, the wind carried murmurs of snow and mountain lions, black bears and rattlesnakes, of Aspens, Joshua trees, old Shaman magic and unseen things.

The wind sighed through the shimmering leaves, rustling up stories about a Bushman lost in Apache country. That feeling would persist for the remainder of the race. Looking back, I can see that it was perhaps

50 A compass and signalling mirror are compulsory gear items, but I have never seen organisers test whether participants are skilled in using these devices effectively. I would guess that at least 50% of any field has no idea how to use either of them.

because I was unmoored between continents, in no-man's land. Rootless and homeless, I was exhausted beyond description and on my last legs.

Our buses arrived at basecamp, which was pitched at 1 600m above sea level on the wide, majestic rim of the Grand Canyon. We rushed to the precipice, eager for the sight we had travelled thousands of miles to see. Below us the Earth ripped open in one long, mighty fissure that cut to the horizon and beyond. Distant bodies of water glistened here and there, like a thousand tiny mirrors adorning the swishing curve of the 1 000ft-deep canyon. There on the shoulder of the Grand Canyon, all nervous banter ceased as we shared a moment of instinctive reverence.

"Hi, I think we are in the same tent," said a tall, athletic, 30-something-year-old German with the disposition of a man you would love to introduce to your sister. He introduced himself as Robin Creswell.

"I am in your tent, too," added a burly man who introduced himself as vegetarian Edgar Palacios of Colombia. He added that he was outrunning years of obesity, heart disease and an unhealthy lifestyle.

One by one, our tentmates gathered around us. There was 54-year old Wilhelm Schneeberger from Austria, who didn't speak much English but seemed friendly, even-keeled and contemplative. There was Jon Bille from Denmark, jovial, nervous and competitive; and Mark Thompson, an intensely focused Brit, who was known for racing easily and then storming home in the final 5km at superhuman speeds; and Grant Monette, a gentle, wiry-framed 61-year-old Canadian, who was in love with the wilderness. Then there was Kim. Kimberly Shadlock was a cowgirl from Saskatchewan in the Canadian Northern Forest, where she farmed cattle with her husband and their three beautiful children. Kim had a dream as big as the vast Canadian prairies, to become what she could be, and to outrun the grief of losing a child.

Meeting there, on the rim of the mighty canyon had somehow immediately brought Kim and I closer. We sat together at dinner, along with 120 other nervous racers, clutching at our paper plates as high winds swirled up from the canyon and ripped at the chequered plastic tablecloths and at the cowboys' hats and leather chaps. The cowboys and one spectacularly beautiful cowgirl lolled easily on their horses. They were real-deal ranchers who had joined the Grand to Grand (G2G) Ultra to work as sweepers on the route.

At the windswept race briefing that followed dinner, it became clear that the race was going to be a killer. What makes the G2G harder than most seven-day desert ultras is that it is run at altitude, and that the elevation continues to increase right until the bitter end. The course covers a massive, cumulative distance of 275km, with 6 000m of cumulative climbing – more than most seven-day races.

The brutal first day covered an ultramarathon distance of 50km, denying racers any 'easing in'. The Long Day of nearly 100km came on the third day, which is uncharacteristically early in the race. Broken after the Long Day, racers had to rise to three more days of racing, of which two were full marathons across impassably difficult desert terrain, with a final sprint finish of 12km and 600m of climbing up the unforgiving Grand Staircase-Escalante.

At the race briefing, I apprehensively scanned the female field. From what I could see, there were no obvious chisel-jawed, lean-machine challengers. I felt deeply relieved. I was already tired in the very marrow of my bones, and I needed that race as a junction – a space within which to decompress and rest after packing up my life – and to reflect on what lay ahead.

I had intended the race to be a meditative, and to some extent, solitary, pause to gently transition to my new life.

Day 1 – Kelsey

50km

My tranquil intention was shattered early the next morning at the startline of the first stage. I had positioned myself in the first row, as usual, slightly behind the leading men, who were already hoofing up the earth.

A lithe, young girl, seemingly not a day older than 20, slipped up next to me. Her name was Kelsey Hogan.

"Hi!" she shrilled with the lively exuberance of youth. She practically had to restrain her lean, toned young limbs from setting off beneath her.

I felt her so close to me that the hairs on our skin touched. I knew with a sinking feeling that it was going to be like that for the rest of the race.

"Hi," I responded, feeling my heart drop into my shoes.

By the look on Kelsey's face, there was not a doubt in her mind that the race was hers for the taking, but it was clear in my heart that I wasn't going to let it go without a fight.

Over many years of racing since that beginners' innocence of running in the Sahara, I had inadvertently shifted my focus more and more towards winning. It was the natural course that the better I did, the greater the pull of the podium. It was also true that the more I focused on performance, the less I enjoyed the experience.

I ran hard out of the stiles, intent on shattering Kelsey's confidence by opening up a gap. Kelsey stayed the course as we careened across the vast, open prairie: 20km of intense shoulder-to-shoulder duelling. I finally dropped her as we started the final 30km climb to our camp.

The hard work paid off as I slowly hauled in the 10th-placed, and then the ninth, eighth and then the seventh-placed man. I caught Dirk Diemont of South Africa 10km before the finish line. We had a kindred moment of connection and agreed to run some of the Long Day together.

I explained about Kelsey, apologised for needing to leave, and went ahead to finish in sixth place overall. The finish-line staff rang a loud cattle bell as I sprinted in.

Not even nine minutes later, they rang the bell for Kelsey. She came to congratulate me on the day's performance, but also to offer a covert warning: "I took it easy today. My coach worked out a whole race strategy for me. He has done many of these."

It turns out that Kelsey Hogan was a 26-year-old, exceptionally talented young protégé who had won several scholarships for track running. Her Canadian county envisaged a bright endurance running career for her and had sponsored her coaching and racing.

To boot, she was the adored family friend of Mormon Utah rancher Terry Madl, who was course directors Tess and Colin Geddes's local benefactor. Terry patrolled the course on his quadbike, and cheered Kelsey on for a family win.

Kelsey was as pretty as they come: Young and bright, with a flick of long, blonde hair that swept down to her buttocks; buttery-skinned; blue-eyed; trim and athletic, and with a smile that could lure a priest into temptation. She drew men like pollen beckons bees.

Kelsey was the outright camp favourite to win – but not in my tent. On the eve of the first day, there was much merriment and congratulations for my win. My seven tentmates had my back, and it made all the difference. We lay about all afternoon, getting to know each other better and entertaining one another with stories of our races and training.

Jon Bille shared that in the bitter Danish winters, he would do half-marathons on the stairwells of an 18-storey hospital in his hometown. Kim described winter training in the Canadian Northern Forest, where temperatures could drop down to –20°C, or even colder.

Kim who runs with wolves

"There is no-one a wildish woman loves better than a mate who can be her equal."

CLARISSA PINKOLA ESTÉS

"The past few winters have been bad, but I don't mind the cold. What makes it difficult are the timber wolves," Kim said.

She saw my incredulous look and the chill shuddering through me. She laughed and took the stories up a notch as she told of her husband driving alongside her, a loaded shotgun at the ready, just in case, and of the day he found the tracks of a large wolf that had been stalking her on her daily running loop. "My hubby saw the wolf skulking through the pines, and tracked it. That lovely man has probably done as many miles in his snow boots as I have done in my Solomons. Bless his good heart."

Kim impressed me more that any athlete I had ever met. She was real and brave, and she trained with wolf's breath on her neck. What impressed me even more was her husband Dave's unequivocal support and guardianship of Kim's running dream. I imagined him there in the snow, beneath his Stetson hat, scanning the trees and the shadows, slit-eyed and alert, while that which he loved most in the world ran a little ahead of his pick-up truck's lights.

I came to know Kim over the seven days of racing, like one can only get to know and appreciate someone's soul in the wilderness. There were no barriers, no facades and no compulsion to hide anything. It was not that we excavated the details of each other's lives, but rather that we came to know each other through the banter and anecdotes, and the things unsaid.

We had both gone through difficulties, challenges, heartbreak, and loss. We were kindred spirits seeking the wilderness for space, self-expression, sanity, recovery and healing – a place of sanctity and becoming.

"Running gave me the freedom to grieve without judgment. I was often surrounded by three small children and too caught up in the chores of everyday life to really have space. In the beginning, when I started running, I ran with all of that grief, pain, guilt and anger until, over time, it began to change. Later came gratitude – and much later, joy. Running really saved me and carried me through some dark places."

When her youngest child was only three years old, Kim had seen a YouTube clip of the Grand to Grand Ultra. She had never run further than a half-marathon, but announced to Dave that she was going to run the Grand to Grand one day.

"Sure. Looks like a fine way to die," he had said.

They agreed that Kim would wait four years, until all of their kids were at least at school. There was no way they could afford the race, but Dave said: "Train as hard as you can, baby. When the time comes, the money will be there."

Her husband sold two cows, fundraised, ranched and worked, and the kids helped out while Kim trained and trained through the bitter winters, despite the wolves. In 2017, her family brought her to the startline of G2G and, no matter what, Kim was going to make them proud.

Day 2 – Downhill is for youngsters

43km

On the second stage of the race, Kelsey had adapted her strategy. We both raced out of the stocks and across the scragland that tilted up into a steep hillside of gnarled Utah junipers and silver-grey sagebrush. I managed to drop Kelsey on the 18km steady climb while working intently to gain a 500m lead, one inch at a time.

I knew what lay ahead. The remainder of the day's course stooped into a fast 25km descent. I ran as fast as I could within the capacity of my creaking joints to maintain the hard-earned distance between us. It was to no avail. Ten kilometres before the finish line, I heard her thundering along the path and soon felt her breath on my neck. I could taste the dust kicked up by our feet and the salt-lick of dried sweat around my lips. We were two wolves loping down the steep mountainside, our necks extended, our gait wide and supple as we sped towards the white canvas tents of camp that beckoned in the distance. The young wolf and old wolf, spit flying, mouths open, eyes watering at speed; we were two women having the time of our lives. She had me.

Kelsey finished 6 minutes, 30 seconds before me. She waited for me at the finish line, where we sat for a while enjoying the afterglow and cheering racers across the line.

At the end of the second day, I had a narrow 2 minute lead on her.

Late in the afternoon, Kim came across the line after a tough day. She crawled into the tent: "I am terrified of tomorrow. And so excited," she said and collapsed on the groundsheet next to me.

Ahead of us loomed the ultimate test of the 85km Long Day. In previous years, the fastest time recorded had been just under 12 hours. It was abundantly clear that the Grand to Grand Long Day had been designed to decimate and destroy. For me, the Long Day held the promise of a 15-hour or more full-tilt sprinting duel with Kelsey. I could not imagine anything worse. The thought of it lay like a sour ball in the pit of my stomach.

The same heaviness lay upon my countryman, Dirk Diemont, who had suffered a spectacular blow-out on the Gobi Desert Challenge earlier in the year. "I don't know what happened. I was running and feeling strong among the front guys for the first half of the stage. Then in the second half, I crashed so hard that I thought I was dying. I never want to live through that again."

The ghost of the Gobi haunted Dirk. I suggested that we run together so that I could pace him, and he wouldn't go out too quick at the start. He gratefully accepted.

Day 3 – Longer than long

85km

We started the Long Day in mid-morning. Dirk and I set off together, Kelsey nipping at our heels. We tore up the first set of red sandstone cliffs at a pace far too quick for what lay ahead of us. Both Dirk and I had used hiking poles, which gave us a massive speed advantage on the steep, technical climbs, but they also came at a significant cumulative energy cost.

We pushed the pace through a magical river valley of lush willows and spectacular sandstone rock formations, where we met Terry on his quad bike, trawling the course.

By the time we hit the 30km mark, Dirk and I had completely lost our young challenger. Our route climbed up and up a 20km Jeep track of red, deep, desert sand. I was beginning to feel the effects of going at about 5% above my sweet spot.

Even such a small percentage outside of the ideal zone suspends easy breathing and pushes one over that thin line, where movement becomes strenuous and the body accumulates fatigue at a much faster rate, producing excess cortisol. I was crossing into territory where there was no more calm running, and where one's focus and the ability to hear the body's subtle cues for food and water falter.

"Dirk, we have to slow down, or you have to go on and leave me to run my own run. I'm going to crash at this pace," I implored.

Dirk protested, saying that he needed to stay with me, or he would burn out himself. The ghost of Gobi rode wide and menacingly on his shoulders. He genuinely looked afraid.

He slowed slightly, but too soon forgot and settled back into his comfort zone – and out of mine. I began to worry as I remembered how I passed out on St Aldems Head steps on that starry night when running ONER, unable to follow on military Christopher's quick heels. Every step alongside Dirk raked and clawed precious energy from me.

Every few kilometres, I would nudge Dirk to drop the clip or to go on alone. He did neither. I could feel myself heading for a fatal energy cliff. At dusk, we exited the deep tracts of desert sand on to a hard-packed gravel road. Last light faded quickly into night. The world got swallowed up in a blackness that felt more complete than I had ever experienced in a race. I couldn't see the stars. The crash was as sudden as it was steep. I felt my energy faltering, my muscles failing, and every bodily system coming to a halt.

"Sorry, Dirk, go," was all I could manage.

He looked surprised and coaxed me along for a kilometre or so, mumbled an apology and headed off into the night, alongside Andrei Gligor from Romania.

I was left for dead, shattered. Broken. I doubled over and threw up, then felt somewhat better, relieved to finally be able to lurch along at my own pace. But it was too late to recover my energy. I had blown wide open and would have to stagger and crawl the final and toughest 30km of the race across the infamous Coral Pink sand dunes.

By the time I reached the dunes and their monster crests mounting against the black sky, the temperature had plummeted to 0°C. The sand was deep and soft and swallowed my legs right up to my knees.

A few times, my shoes came off and got lost in the deep sand. I dug desperately, like a deranged desert beetle in the darkness. Fearing a failed excavation, I took my shoes off, attached them to my hiking poles, and crawled my way barefoot up and down 12km of ever-deepening crests and troughs of icy-cold dunes.

My feet turned blue, even bluer than my mood, because I knew that at that pace, Kelsey was gaining on me every second. She would certainly catch me long before the finish line.

At the final checkpoint, an hour before the finish line, Kelsey caught up with me, where I sat hunched over and broken at the campfire. She was as cheerful and blossomy as she had been on the very first morning of the race.

"Well done, you little trooper," I thought. I was most impressed by her performance. She had raced the stage like a seasoned long-distance runner and had kept the stallion's kick for the end.

I finished just under an hour behind Kelsey. She won the Long Day stage superbly and had slipped into the lead by 58 minutes.

There were only three days left to race, and the likelihood of me erasing a gap of nearly an hour was slimmer than the thin blue line of first light above the black horizon. I fell asleep just before dawn, with a feeling of sweet surrender and the stress of performance pressure exiting my body and mind. Finally, I could use the remainder of the race to rest up for my arrival on the shores of my new life.

Throughout the morning, racers trickled in across the finish line. Kim came in 26 hours, 39 minutes after leaving the startline. Beyond exhausted, she still exuded that wild will and never-give-up of the best racers. At 29 hours, 19 minutes after starting the stage, 63-year old Pierre-Louis Besson of France staggered across the finish line, escorted by two fellow racers and followed by a cavalry of cowboy-bearing horses. It was like a scene from the movies. Pierre-Louis was doubled over from exhaustion, the left side of his body limp and seemingly collapsing to the ground, as if in the grips of a stroke. Everyone had gathered to cheer him in. Around me, people stared in shock. Many racers had their hands clasped over their mouths.

There comes a point when perhaps we drive the body too far. Who knows where that point is and when it will come? The eternal occupation of the long-distance runner is to keep pushing against the edge, to see how much more there is to go. Who can say what is too old, and who can judge Pierre-Louis for showing up, at 63 years of age, with still enough life left to try?

I stood there watching him, half-hoping that I would one day have his same will and guts, and half-wondering whether it was worth it. The older I get, the more I wonder.

Day 4 – A day of rest and Coca-Cola

Our rest-day camp was pitched on a spectacular prairie of yellow grass. In the far distance, one could see the white-and-pink cliffs we had just traversed. We lay about, our feet elevated, eating through our daily rations and resting.

By late afternoon, Colin and Tess rolled into camp in a big-wheeled 4x4, carrying a large ice-filled cooler box stacked to the brim with 500ml cans of ice-cold Coca-cola. Each racer was allowed one unit – a welcome reward at the end of the Long Day.

Some people downed their drinks in a gulp; others savoured them slowly. The sweet, dark bubbles burned icy-cold down my breath-scratched throat. As we sat there, clasping our precious red cans, a purple veil of soft rain sifted over the distant mountains and trailed behind it the wide arc of a rainbow. The air smelled of upturned soil, aromatic sagebrush and wet dust.

Colin and Tess put on the best of shows to keep us entertained. A country and western singer, decked out in his Stetson hat and chaps, sat on a low stool against the backdrop of the rain-purple sky and strummed out sweet ballads for all the prairies to hear.

Just before supper, the handsome cowboys and cowgirl rode into camp and set up a wooden horse on which to teach us the art of lassoing. Before long, the wooden horse had been abandoned and racers had been challenged to try to escape their expert, whirling loops.

Eric Claverly, a 37-year-old Frenchman and the leading male, volunteered. The cowboys caught his ankles in full sprint and brought him down with a thud. It was my turn. I hopped and dodged and leaped and felt the swoosh of the rope slip just beneath my feet.

It was in that moment of leaping clear of the noose that I felt it in my bones: A bounciness, a certain quality of energy. A brimming vigour. I knew that feeling well. I was getting into an optimal long-distance burn and could feel my energy reserves surging. It was a good omen for the tough course and long distances that lay ahead. If all manner of things aligned, I would be able to claw back some minutes on Kelsey. There was fight in me still.

As dusk fell, Colin and Tess published the race standings. Racers flocked around the pinboards with headtorches to search for their names and cumulative timings. Dirk was in the front of the crush. He had done well and stormed home in sixth place on the Long Day, escaping the Gobi ghost for good.

He was beaming as he trotted over to where I was slowly savouring some hot pea soup.

"Erica! You're still ahead of Kelsey! You have a three-minute lead on her!", he half-whispered, grinning with delight.

"That's impossible! How?" I was incredulous, but Dirk explained that Kelsey had dropped a water bottle during the dune stage.

"Apparently she had tried but couldn't find it, so just kept going. The sweepers picked it up. She got an hour penalty."

I felt for Kelsey. She had earned her lead, but we were back in a neck-to-neck race, compelled to push each other to breaking point. I sidled over to the boards to check for myself. Kelsey was there, doing the same.

"I guess we are back at it tomorrow. I was almost glad when you opened the gap," I said, having confided in her even on the first day that I came to the race to recharge for my transcontinental relocation.

She gave a wry smile. Her eyes were bloodshot. The exhaustion was printed on her body, in the slight slouch of her shoulders and drooping limbs.

"And I have the worst pantyline rash," she groaned.

We stood there in the failing light, in kinship and admiration of each other, the old wolf at the tail end of her running career, and the young wolf, just starting out.

"Definitely turf the panties. You will be much better off without them," I offered.

"Thanks," she grinned. "You are a machine up the hills."

"And you, on the downs," I reciprocated. "One day you can teach me."

It was her first-ever seven-day race, and she was gaining invaluable experience, actively learning and absorbing what she could. She was a smart lass who watched with an eagle eye for race tactics, mental strategies and every other way to boost resilience and wire the body for the long haul. Young Kelsey Hogan had a bright running future ahead of her, and she was willing to work for it. As she walked off to her huddle of cronies, I quietly wished her every success.

Day 5 – Sprint finish

42km

The sting of the Grand to Grand is in its tail. The final three days of the race exact the steepest and longest climbs of the entire race.

Just before our race start, four of the older female racers huddled around, hugged me and said: "Do it for the older ladies. Please!"

It was a moving plea. I had not anticipated that outside of my tent, there was a sub-group who wished a win for me.

Stage 4 was a killer day. Its elevation profile looked like a rearing anaconda – one relentlessly sheer climb-and-plummet after the other, in and out of Zion Canyon, getting steeper and steeper towards the end. The course stacked the odds equally for Kelsey and me. I braced for a head-to-head race.

Kelsey set out hard from the line, with me right on her heels. I hung on for dear life as we careened down the first giant descent. On the subsequent monster climb, I gained on her, until I overtook her, and with great effort opened up a few more metres between us. Once ahead, I lengthened my stride to the technical rope section, where I knew I could gain a few seconds on her.

My adventure racing years locked into gear, and I hurtled down the small abseil and technical rope section, only touching the rope here and there. But it was too brief a technical section to gain an advantage. Kelsey blew on my neck, and on the downhill, she overtook in a swirl of dust, but did not manage to widen the gap.

At 30km, we were still in full sprint, shoulder to shoulder, until we started up the final and longest 10km uphill.

I had her!

On the blood-curdling steep climb, I came after her like a badger, remorselessly reeling her in. Once I passed her, I bent myself double into it and gained a metre at a time. She huffed after me, refusing to relent.

A river of sweat streamed from my body, every alveolus in my lungs bursting for oxygen, my legs faltering from exhaustion and the acrid build-up of lactic acid. After what felt like an eternity, I felt her slip behind. I opened a 100m gap and lost sight of her in the Utah junipers and scraggly pinyon pines. But not for long. As I topped out on the climb, it immediately tilted into a steep 4km downhill towards Rest Camp 5.

Kelsey was not giving up without a fight. She accelerated and tore past me on the downhill, quick and swift and with the flexible kneecaps and fearlessness of the young. In comparison, I teetered after her. I was nearing my 48th year on the planet and had accumulated hundreds of thousands of kilometres in my joints.

By the look of things, I had zero chance of catching her before the camp.

I thought of the four older women's plea to keep ahead of young Kelsey. Their appeal propelled me. It was the order of things: Old wolf, young wolf. I still had fight left.

Ignoring the agony in my body, I pressed forward – harder and faster, keeping my eyes on the little flags in case I lost the tricky trail that kept switching back on itself, left and right. I noticed a swirl of dust to the left of the path, 200m down the valley. It was Kelsey. She had missed a turn and was heading back up the mountain to recover the trail.

I engaged a gear I didn't know I had, and thundered down the correct gravel track and caught up with Mark, my super-swift tentmate. In the final sprint, he was an unbeatable and formidable racing machine.

He liked Kelsey and had spent many afternoons among the adoring drone of men who had hovered around her, but now his loyalty became clear: We were tentmates and had bonded on the long afternoons of rest and idle chatting.

"Come behind me! I'll slip you!" he urged and clicked his speed up a notch.

I ducked into his slip. Our legs wheeled faster and faster, on the brink of losing control. Our chests widened, gulping air. We became blood and lungs and sheer, dazzling speed. We sprinted across the finish line at a speed of just over 15km/h, flushed and exhilarated, and having dropped Kelsey more than a kilometre back.

Tailing Mark had bought me a precious 4 minutes, 11 seconds to add to my slim lead of only 3 minutes.

My brave, young rival came across the line heavy-limbed and with a look of disbelief in her eyes. She had not expected me to fight for it. Nor had she realised that I would grow stronger by the day.

I was looking forward to the next stage. It was an arduous 43km, technical and relentless climb. Statistically, the odds were in my favour.

Day 6 – The big climb

43km

We shot out of the starting blocks at tremendous speed. Frenchman Erik led, followed by another Frenchman, Benoit, and then me, French by ancestry. On our heels were Frenchmen Olivier and Christophe and then little Kelsey, forming the head of the swan formation. Trailing behind us, the dust-kicking pack of chasers fanned out across the scrub and deep sand tracks.

What a sight it was.

Our swan formation filed down and spat us out one by one into the excitement of narrow slot ravines. By the time I had been flushed out of the red-and-ochre-swirled channels, I had dropped Kelsey and most of the pack.

High on adrenaline, we clambered out, on the other side of Zion, and laboured relentlessly towards the white and grey cliffs that loomed in the distance.

The course meandered up and up along a mountain stream and on to a deserted plateau. My ears pricked up and my footsteps lightened, becoming almost inaudible as I stole through the hardy and gnarled ponderosa pines. My body settled into the vast solitude and silence. All the while my energy surged, as if being fed by invisible energy-arteries of the Earth.

I trotted with unwavering focus: A quiet mind and quiet breathing, knowing that the young one would be chasing steadily in my spoor. With 10km to go, I caught up to Robert Harrison of the UK.

We didn't talk much. As we fell into a rhythm, our combined energy created a reservoir greater than the sum of its parts. Robert and I shifted gears and clicked up the pace; up and up the trail that inclined ever more steeply towards the horizon.

A race photographer had hidden himself in the pines and captured the moment. The deep and intense alchemy of our combined focus is evident in the perfect pendulum-synchronicity of our limbs, the equal frown on our brows, and the mirrored forward tilt of our bodies.

The further we ran together, the more Robert fell into a meditative trance of euphoria. By the time we blasted across the finish line, he had run the fastest stage of his entire five-day race career, and more than a third faster than his Day 1 pace.

He flung his arms around me and hugged me tight. Salt, sweat and tears. We had shared something magical, a remarkable moment of deep energetic connection that is difficult to translate into words, and even harder to maintain in the glare of day-to-day life.

The end-of-stage bell tolled for Kelsey 17 minutes later. I saw in her eyes the look of an animal run to exhaustion. The gap between us had widened to 24 minutes. All that remained was one unforgivingly steep 12km stage, in which we would climb from our final camp at 2 000m above sea level into the thin air of the Grand Staircase-Escalante at an altitude of 2 600m.

Kelsey looked broken. I, too, could feel in my bones that I had only one day of strenuous racing left in me. The increasing altitude was causing my face and hands and feet to swell with cumulative oedema.

Only a fool would count the race as won.

Day 7 – A woman and her pack

12km

On the final morning, Kelsey did not let me down. From the word go, she charged after me as we wound our way up and up the forest trail.

We hurtled at full tilt past ochre cliffs and through fresh, sharp-smelling forests of spruce and pines, and past lines of spectators who had come to see the end of the race. Up and up we went into thin air.

I broke the ribbon three minutes ahead of Kelsey, in a hard-won eighth place overall and as the first lady home. Eric Claverly took the men's title. Four of the first five podium positions were won by Frenchmen.

Dirk finished in sixth place, and Kelsey in ninth overall. By mid-morning everyone had crossed the finish line.

In truth, once the race was done, the last thing anyone cared about was placing. We sat in small groups on the edge of the world, looking back across the layered landscape we had just crossed. We laughed and cried and bade our farewells with elaborate promises of intercontinental visits and joint race entries.

"You must come run the Wolf Run in Canada with us one year," Grant said. He was as thin as a rake and hollow-cheeked after the week's exertion. Wilhelm and Jon, from my tent, shared a beer together. Robert Harrison came by to thank me for the best run of his life. Kim brought her family over to meet all of us.

Dave, her husband, was exactly as I had imagined him: Strong, stout and quiet beneath his Stetson hat. Her two boys were carbon copies of their dad, and her beautiful blond-haired girl stared at the racers with a glint in her eye.

"She wants to be a runner," Kim said, the same bright light shining in her eyes. She lingered. I could tell that she wanted our tent camaraderie to last a little longer, but just as we would all soon be, she was being swept back into the gravity of her normal life.

Later I looked across the lawn and saw Kim leaning back against her husband's chest. Her eyes were closed, and her face was tilted towards the sky in a moment of overwhelming emotion. Their three children sat in formation around them, basking in the afternoon sun. It was the most beautiful thing I had seen in the 10 days I had been in Utah.

"That is how a love relationship is meant to work, each partner transforming the other. The strength and power of each is untangled, shared. He gives her the heart drum. She gives him knowledge of the most complicated rhythms and emotions imaginable ..."

CLARISSA PINKOLA ESTÉS

I observed Kim and her pack with great awe and wonder, and a deep, archaic longing. What they had was my heart's deepest desire and hope. It was the fuel for so much of what I pursued, and it had, in so many ways, shaped the person I had become over the course of my adult life. That longing echoed loud and clear from the Grand Staircase rim and across that vast Apache prairie.

As I boarded the plane in Las Vegas, my orange-swirled Utah-stone trophy clutched under my arm, my mind was not on running. All of my soul hankered for homecoming. I was going back to my motherland, to Africa, to start Thrive Guru and to build a Nature tribe. I was flying south for love, to find my person and to make a family. I had grand dreams. I was going to build something beautiful for someone. An African Taj Mahal.

That someone was already calling for me in a beguiling voice, and her name was Thandi. I was running towards her like a thirsty beast to water.

"I closed my eyes and spoke to you in a thousand silent ways."

RUMI

13

AN ODE TO ENDURANCE RACING, 2017

"The struggle alone pleases us, not the victory."

BLAISE PASCAL

One night, 12 years before running in Utah, when I was still adventure racing, my team and I had crested on to a high, marshland plateau in the Drakensberg in Lesotho. We had not slept for 72 hours. Our bodies were on the brink and the air felt thin and sharp at an altitude of 3 500m. A thick mist lay wet and heavy across the moonlit vastness.

Suddenly a herd of wild horses galloped out of the moon-white swirl, saw us, and stopped. We stood there, four racers on the nether end of our endurance, the 10-fold wild herd necking the air. We stood like that for what felt like the longest time – an eternity. In real time, it was perhaps two minutes. The pack leader snorted, flicked his mane, turned, and galloped off into the moonlit mist, his herd hurtling on his heel. My teammate, Brian, vomited loudly. He had been puking all day from altitude sickness. Team captain Kobus laughed and patted him on the back. We picked up after the horses. No one uttered a word about what we had just witnessed. No words were big enough.

Throughout my endurance-running years, I had experienced a thousand moments like that – moments in Nature so extraordinary that they changed me forever.

"I went to the woods because I wished to live deliberately, to front only the essential facts of life, and see if I could not learn what it had to teach, and not, when I came to die, discover that I had not lived."

HENRY DAVID THOREAU

Thoreau wrote the above words before he sold all he owned and went to live a simple life on the banks of Walden Pond: To think, write and clear himself of the clutter that had become his life in industrial, urbanising America. Leaving London, I followed in his footsteps, because the call of the wild had become louder in my heart than the call of getting and having.

It was in endurance running that I first understood so keenly that what we need in life can be contained in a little backpack. Thoreau said: "*As you simplify your life, the laws of the universe will be simpler; solitude will not be solitude, poverty will not be poverty, nor weakness. What I found in simplicity was fullness.*"[51]

I was seeking Thoreau's fullness. The spiritual teachings of the world's main religions pointed in the same direction: Surrender. Non-attachment. Cessation. The death of self.

By leaving London, I was letting go of many things that defined my life. The thousands of miles of endurance racing had made me resilient enough in my mind and heart to step into an unknown where I bore no title and had no foothold. Endurance racing had taught me the guts to try, to reach far, and to be my own person, despite the fear.

Above all, it had taught me to risk trusting others. It was through endurance sport that I saw deep into the human soul. In those moments when all of our pretences have washed away in exhaustion, when we are stripped naked of our thin facades; in those moments when we can access each other directly and to the core, I found no shame, but instead a shared humanness. In that harsh x-rayed nakedness I discovered an unbearable beauty and bravery, and a sense of how irrepressible our need is for that upstream-thrashing against the tide of our limitations and imperfections – all of us somehow broken, but never beat; all of us

51 https://www.brainyquote.com/quotes/henry_david_thoreau_107811 (Accessed: 11 July 2021)

fighting on to the very end, like egg-fat salmon driven by one singular urge to become what we can.

It was in those moments of pure, connected experience and camaraderie – sweating, struggling and stinking together on the long, dark trails through the night – that I understood how achingly similar we all are. I saw so clearly that the stark gender, cultural, national, or whatever other identities we subscribe to, are a distraction. The truth is that there is far more that unites us than separates us.

Scientific research reveals that outdoor activity in groups bonds people deeply.[52] It shows how physical challenge in a group setting can help bring back teenagers from the brink on to a constructive life path. It shows how exercise and running in the outdoors alleviates depression and feelings of hopelessness. It shows how runners more often than not build a deep kinship across cultural, racial and socio-economic boundaries. Running unites.

I have a friend who grew up in poverty in Soweto. Her name is Khanyi Chaba. She now stands glittering and well-heeled on influential stages of the world. She says: "Privilege is not a sin. It is not something to be ashamed of. Your privilege is responsibility."

Khanyi is a 10-times Comrades runner and a mountaineer. She describes how climbers are roped up together, each attached to the other's fate. Each one is equipped with an ice axe. When one person starts to slide, it is the job of all of the others to dig their axes hard into the ice, to arrest the fall.

Khanyi stands there, and with a sea of eager teenagers turned to her like rain-fresh daisies to the sun, she says: "Use your privilege like an ice axe. When you see a friend about to use drugs, dig in your axe and say: 'No!' When you see someone bullying another, or using racist or sexist language, dig in your axe. Say: 'No!' When you see a man battering a woman, say: 'No!' Dig in your ice axe. Use your privilege to stop others from falling."

Years of endurance racing had awoken in me a desire to take others with me; to take the privilege of my health and my will and to inspire the people who need to move for the very sake of their life to take that first

52 Eigenschenk, B., Thomann, A., McClure, M., Davies, L., Gregory, M., Dettweiler, U. & Inglés, E. Benefits of Outdoor Sports for Society. A Systematic Literature Review and Reflections on Evidence, *Int J Environ Res Public Health*. 16(6): 937, March 2019.

high-inertia step, and then the next one, and the next, until they in turn shine out like lighthouses and get others moving.

In the end, it is not really about running; it is about who we become and how we show up in our lives, and about the positive ripple effects we leave in the world, if we so choose.

Endurance sport had, in a myriad ways, tempered me. It taught me that in the long run, gentle ways always trump brute force. In my dire moments, I have seen into the heart of my own fallibility. It has taught me grace to forgive and accept, and to love.

I started out as a newbie runner, stumbling through my life, making unintentional mistakes. Through running, I found a better path, one little step at a time. Looking back, I could see that the crooked path had evened out. More importantly, I could begin to pay forward that which I had gained.

As I left the international running stage, I had no way of knowing that some of the best running of my life was yet to come, that the wide arc of the African sun, the smell of camel thorn trees and the scent of one particular woman would shake off my cumulative fatigue and shock my running-heart back to life.

14

COMRADES SHOOTING STAR, SOUTH AFRICA, 2018

"Your heart knows the way. Run in that direction."

RUMI

Our dreams are what propel us forward. Like hot air balloons, they rise above the banal of the every-day and colour the sky, floating somewhere to a place we call hope. The small seed of hope lifts, drifts and falls where it will. It grows, bears its fruit and dies. And then we do it all over again. We never quite arrive anywhere.

I was going home to find love. I was aiming towards a final destination, a secure and forever resting place with someone I would love above all else. What I learned instead was that life, by its very definition, does not offer final destinations. Like all of creation, we ride the wave of inexorable change: Night follows day, the tides turn, the seasons shift, what is born must die, and what begins must at some point end. Change is the only constant, and in its discomforting, irresistible rhythm, it carries the creative energy that is life.

I arrived back in Cape Town in October 2018. I expected summer, but instead the wind howled like a deranged woman around the corners of my small, short-lease Mouille Point flat. The sky remained grey, and I realised suddenly that apart from my mom and sister, and my sister's son, Bandile, all of my life and all of my friends were on another continent.

After all of the high expectations of coming home, I felt like a foreigner washed up on the shore – exhausted and alone. The urge to belong, to be part of a group and to connect, is our deepest human need. An American study with 181 000 adults showed that loneliness has the same impact on mortality as smoking 15 cigarettes a day, making it even more dangerous than obesity.[53]

And so, when I met Thandi on a blue, full-moon night for a drink at Lily's in Mouille Point, and she introduced herself as a running-geek and lover of all things running, the magnetic pull was too great for either of us to resist.

On our first date she said: "Freedom or whatever – not sure what I want; aspirationally bisexual; impulsive; definitely a loner."

I said: "Definitely marriage … and someone to live in the Taj Mahal with – forever … not for satisfying a straight-girl curiosity. Please."

I knew from the start. The answers were clearly there. I should have stayed away, but her pursuit was as thoughtful as it was ardent. She bought me a bike light. "Please don't ride in the dark without a light," she said.

She offered to drop me at races and pick up my race numbers and do my race laundry – all of which I refused – as was the decent thing to do. Above all, she was as unwaveringly keen to trek into the wilderness with me as Billy had been so many years before.

We dreamed of the same escapes: A small tent, maps, long days in the mountains, good coffee and Spartan simplicity. For both of us, two-minute noodles on a far-flung mountain trumped any Michelin-star meal. I took her on her first-ever wild-camping adventure. We talked in brilliant multi-colour, our minds feasting on each other's cleverness and bright thinking, and on all of the hiking plans we were making together.

Thandi was the wilderness mate I had longed for. Before long, I capitulated.

She was complex: Feminine and mild-mannered, hard-edged and pitiless. She was eager to please and would do anything one asked of her, and

---

53 Holt-Lunstad, J., Smith, T.B. & Layton J.B. Social Relationships and Mortality Risk: A Meta-analytic Review. *PLOS Medicine* 7(7): e1000316, 2010. Visit https://doi.org/10.1371/journal.pmed.1000316 (Accessed: 12 July 2021)

more; generous to a fault; emotionally austere; frugal in sympathy and suddenly abundant in showers of affection. She was abundantly tactile, "with you only", she said, and then without warning, distant and withdrawn. While mostly as calm and soporific as a sleeping child, to me my Thandi was as unpredictable as a grenade.

A driven and time-pressured professional, she always found time to fastidiously hang her freshly laundered, double-rinsed bedsheets out to dry in the sun. Thandi inhabited the space of her life with a private elegance, and she was beautiful in the way desert women reveal their loveliness – sparingly, and only to some. Behind closed doors, she dropped the veil. Only for me. And that was the magic.

She was a mom to a beautiful 11-year-old boy. Rhadi welcomed me into his life with the brightest, toothiest smile one could ever hope for. Before long, he and I had become the best of surfing buddies. Still too young to be teenage-shy, he would call across the water: "Did you see my wave?".

God alone knows, I had arrived in paradise. I fell for the pair of them wholeheartedly, and without reservation or caution, I gave them my soul.

In the first year, Thandi's adoration for me seemed bottomless. "I am your number one fan," she would say as she drove me to races in the wee hours of the morning and cheered me across many finish lines.

She had read every book, knew every fact, could offer up the statistics of every name and every race that ever held any esteem in running. She knew the theory of what I did by instinct, and was completely incredulous that I didn't know my fastest marathon time – as incredulous as I was that she actually wanted to attend the start of my early-morning races at the most ungodly hours.

Her fascination with running rekindled my enthusiasm for the sport. She gave me a reason to run because, above all, I wanted to remain her champion. For that, I trained like a beast.

Comrades Marathon, 2018

89km

In June 2018, six months into our relationship, I ran the Comrades Marathon for the first time in 15 years.

The Comrades Marathon is a rite of passage, described as "the ultimate human race". It is a loud and colourful affirmation of the human spirit. As the world's largest and oldest marathon race, it is 89.9km long and has a cumulative elevation gain of nearly 2 000m. It is all run on road, between Durban and Pietermaritzburg in KwaZulu-Natal, South Africa. Every year, the race changes direction – either uphill to Pietermaritzburg, or downhill towards Durban, and it has a strict 12-hour cut-off.

Every year the race draws millions of spectators to their television screens to bear witness to the 12-hour-long human ordeal, to share in the agonies and ecstasies of the runners, in their stories of sheer will and determination, and in the heartrending disappointment of the near-finishers.

All South Africans have, at some stage, sat at the edge of their seats watching the finish-line referee raise his gun at 11 hours, 59 minutes and start the 60 second countdown, while the camera pans out to throngs of broken runners, stumbling, crawling and limping hard towards the finish line. In the final 10 seconds before he fires the gun, the referee turns his back so as not to see the great heartbreak of the stragglers who will be just one second too late.

Two nights before the 2018 Comrades, Thandi and I flew into Durban. As we drove to our hotel, a bright shooting star trailed its long tail across the skies. We were silent in the dark night, content in each other's company.

"What is your deepest wish?" I asked, knowing that mine was for us to be together forever.

Six months into a new relationship, we both knew it was foolish and too soon to speak such words out loud. Right there, we each wrote a cryptic email to ourselves on our phones and agreed to reveal them to each other one year on, at the next Comrades.

On the morning of "Down" Comrades 2018, my beautiful Thandi, still in her pyjamas, drove me to the mouth of the Pietermaritzburg starting line and kissed me goodbye, her breath smelling of warm sleep and a sweetness I had come to know as home and everything that was good in my life.

I watched her drive off, and along with 20 000 other hopeful runners, crammed into the overcrowded running chutes.

It was a cold morning, not even 5am. Vapour streamed from our breaths and the air smelled of nervous excitement, sweat, deodorant and menthol rub. Around me towered a group of tall and animated Zulu men. One of them pulled me towards him and created a safe space for me under his armpit, to prevent me from being face-squashed against the fence.

As we neared the countdown, South Africa's national anthem played. Thousands of voices lifted in unison as we sang *Nkosi Sikelel iAfrika* in Xhosa, English and Afrikaans. We sang it with fervour, giving voice to our longing for unity.

My body broke out in goosebumps. I had a lump in my throat, and without shame, tears welled up in the eyes of men and women around me. There, in our slight running shorts on the startline of Comrades 2018, beneath the brilliant red-and-white fireworks exploding against the night-black sky, there was no separateness. We all belonged to a tribe of dedicated runners, and the love ran through us like a blessing.

I have run in many countries and among many cultures, and I have repeatedly witnessed how running can be a centre point for building unity. On that morning, it did not matter who you were or where you came from, Comrades gave us one flag under which to stand.

We set off into the darkness, nearly 20 000 of us, heaving forward across the startline, cautioning each other against discarded bottles and cat-eyes and other obstacles in the road, pushing on at 12km/h with only one thought in our minds: "89km to go."

In the first hour, we ran in silence, breathing hard and frowning into the darkness: Sweating, worrying about the niggles – the tight hamstring, the tender Achilles tendon, the niggle of ITB, and looking for our appropriate pace group with whom we would stay for the rest of the race.

I hunted for my pace leader, scanning ahead across the heaving mass of bodies for the bobbing finishing-time boards that the pace leaders carried aloft on long sticks. As dawn broke, I pulled into the 9½ hour bus and settled into a group of 200 runners or more who hoped to finish at the same time. I kept my pace at a steady 5 minutes, 30 seconds per kilometre and concentrated on my breathing, cadence, posture and body signals for food, sugar and salt.

Alongside the road, crowds roared and cheered us on, calling us by the names pinned to our running vests. Nearly half a million spectators of every race and creed willed us on. Every 3km, a sub-set of the total

40 000 aid station volunteers fed and watered us, ensuring that we wanted for nothing. We were carried forward by a rainbow nation of voices and goodwill.

Thandi was there among the thousands of supporters. She drove like a wild woman to catch me at three spectator points along the 89km course. She first found me near the 30km mark and appeared, beaming with excitement. It was her first opportunity to support at a Comrades, and it was something she had wanted to do for many years. Just seeing her face made me straighten up and quicken my pace. All for love.

At 40km, the wall of runners started thinning out, and the banter and laughing resumed. The first marathon, and nearly half of the race, was done. We started relaxing into the run.

"Eeasy, eeasy, aaalright, eeasy, eeasy," chanted my pace leader, to keep us together to the rhythmic beat of our pounding feet.

At 60km, the worst pain began. It would gather force from thereon in. I needed space to deal with what was happening in my body, so I pulled ahead of my bus.

At Cato Ridge, 20km from the finish, Thandi appeared out of the throng of spectators. She ran alongside me for two kilometres and kissed me. The pain lifted out of me, and I upped the clip a few notches.

In the final 10km, the pain returned with overwhelming intensity. Desperation and brute strength drove us runners forward. Those who could, ran harder, to end the agony.

At 85km I passed a young runner from Soweto who was limping painfully, his face contorted with suffering. His tanks were clearly empty – of both energy and will.

"We can do this. Come with me," I said, urging him to start jogging again.

The two of us egged each other on, and in our final 4km, ran our best time splits yet. We charged into the Durban stadium together and across the finish line in just under 9 hours, both earning Bill Rowan medals. The young man embraced me and disappeared into the finish-line crowds.

Exuberant Thandi was there waiting, looking so happy to see me. We drove directly to the airport in our bubble of love and glory and flew to

Cape Town. That same night, we took Rhadi out for a celebratory dinner. There was no exhaustion, only euphoria – and a happy family.

Otter Challenge 2018

41km

Three months later, Thandi accompanied me on the long drive to Storms River Mouth in the Eastern Cape. I had unexpectedly won a ballot entry to the much-contested and internationally popular Otter Challenge, another iconic race on the South African race calendar and part of the Ultra Trail de Mont Blanc golden triad. The race spanned the entire distance of the five-day Otter hiking trail and had a scanty cut-off time of six hours.

Not having had enough advance notice to arrange our time off work and our travel to the race, we arrived too late for the prologue event. The prologue was to calibrate racers into their starting chutes, and it was a requirement for an official podium finish. It seemed irrelevant, as I never thought I would podium and was merely attending for the sheer beauty and exclusivity of the acclaimed course.

That all changed as we stood in the race-briefing hall on the eve of the run. Race director Mark Collins warned racers to take utmost care in negotiating the challenging river crossings, strong sea currents and the sheer cliffs. As I watched the slideshow of the terrain playing out behind Mark, something deep in my body surged, like the shudder in a horse's flank.

I leaned into Thandi: "I think I could do well tomorrow," I whispered. It was a visceral knowing in my blood.

On race morning, Thandi came to the start at Nature's Valley beach. There, against the backdrop of white sand and the powder-blue sea, she looked so beautiful and young in the early-morning sun. My heart felt full. I was her hero, and she was my running muse. I loved her more than I had ever loved anyone in my life.

I ran sure and steady from the get-go, meeting the 41km of cliffs, sharp rocks, steep valleys and climbs and the swirling river crossings and riptides with the running ease of an animal. I passed a myriad racers, but didn't think much of it. I was completely in the zone. All that existed were my sinew and muscle, my breath and the path beneath my feet.

Thandi walked out on to the path near the finish line.

"Wow, you are in the top three women!" she grinned.

I didn't quite believe it, but on the 600km drive back to Cape Town, Thandi scrolled through the results.

"Oh my God! You won!" she exclaimed.

It was a good omen, because early the next morning I was scheduled to leave to participate in the iconic, beastly-hot and challenging Kalahari Extreme Marathon, colloquially known as KAEM. I was going to defend my 2002 title.

Kalahari Augrabies Extreme Marathon, 2018

When I finally arrived at the Augrabies National Park, it was clear that word of my Otter Challenge win had spread through the camp faster than a veld fire.

Most of my fellow racers considered it insane that I had just raced a challenging ultra on the southern-most coast of our vast country, and then driven a cumulative distance of nearly 2 500km to immediately start a 250km race in the desert.

I noticed a few slit-eyed glances from the top dogs. They had marked me: "Gotta beat that girl."

I wished that I had remained incognito. There was swelling and inertia in my legs from dehydration and the long drive.

But beneath the swelling, my body told a different story. There was a distinct body sensation that by doing the Otter Challenge, I had blown the mitochondrial cobwebs from my cells and put my body directly into that super-efficient, blue-flame energy-burn that only comes on the second or third day of multi-day races. The Otter race had put me into early ketosis.

It was a gamble, but my ramp-up race had paid off well, because right from the outset of KAEM, I felt strong and in charge of my body's output. On the first day, I opened a half-hour lead on the second lady, and widened the gap day after day.

On Day 3, the race director came to the racers' marquee bearing a sealed envelope. My heart leaped because I recognised Thandi's handwriting. Mistakenly, the entire contingent of racers burst out singing: "*Happy Birthday*", after which I had to explain that my partner had shipped a letter of love into the desert with one of the support crew. I read it a hundred times, and it made me work even harder for the final finish line.

After seven days, I crossed the line, the first woman home by a long margin, having successfully defended my 2002 title.[54] I was on a winning streak I could never have foreseen when I had left the UK a year earlier.

Immediately after the race, still dust- and sweat-streaked from seven days of living and running in the desert, I kissed the race owners, Estian and Nadia, and all my new running friends goodbye, skipped the prizegiving, climbed into my car and drove 900km to Cape Town almost non-stop to get back to Thandi.

After KAEM, and partly inspired by my unwavering belief in her, Thandi ran her first marathon in six years. I ran the last 3km with her, and to this day those few kilometres seem to be some of the most meaningful of my running life. There, next to her, my heart had never felt fuller, or my life more complete.

Comrades Shooting Star, 2019

In 2019, Thandi and I travelled down to Durban for the "Up" Comrades Marathon. It was our second Comrades travelling together, and having her by my side seemed more important to me than the race itself. Thandi's mood determined whether I ran well or not. I should have heeded the warning in that.

The night before the race, we shared with each other the star-struck wishing notes that we had written the previous year and emailed to ourselves as a record. I had filed her beautiful email under "*Comrades Shooting Star*". It is exceptionally painful to read the message now.

54 In 2002, I walked and partly jogged KAEM alongside one of my adventure racing team mates as a training session rather than a race.

She wrote these words: *"Stream of consciousness as it popped into my head, clumsy phrasing and all: I wish we get married and stay together for a long, long time."*

I believe there was a time when she really felt that way.

During the race, Thandi met me at four spectator points, having perfected the art of missing the crowds and the inhuman traffic jams on the N3. I ran into the stadium at Pietermaritzburg in under 9 hours, faster than the year before, because Thandi was waiting at the finish line and because she had said: "I am yours."

Thrive Run Club

It was during that golden period that I started Thrive Run Club.

Run Club's founding mission was to get people off the couch and into a lifelong, passionate affair with running. It started as a small club with a big heart, built around a central belief that, no matter the body shape or level of running ability with which you were born, everyone can learn to love running and learn how to run better.

The club became my family, a tribe to which I belonged, heart, body and soul. I had no way of knowing that one of my club members would, through his encouragement, save me from quitting the 2019 Kalahari Extreme Marathon when I would run into dire trouble.

Towards the tail-end of 2019, every system in my body and in my life seemed to be heading for shipwreck.

"You have to keep breaking your heart until it opens."

RUMI

15

RUNNING INTO TROUBLE, KALAHARI DESERT, 2019

"The wound is the place where the light enters you."

RUMI

In the brevity of our over-used idioms lie thousands of years of collective wisdom: Trust your gut.

When I arrived at the 270km Kalahari Augrabies Extreme Marathon, my gut was a mess. I had arrived at the race on one knee, weak from a general low mood and a strange muscular weakness. Then the hot flashes began, setting my bedsheets on fire and repeating every 90 minutes, leaving me broken from sleep deprivation and a listlessness in the marrow of my bones. Then came an abnormally bloated stomach and three days of vomiting, during which I felt too ill to manage even a slow 5km pre-race trot.

My doctor diagnosed it all as the onset of menopause. "Your symptoms are common – nothing to worry about. I know its bad timing, but when you come back, we will start treatment. Good luck for the race."

I didn't feel consoled.

Arriving at Augrabies National Park, the race doctor conducted a medical check: I weighed in at 53.5kg – 1.5kg over ideal race weight, and my blood pressure was low.

"A bit of gastric flu last week, but I think I'm over it." I brushed over it, not wanting to prompt additional checks. The doctor made a note.

The kit marshal, albeit a little incredulous, signed off that I had met the compulsory equipment requirements. My backpack weighed in at a slim 5.5kg dry and 6.2kg wet. It was by far the lightest pack in the race, and it afforded me an enormous advantage on the first two days, when everyone else would be labouring under mule-heavy packs.

Over a 250km desert course, two or three kilograms of extra weight in one's pack can add as much as one to three hours to one's overall finish time. If one is racing for the podium, one could lose the race even before leaving the startline.[55] When I packed for the Kalahari Augrabies Extreme Marathon, it was a ruthless game of shaving off the grams. Ultimately, endurance racing is a discipline of increments, of micro-efficiencies that accumulate into superior performance.

I have won more than my share of multi-day distance races, but not because I've been faster or stronger than my competition. I have won because I've taken care to gain every micro-advantage possible. I have done this, for example, through the deliberate manner in which I place my feet; by seeking with every step the hard ground and the inside corner; running with the slant of the grass rather than against it; running through the water where the mud is thin, rather than getting sucked into the heavy mudbanks on the side paths. Every single step counts.

Micro-gains are begotten through swift checkpoint transitions: Pre-planning them, counting the seconds spent there, and whenever possible, avoiding the stops altogether. They are gained by keeping one's core temperature low. In extremely hot deserts, as I had first done in the Sahara, I wear white cotton gloves and keep them moist, whether with water or sweat to cool my ears – as crisp and minty, as if having suddenly switched on an airconditioner.

Some of my greatest efficiencies are gained through how and what I eat[56], keeping the sugar load low and eating nuts for fat, and eating far less

55 Scan the QR code at the end of the book for a detailed description of the contents of my race pack.

56 The QR code includes an autopsy of my race nutrition which, if optimised, gives an athlete superpowers of performance. Some recipes by LANGPAD for super-nutritious, long-distance race food, have also been included.

than one would imagine necessary. By so doing, I activate fat burning for greater energy efficiency and reduce free-radical damage.

I gain efficiencies by how I breathe to incite a deep body calm, and so keep cortisol production low. On a run, I constantly remind myself to keep the out-breath long and to relax my body.

Efficiencies are also gained through the quality of one's thoughts. What I think, moment to moment, pushes me into an upward spiral rather than on a downer of worry, terse competing, or stress.

On the eve of KAEM 2019, I lay in bed staring at my little backpack of rations, nauseous and fully realising that I was going into battle stripped of my strength and my good stomach bacteria, wholly robbed of that forcefield of confidence that comes from feeling fit and strong.

And what made things a thousand times worse was that I had gone into the race sensing a chink in Thandi's wholehearted support.

Our relationship had developed some unsettling challenges. Twinned with the moments of passionate love came gargantuan blow-ups and the steep crevasses of conflict and unintended hurts. The misunderstandings and frustrations had accumulated because, as much as we tried, we failed to find a common language in which to diffuse our disagreements and in which to build a safehouse.

Thandi disliked my friends – every last one of them. I saw them less and less and failed to notice the peril in that. I loved Thandi more than life, and I had no doubt that we would make it through.

Day 1 – Meeting Helen

25km

In the morning, I forced a little ProNutro porridge past the nausea that had wedged in my oesophagus. My stomach roiled with the sludge as I jogged to the startline.

National flags from 18 countries hung motionless in the still heat. It was only 7am and the temperature had already climbed to well above 30°C. Cicadas chirped with insane intensity.

Among the milling, nervous racers and many old friends, I spotted my competition. She sat dead-still in the shade, long-legged and lean, her eyes a piercing blue above the set jaw of someone who is accustomed to a life of unyielding discipline. She didn't chat to the others, but instead scowled beneath her Comrades Marathon cap. My stomach gave a little heave and pushed back the rising porridge.

I never set myself a race-pace objective. Neither did I read the biographies of other entrants – not because I am not competitive, but because the pressure of knowing doesn't serve me. Fretting about another competitor's performance is nothing more than an energy thief. As far as possible, I try to arrive at every race with a sense of curiosity and a singular focus on running my own race. The more I can maintain that spirit, the better I perform. In 2019, the KAEM title was mine to lose; and seeing my edgy competition so poised for the start-gun greatly added to my biliousness.

At 8am, Nadia and Estian, the race owners of KAEM, set us off on the 20th edition of the race. Seventy-five racers leaped across the hot, flat rocks of the Augrabies Falls and disappeared into the hot vastness of dust, drought and desolation.

I ran hard on the heels of Hylton Dunn, a formidable runner and the leading man who was touted to win the race. I wanted to make the most of my pack-weight advantage and build a reasonable buffer between myself and my chasers. There are few things that give one a greater psychological advantage right at the outset of the race, and I needed every gain I could get.

The race route cut through a cluster of camel thorn trees and past three long-lashed giraffe. They continued their chewing and stared undeterred at me across the treetops. I inhaled the sweet scent of the trees, the dust and the scraggy veld, all baked to a cinder under the hot African sun. In a single moment, I experienced the most comforting sense of belonging, of being home, of have finally arrived where I knew the Earth. I felt that somehow it knew me, too. For a while, it made me forget about the chasers.

The girl in the Comrades cap was nowhere to be seen and the first checkpoint came swiftly at 10km.

Then came Checkpoints 2 and 3.

Shortly after leaving Checkpoint 3, I heard Russell Nugent, a local from Upington who was chasing hard on Hylton's heels to win the race, and

Fergus Wall, a tall, lean, Irish racing machine, closing in. They caught me, lingered a while, and accelerated past, leaving behind a trail of Irish banter and friendly profanities. I upped the pace and stayed in their footsteps. We were 18km into the race and miles ahead of the pack.

At 23km, we turned a sharp left up a sandy riverbed into the belly of a narrow desert gorge, laced with black lava rock. Everything had been baked to 45°C by the merciless African sun.

I sprinted into the finishing strait in fourth position overall, swallowing hard at a sudden rush of bile. I strode directly to the medics' tent, but then decided against telling them about the increasing nausea and discomfort in my roiling intestines. I was sure it would pass.

Alet Maartens, who headed up the medic team, sat astride on her veld stool. She is the kind of woman you would want next to you in the trenches. An ex-pastor and a gifted paramedic, she is able to pick out the ill and diseased even before they mention a word of their aches and pains. I had met her at KAEM the previous year and had immediately connected with her.

Across from her sprawled a woman dressed in khaki combat trousers, wiping at the lens of her massive camera. She had been a KAEM race photographer for many years, and was as permanent a feature as the heat. One would often come around a bend and find Hermien Webb splayed flat on the ground, balancing the camera to get a good shot.

The top of Hermien's khaki bush hat had been lopped off to make space for a cascade of blonde hair, strands of which had turned an attractive grey.

"I am not going to fucking dye my hair! Ever!" Hermien exclaimed in her larger-than-life manner.

The conversation turned to menopause and women's challenges in general.

"Have you any idea what women go through?" asked Hermien, addressing Cuddles, a 24-year old medic with a saintly face. He unfortunately shook his head, thus inviting the gender education of his life.

Hermien and I took turns chronicling the monthly female hormone cycle that left us simultaneously grumpy, moody, sad and mad, and utterly incomprehensible to the men in our lives. What men may not know is that, when our menstruation cycle strikes, our blood pressure drops off a cliff, leaving us dizzy and weak. At a biological level, our haemoglobin count drops, severely compromising our VO2 max[57]. Our oestrogen drops, which plummets our dopamine and serotonin levels, making us feel psychologically low, seemingly without reason. Our core body temperature elevates, we lose vast amounts of iron and generally experience the extreme pain that goes along with one's uterus lining tearing free. And then there are the compromised bowel movements, the elephant legs from retaining so much water, the sensitive, enlarged breasts and abdominal swelling.

"Try running in this state, while bleeding copiously, which causes all manner of additional chafing and discomfort. God forbid, let it not be on the long stage of a race," I added, remembering the bitter Long Day on the Lycian Way, next to a disenchanted Hasan.

Hermien had by then become red in the face, as in the grip of a hot flash, and picked up the baton.

"We go through this once a month for 40 years, until we hit menopause. And then, instead of relief, we enter 10 years of insomnia and hot flashes. I can't even have a glass of wine without spontaneously combusting!" she groaned.

Cuddles looked a little pale.

Alet took over: "And let's not forget about pregnancy and giving birth!".

She described the crazy cravings, the staggering changes in body composition and the inexorable creep of body fat, the sleep patterns that change for life, not to mention the excruciating pain of childbirth, which could be likened to passing 10 gallstones all at once, resulting in all manner of permanent skin-stretching and vaginal tearing.

"In my next life, I am coming back as a guy," Alet grumbled.

We all had a good chuckle. It was funny, in a way, but not. It is seldom talked about on the race circuit, and there is too little appreciation for what women must overcome just to make it to the startline of races.

Loud cheering interrupted our conversation. The finisher bell rang. The Comrades-cap-wearing woman strode into camp a mere 13 minutes after me, looking chisel-jaw strong. Without doubt, it was going to be a hard race, and uncomfortably close to the bone.

57 The amount of oxygen one's muscles can use per kilogram of bodyweight per minute – one's combustion capacity.

For the rest of the afternoon, all of the racers lay in that hot gorge under the white, canvas marquees. Trying to avoid the death grip of the heat, I sought the shade of an acacia tree, where I found my opponent doing the same.

"Helen." She introduced herself in as few words as possible, yet beneath the brevity, she seemed open, inviting conversation.

Helen and I had known each other for little more than half a day, yet we openly spoke about love; about love lost; heartache; mistakes; divorces, and of healing. My heart softened towards her. It is the way of the desert; it opens the heart and breaks down the toughest exteriors.

Sitting there with her, I had a visceral premonition that she was going to beat me, and somehow it was the last thing that mattered under that cobalt-blue bowl of sky.

By evening, a migraine had gripped its iron fist across my skull – and it squeezed until I felt I would pass out from the pain and nausea. I lay weak and miserable among my unsuspecting tentmates, waiting for night to fall, and knowing better than to make a scene – partly because almost everyone has some form of misery to complain about after the first day's racing, and partly because loud protesting is to discomfort what wind is to fire. I had no desire to give my increasing physical discomfort a name, or any fuel to gain force.

Day 2 – Death Valley

41km

By dawn, the coolness of the night had already fled before the desert's heated breath. I wrestled down my ProNutro.

Alet was watching like a hawk from the medics' tent and called me over. "What's wrong, Erica?"

I was taken by surprise "Just a bit of nausea. From a migraine. It will pass," I said, also aware that medics have the unfortunate duty of removing poorly participants from the race, if need be.

Alet gave me a thimble of Jamaica ginger and two paracetamols. Neither remedy made any difference.

We had a staggered start and set off in batches, from slowest to fastest. At 8am, Helen and I set off together with the three leading men into a furnace of heat.

Now familiar with the terrain, Helen opened full throttle. I stayed on her heels until Checkpoint 1, at 9km. She upped the pace, making me work even harder to stay with her until Checkpoint 2 at 20km. I was determined not to forfeit any of the 11-minute lead of the first day, but after 25km, Helen tore off into the heat-shimmering distance. I was in no shape to follow.

As I turned up the sandy gorge of Death Valley, the young medic on duty pressed an anti-nausea tablet into my hand. "Alet let me know you're having a tough time."

I swallowed and gagged.

"Keep it in," I muttered to myself, desperate to avoid vomiting and the subsequent doom of electrolyte loss.

I fought my way up the sandy trail as it slanted steeply upwards towards the escarpment, and on to sheer sections of oven-hot stone slabs.

Scrambling up over a blind rise, I bumped headlong into the decomposing carcass of a gemsbok, its long, straight horns pointing heavenward, and its chest cavity hollowed out by maggots. My stomach heaved. The desert floor responded with a broil of hot air rising into my face.[58] I bent over double and hurled, violent stomach contractions spilling out two days' worth of half-digested food and bile on to the hot sand. God, I felt awful.

I rose from my knees, unsteady and trembling, and staggered on through the heat.

A few hundred metres further, a fresh zebra carcass obstructed the way. Around it was a spray of blood.

"Haemorrhaged to death, poor bastard," I thought with great sadness for the animal.

The canyon echoed with my retching. Three racers passed by, each in turn offering their help.

I waved them on. "I'm okay, just taking it slow through the heat."

I was ridiculously sure I would still bounce back.

---

58 In 2019, checkpoint volunteers measured ground temperatures of 60°C in Death Valley.

Dizzy and disorientated, I came upon another zebra carcass, half-decomposed in a putrid pool of purple water and rotting flesh. My stomach lurched and spewed.

I fell, thinking: "God, I can't pass out in this heat. I will die." Drawing on my last strength, I crawled like a wounded animal under a rocky overhang for respite from the scorching heat.

I remember a feeling of bliss washing over me and I passed out.

When I came to, after I don't know how long, the distant silhouettes of two racers floated by on the hot haze. My tongue was thick and hot in my mouth and my water bottle was empty. Hidden from sight, I knew no one would find me if I passed out again. I crawled out into the blaze and staggered in the direction of the checkpoint. A surreal mirage of three, elongated white figures appeared on the horizon.

When the three medics got to me, they half-carried me to the checkpoint. All I remember is a scene of profanities and frustration, and much pain as the checkpoint nurse failed four or five times to find a vein plump enough to insert a saline drip.

"My dear, you have to drink at least a litre-and-a-half of water before we will let you go," the nurse concluded.

It was a bitter struggle because every sip I took was retched out a second later. Everything happened in a daze of confusion. The nurse rolled me on to my side and injected me for nausea. Someone doused me in water; someone washed my hydration pack and pipe with disinfectant – in case I was carrying a virus in the hot, tepid plastic. Someone else peeled me an orange. Even the smell made me gag. Another medic took my blood pressure and said it was way too low and that I would probably not be allowed to continue.

Medical science tells us that blood pressure is controlled parasympathetically and can't be manipulated by our thoughts. God only knows, there on that desert floor I willed my blood pressure to climb.

With every passing minute the gap between Helen and me grew. I knew I was on the mend when I began worrying about the distance that was mounting between us. At the end of a litre-and-a-half of cyclical drinking and retching, the medics finally released me. They recruited a fellow racer to escort me to the finish line.

"Simone, she is not allowed to run, she must walk." Simone nodded dutifully and, bless her soul, the moment we were out of sight, she settled into a slow hobble of a trot next to me. She was clearly in excruciating pain.

"My feet are so swollen that I can't fit them in my shoes any longer," she said, trying to hide the emotion in her voice.

Simone and I stumbled into camp more than two hours after Helen.

I had fallen from fourth to 12th place overall and had, in terms of distance, fallen 16km behind Helen – 16km!

Helen was getting stronger by the day and I was down on my knees with some inexplicable illness. For all intents and purposes, the bell had tolled for me. My chance for top podium was over.

Where the other medics failed, Alet expertly inserted a drip right into an eager blue vein. I lay there, more grateful to be alive than sad about what had happened, feeling the cool of the drip plumping up my cells, and missing my mom and Thandi.

Simone slowly and painfully peeled off her socks. Every single one of her little toes was bashed black and blue from repeatedly hitting the front of her shoes. Her feet, angry, red and swollen, were covered in a multitude of fat, painful and waterlogged blisters. I held her hand while Alet patiently punctured and ran a thread through each blister to drain them. She then injected the worst ones with purple methylate. The burn was as intense as a branding iron on the tender inner flesh of Simone's battered toes. Silent tears ran down her cheeks.

As per the experts' recommended way, Simone raced in thick, woollen socks and gaiters, which is, in my opinion, the perfect way to cook one's feet and soften them so that even the slightest friction causes a blister.

I watched in horror as more racers limped into Alet's bush surgery. It was only the second day and already there was a carnage of foot problems of every horrific kind: Blackened toes under which pussy infections had begun to fester; heels coming off in thick, bloodied masses, and balls of feet that had such large and deep blisters that Alet had to cut away all of the skin beneath the ball, leaving raw, fleshy stumps on which racers had to limp day after day; large pieces of skinless flesh that would invariably get full of sand and grit, until it all turned into a painful, bloodied, pulpy mess.

Even after seven days of running in the desert, I have been blessed with escaping every foot affliction that plagues so many racers. It has been like that for 20 years of endurance racing, and I wonder whether I was just lucky, or whether it had paid off that I have broken away from the conventional wisdom of trail-running footwear.

I wear super-thin, no-name-brand anklet socks and light, super-breathable, short-distance road-running shoes. They help me to stay light on my feet and maintain connection with the changing ground surface. The soles are flexible and the meshing is soft enough so that my feet never have to fight the shoe. I wear my lacing as loose as possible to allow oxygenated blood to flow freely to my feet. I run light, as far as possible with quick cadence, which reduces the degree to which my feet have to dig in and graze against my shoes. I also try to avoid walking, which is the highest friction foot-movement of all.

Later that afternoon, I found Simone in her tent. "You need thin socks. And dump the gaiters. They are just cooking your feet."

I gave her my only pair of spare socks, and just hoped and prayed that the big-toe holes that had already formed in my only pair of racing socks would not grow any larger. I made a cunning plan to swap the socks on my left and right feet so that the holes would be opposite my pinkie toes.

For the rest of the day, I lay in my tent, the nausea unabating, and forced down morsels of food. Eat or fail. It is the irrefutable law of endurance racing.

My mind continued a treasonous downward spiral: "You are feeling so awful. Just quit. Go home to Thandi and Rhadi. It will be time much better spent than lying around in the desert for days feeling sick." The sirens of quitting goaded me all afternoon long, and I felt myself losing heart. That is the singularly most dangerous thing that can happen to a runner.

In the late afternoon, a marshal came by with our daily desert post. I set upon my stack of printed email messages from my mom and friends and Thandi – precious beyond measure for the boost in morale they brought. The contents didn't matter, because for us racers out in the desert, it is not so much the words we are after, it's the names on the pages and the knowing that someone cares.

There was an email from Siraaj, a new member of Run Club, whose passion inspired everyone with whom he ran. His words shot through my spine and made me sit up straight.

"Dear Erica, thinking of you in the desert. Thank you for everything you have done for me, for getting me running, for inspiring me to do my best. Good luck for tomorrow. And remember … NEVER EVER GIVE UP!"

I stared at Siraaj's email. How could I not continue the race? Those powerful few words incinerated all my wavering. Walking away from the cyber tent, I decided to stop complaining about my nausea, to lift my spirits as best I could, to socialise, and to eat every last morsel of my rations.

Once I got my head there, my heart followed, despite the overwhelming sick feeling in my stomach. I was back in the race – and I was going to finish, no matter what.

During the night, hot and cold shivers racked my body. By 4am, the desert temperature had plummeted. In a moment of desperation, I folded my foil emergency blanket around my aching, quivering body.

Rustle-rustle-rustle.

Glittering in the moonlight, like Priscilla Queen of the Desert, I finally drifted off for one meagre hour of sleep.

Day 3 – Never ever give up

42km

The first people set off at 5am in staggered starts. I set off with the top-10 batch at 7:30am, dragging my legs like waterlogged tree trunks. My body felt completely devoid of energy, as if none of the food I had forced down the previous day had digested. Instead, the bulk of it had festered in my distended stomach.

The men in the top 10 batch noticed my laboured plodding and came after me, each one aiming to move up the ranks. I fell to the back of my batch and watched the top 10 guys disappear over the horizon, grateful to be alone in my misery.

Once I was out of earshot, I called out to the vile affliction in my stomach: "Whatever you are, I command you to get out!" and in desperation added: "In the name of Jesus, please!"

The failed exorcism made me seem as deranged as I was despairing. Hearing myself so out of sorts, and remembering Siraaj's email, I followed with a sterner: "*Kom, meisie*, pull yourself together!"

At Checkpoint 1, Irishman Fergus sat slumped under the marquee. He was as white as a sheet and complaining of cramps and nausea. Since the first day, he had been running hard to keep up with Russell Nugent.

Fergus had kept a steady third placing overall, but the previous night he had said he couldn't stomach his food. I felt for him because I understood from the mess in my own gut how dreadful it is to run these distances with stomach problems.

I left the Irishman there, and warily wobbled on to Checkpoint 2 at 19km, and Checkpoint 3 at 32km. Helen was nowhere in sight. I imagined that she had blitzed the course in record time.

I felt awful, and deliberately turned my mind from it. I focused instead on the fundamentals: My cadence and posture; relaxing my body; wetting my ears; exhaling deeply; pushing away morose thoughts of self-pity; thanking the slight tailwind; gently rubbing my distended belly, and eating a small bite of dried banana and coconut flakes every 45 minutes. I was just ticking over. One step at a time.

It paid off.

Somewhere after the 35km mark, I noticed that the blue sky had taken on a magnificent silver sheen. New puffs of hot-white clouds drifted dreamlike through the sky and cast a herd of shadows over the vast, ochre landscape. The entire desert opened for miles and miles towards the green, thorn-tree-lined spine of the Orange River.

Camp was only 8km away. It was then not far to water. And to rest.

Buoyed by the slight drop in temperature, the awe-inspiring sight before me, and the prospect of lying down, the nausea exorcised itself. My legs loosened themselves of the dead weight I had been dragging all day. In that moment, the Kalahari Desert seemed the most magical place I had ever been.

For the final, heavenly few kilometres, I careened down the dusty track to our river camp, and to where I believed, beyond belief, that there would again be a mid-way letter of love from Thandi.

At the finish line, Dangerous Dave, one of the KAEM photographers, hoisted his camera.

"How did it go?"

I looked past the lens and saw in his pale, blue eyes a genuine concern.

I saw him clearly: Dangerous Dave, who used to be obese, who started running and gave up drink and smoking, and who now lives for the spirit and the adrenaline of outdoor adventures, following runners day and night on his quadbike across desolate deserts, recording and getting a vicarious kick from their struggles and victories.

"I just made it!" I laughed, and met his bright smile of shared triumph.

It is the nature of love that it can exist in a micro-moment between two strangers, as pure and perfect and whole as between two people who have shared a lifetime together.

I went straight to the cool, deep flow of the Orange River and soaked my weary body and rancid clothes until cold shivers took over every inch of my body. On my way back to camp, Jenna, who manned the finish line and cyber tent, called me over to collect my emails, "By the way, Helen came in just 12 minutes before you."

"That's impossible. I ran as if I had one foot in the grave today."

She laughed: "That's why I am telling you. You may be able to make up the time."

Just 12 minutes! And there it was again: That shy hope, and its cautious twin: The wisdom and discipline to keep hope bridled and keep the eager eye on one prize only – finishing the race.

In the late afternoon, we heard that Harry was bringing in Fergus. It was infamously loud, loved and boisterous Harry whom I had first met and shared a tent at the Runfire Cappadocia race in Turkey. One could hear Harry's voice a mile off – hoarse, raspy and full of mirth.

By 5pm, many hours since we had first received news that they had been struggling, Harry and Fergus staggered into camp. Harry looked shattered, but not as bad as hollow-cheeked Fergus, who had taken on the skeletal look of a prisoner of war. Both men collapsed under their tent and remained prostrate for the remainder of day.

In the early evening, as we gathered around the kettles to eat, we all went quiet as Phil Waudby's wailing rang plaintively across the desert. Alet was on the 15th hour of her shift and stoically cutting into Phil's infected blisters, speaking softly to ease the 70-year-old man's agony.

We all had the same thought: How will he manage the 77km that lay ahead the next day – 55km of which promised to be a relentless ascent along sandy riverbeds and stony game tracks? It was going to be a killer of a Long Day.

In 2012, Phil had run 1 200km from Johannesburg to the startline of the 250km KAEM to honour his mother's passing, and to literally run the grief out of his body. Two months after successfully completing the challenge, his wife passed away.

"I have never been the same since," he had said to me the previous day.

"Now I run to raise funds to stop the bastards from massacring our Black Rhinos," he said and proudly pulled up his sleeve to reveal a giant rhino head tattoo on his right shoulder.

The body is a faithful history of one's life. Joy and grief is written into one's cells. I believe that running helps us access that which we have yet to process. It opens the difficulty in a gentle way so that healing can happen. Perhaps the motion of running is reminiscent of being rocked in loving arms; perhaps there is something in the comforting rhythm that reminds us of the safe place of the womb. Whatever it is, running has the power to heal.

When I listen to the stories of my friends and fellow racers, and when I think of my own life, I realise how running has been an unfailing lifeline for many of us. It has helped us to climb out of the pits of despair after illness, divorce, trauma and loss; every day helping us to walk out of the dark woods of depression and stress.

One of my favourite scientific, randomised trial studies – which is just a clever way of saying that the research was conducted in a proper and unbiased way – divided 156 adults with severe, chronic depressive symptoms into four random groups. One group was treated with antidepressants; another with aerobic exercise for 40 minutes three times a week, and the third group with both exercise and antidepressants. The fourth group didn't get any treatment.[59]

The findings were that all three treatment groups showed the same degree of recovery after 16 weeks, and even more significantly, that 10

59 Babyak, M., Blumenthal, J.A., and Herman, S. et al. Exercise treatment for major depression: Maintenance of therapeutic benefit at 10 months. *Psychosom Med.* 2000.

months later, the relapse rate was 50% less in the exercise groups than in the medicated group.

Whether one is a 5km-once-a-week-jogger or a long-distance desert racer, running gives one a track on which to keep one's life together. It calls on one to show up, irrespective of the weather, regardless of our life circumstances, and whether we feel like it or not. And as we step up, day after day, to 'just do it', we slowly but surely become improved versions of ourselves.

It is not at all far-fetched to say that running supports our success in other areas of life. A fascinating longitudinal study[60] of 1 500 listed companies in the US showed that marathon runners made better CEOs. Fit CEOs created 5–8% more value for shareholders than unfit ones, primarily because of greater job performance, better stress-coping and enhanced cognitive functioning.

The same holds for employees. Doctor Wendy Suzuki, a neurologist in New York, has provided compelling evidence that running makes employees smarter.[61] It increases concentration for up to two hours after exercising, improves memory and increases creativity.

Running was all of that for me, and more. It had been the bridge that brought Thandi and me together.

As the evening wore on, I realised with a sadness as heavy as my fatigue that there was no half-way, Day 3 letter from Thandi. I turned my mind from it and tried not to ruminate, for the weight of the knowing that was settling in my gut had a power greater than any other to end my race.

Day 4 – A long, beautiful day

77km

In the black hours before dawn, the first batch of racers started preparing for the 77km ordeal that lay ahead. The rest of us lay in our sleeping bags, noticing the frowns under headlights, and feeling sorry for the folk who

60 A study conducted between 2001–2011, Limbach, Sonneburg, 2015, https://content.tcmediasaffaires.com/LAF/lacom/CEO_fitness.pdf (Accessed: 12 July 2021)

61 "Exercise adds up to big brain boosts, Cognitive Neuroscience Society, *ScienceDaily*, 25 March 2019, www.sciencedaily.com/releases/2019/03/ 190325080354.htm

had been the last to arrive the previous night, for they had had barely any time to refuel, rest and receive medical attention before they had to get up and set off again on what would be a 25-hour-plus stage.

The first group set off at 5:30am under the bright light of Venus, just as she was dipping towards the horizon. After that, a batch of runners left every hour. These are the longest mornings of one's life.

We had breakfast. Then we packed. And then we waited.

Around 7am, Fergus came to bid us goodbye. He looked emaciated. Unable to bear even the thought of repeating the suffering that he had endured the previous day, and with a good 170km to go, he had withdrawn from the race – but not without one last spectacular show of Irish humour.

He described how Harry had carried him over the line the day before: "Harry did me good and proper yesterday. He gave me the King's Lawnmower treatment. He commanded: 'Young man! Drop your pants!'"

Fergus proceeded to describe a spectacularly unpleasant sequence of highly invasive anatomical manipulations that are sure to get any soldier running for his life. We roared with laughter and Fergus collapsed in a heap, exhausted by this final show for our amusement.

We were sad to see him go, and even more sorry for what we knew would assail him once he started feeling better back at the Augrabies Falls Lodge. There is no amount of beer, good food or rest that can erase the disappointment that lingers for days, and sometimes for months or even years, after having to throw in the towel.[62]

By 10am, the volunteers had packed up the large canvas marquees but for the one under which we sat. The medics had departed for Checkpoint 3, and there were just eight of us remaining.

Waiting.

At 11:30am, I wet my head and my cap. My time had come. At last. Helen, Russell and the leading man, Hylton, were in the final batch and would start an hour after me.

I set off on a relaxed, meditative shuffle, grateful for starting in a slower batch and at a gentler pace.

62 Once he did feel better, Fergus showed up at checkpoints to support his fellow racers – a true champion rising above circumstances.

My body was still weak from the second day's collapse and my stomach remained uncomfortably distended, but my mind was a blue blaze of resolve. At its centre was a white-hot stillness.

"Run your own race. Easy. Just breathe. Relax." It was a good mantra for the Long Day.

With every step, I stoked up only good thoughts to calm my body all day long and to lessen the cumulation of cortisol. Our bodies follow faithfully where our thoughts lead us – on long runs, one's thoughts must be fire, not fog, lighthouse or storm.

Within the first 500m, I eased ahead of my batch and soon disappeared into the heat-shimmering distance – *trot-trot-trot* – animal-like, eventually devoid of all thought but those of food, drink and motion. Just being, and utterly in the moment.

At 15km, I passed a large, male gemsbok drinking at a watering hole. He darted off into the thorn thicket, stopped and turned his beautiful superhero-like face towards me: A dazzling white brow and a long, black marking over either eye. *Geheimsbok*,[63] the Dutch called them for their masked appearance.

His gaze made me slow down and stop. We stood together like that for a few seconds. "Hello, gemsbok!" I said and veered slightly off the trail so as not to startle him.

"I am just passing. Thank you and good luck." I watched him from the corner of my eye where he stood under those splendidly straight horns. He seemed at ease as he gazed after me while I *ploffed-ploffed* up the steep, sandy road.

The interaction filled my whole being with a deep sense of the familiar, of coming home, as if, at the dawn of time I had stood before a gemsbok like that, perhaps as a Kalahari Bushman hunter. I felt it in every cell and sinew of my body.

The First People, the Bushmen of the Kalahari, the San – choose what name you wish, with respect – were a people with whom, for many reasons, I have come to deeply identify. My grandmother called me "*Boesman*" from

63 "*Geheimsbok*" means "secretive antelope".

as early as I can remember. It was a nickname I cherished, as it bestowed on me every human quality I thought worth having: Being in tune with nature; respectful of life; wise in the way of the veld; resourceful; hardy; resilient; communal; deeply spiritual; animist, and a people who could run extreme distances beyond imagination. There is great power in a name. Maybe my grandmother unwittingly created a mould for my life, and, without knowing it, I grew into it little by little.

There, plodding away from that gemsbok, after so many years in the bitter winters of the United Kingdom, it felt as if the great Kalahari Desert was calling me by name: "Boesman, welcome home."

I ran from checkpoint to checkpoint, never thinking further than the next section to come. I had faithfully memorised the nine distances that separated checkpoints along the 77km course, and then grouped them into three distinct segments. It helped me eat the monster-distance one bite at a time.

I repeated the sequence to myself: 9-9-8-9; 10-10-8; 7-5. Done! It was a mantra that trivialised the harsh, physical reality of each leg. It was like being in a video game – surreal and out of-body, which made the physical pain more bearable.

As the day wore on, I caught up to everyone who had started ahead of me, and I bore witness to their races and dogged perseverance.

I shuffled past British Edward, 69 years old. He was a large, square man with the longest arms, dressed in an oversized sweater that made him look like a desert version of Edward Scissorhands. He told me that he came back to run KAEM year after year, because the people there had become his only family in the world. He told me a story about a young racer named Gabriel with whom he had become close, but he had subsequently passed away.

"You know, on Day 2, when it got impossibly hard in that hot Death Valley and I was failing, I felt someone's hand on my back, encouraging me forward. I am sure it was Gabriel coming to keep me company," he said.

One thing I know for sure about running in the desert: Out there, we are able to get in touch with that which is greater than us. The vast spaces that surround us, and the pain of physical exertion washes away our sterile cynicism. Being there in that direct and vulnerable way opens us to the miracle of life beyond what we can see, and far beyond what we are able to access in built-up, noisy, information-overloaded cities. Out there in the desert, we awaken.

I caught up with a bus of 10 back-markers, who were playing an ingenious mind game to pass the long hours. The front runner proposed the baking of a cake, and in turn each runner added an ingredient. Someone mixed, someone waxed the cake tins, someone else put the cake in the oven and set the timer for 45 minutes.

Everyone watched the clock.

Once the cake was ready, there was a whole ceremony of cutting and devouring; and then they started all over again. I passed them in the mixing stage of their second baking session and marvelled at how strange and super-adaptive human beings are.

Not long after, I passed British Lorraine, whose feet were in such bad shape that she was practically hobbling on bloodied stumps. She still had 55km ahead of her, but in the way she moved and from the expression on her face, it was clear that her spirit was far from broken. As I passed her, she cheered me on with the enthusiasm of a football fan.

Between midday and late afternoon, the heat grew as intense as wrath – a red-hot rage that swallowed us whole and seared the skin from our bodies. At 45km, nauseous, dizzy, and on the verge of passing out again, I slowed my pace and drank a medicinal electrolyte, wet my ears and stumbled on through the blinding heat. Somewhere from deep within my interior arose a silent plea for help. Alone in that deafening, dead-heat silence, I knew that my strength was failing me. I called to the Earth beneath my feet, "Spirit of the Great Kalahari, carry me."

I geared into autopilot, emptied myself of thought, and settled into survival mode, one step to the next.

At 50km, Russell Nugent thundered past me. I tried for conversation, but he told me later that he had been shattered and running on reserve, protecting his energy. He was doggedly focused on the path ahead, too tired to talk – *pat-pat-pat* – running for his life.

Like him, I was chasing to make the most of daylight. I made it to Checkpoint 6 at 55km just before sunset and sat down for the first time after 8.5 hours of running.

"You look terrible," Alet remarked, as if I didn't know.

The semi-shocked look on her face told me enough. She was accustomed to seeing me race from a place of joy and composure – not staggering into checkpoint without banter and looking like hell.

I ran off, intermittently gulping down nausea and forcing down handfuls of salted coconut flakes. Eat. Eat. Eat or crash.

Shortly after the checkpoint, the path firmed up into a smooth, hard-packed single track. I rested into the long forgiving descent from the high plateau towards the Orange River Valley. The evening cooled and a great peace settled across the desert. My nausea eased.

I was utterly alone on that plane, a runner silhouetted against the blood-red ball of the setting sun and the black silhouettes of Kalahari quiver trees.

I slowed my pace and watched in awe as the magic of the night unfolded. The first stars appeared, and the darkness deepened. Stars multiplied and spilled in their billions from the shimmering gyre. The Southern Cross hung low and bright and achingly familiar in the night sky of my childhood. Despite the discomfort of feeling unwell, I had never felt more whole in my life.

I refrained from switching on my headlight and ran by feel. Gently, the Kalahari spirits picked me up and carried me across the land.

A few minutes into my reverie, I realised that I hadn't seen a route marker for a good kilometre, and I started to worry. Had I missed a split in the road or taken a wrong turn? I had been lost in the Kalahari before. I flicked my headlamp on and turned back, carefully retracing my spoor in the sand.

In the distance, I noticed a light bobbing towards me. Whoever, or whatever it was attached to, was running at a furious clip.

My heart sank as I enquired into the night: "Helen?".

No answer.

"Hylton?" He burst through the darkness like a rhinoceros in full pursuit.

"You are doing really well!" he huffed. He stayed by my side for a minute and then charged off into the black night.

The ox-blood-red giant, full moon rose, eclipsing every star in her path and bathing the veld in yellow light. I again switched my headtorch off, and for the next 7km, I ran wild and free into the moonlit wilderness.

The nausea steadily returned, that time twinned with a deep exhaustion – deeper than the marrow in my bones.

I had been alone all day. I needed company and encouragement, and above all, someone to help me step out of the little puddles of self-pity that had begun to accumulate around the pain. I spoke to myself in a loud voice: "*Troepie,* pick up your knees! Higher. Don't be so useless. Come on! Are you made of chicken *dinges*?! No, you are not. Higher!".

"*Ja, Korporaal!,"* I answered double-quick, running taller and quickening my step.

It filled me with almost childlike delight to play *Troepie* and *Korporaal* under the starry sky with not a soul for miles around. It helped speed up the kilometres and gave me something other than my aching feet and the bacterial frothing in my stomach on which to focus.

As I entered the Orange River Valley, Dangerous Dave came roaring out of the darkness on his quad bike.

"You, again! I am going to give you a good spanking," he yelled gleefully, so immeasurably glad to see me.

"I can't wait! Race you to camp!", I teased back, fighting through deep river sand towards the finish line.

I felt no pain or fatigue in those final few kilometres – only love and awe, bliss and euphoria. At the end of a long 77km and a good 11 hours on my feet, I had hit a boundless runner's high of endorphins and a sense of great relief that I had made it.

I ran into camp right on the river's edge and rang the unmanned finisher's bell. I was home. It was done.

In the privacy of darkness, I stripped off and stepped into the swift, dark water, letting the coolness rush over me, and the rancid sweat, the old, dried blood, dust and all of my muscular tension rush down the river. I sunk below the silver, shimmering surface in a moment of complete bliss. Then something enormous bumped against me, swishing past my thighs and thudding its way back upstream towards me.

I leaped from the river, screaming, and fumbled for my headlight to see an enormous barbel cut the water like a shark. It was then that I noticed that the river shallows were fat with fish, splashing and slapping their tails, eating and spawning in the thick, black starlit water. It was like arriving in paradise after days of wandering in the merciless desert.

Helen came across the line 1 hour, 17 minutes after me. She said she'd had a good day and felt strong. We had both raced well, but the day's small triumph was mine. I had bagged the prize of first lady on the Long Day.

Day 5 – Rest

The Long Day was over. At 8am, the last racers finally crossed the line after 26 hours of battle. Lorraine collapsed next to me, her feet looking like those of a leper: Bandaged, bloodied, and swollen beyond recognition. She fell into the deepest, sweetest sleep for the remainder of the day.

We had a whole day to rest, swim, eat and recover before we had to face the final 73km to the finish. All day we lazed together under the hot marquees, talking nonsense, telling stories and sharing our meagre rations of food as acts of great generosity. On these races, by the fifth day, food is bitterly scarce.

Ayob brought me a rusk – a hard biscotti-like, quintessentially South African biscuit made for dunking. I shared it with Helen. Richard gave me a few sticks of sugared, dried fruit. We call it mebos. It was a lifesaver when my stomach refused everything else. Morgan arrived with gifts of delicious oatmeal bars, which saved me from having to gag on oats for breakfast. Hong Tan from Singapore gave me two rice cakes. They must have been the most delicious things I had eaten all race – bland, light and forgiving on my stomach.

A desert race is made up of the sum of a thousand small kindnesses. Our shared adversity opens us to each other. We share our precious morsels of food; we hobble to the kettles on sore feet to fetch hot water for the fallen; we give away our last pair of socks; we rub each other's painful shoulders and offer to cuddle up for body heat against the cold desert chill.

Evening cooled the Earth. Fireflies darted back and forth over the swift, black river, and arced lighting silhouetted the distant mountains that we had crossed on the Long Day. The air smelled humid and rich with the promise of approaching rain.

By 10pm, desert rain had arrived on the tail of a dusty storm. The tents flapped dangerously, and after a volley of fierce gusts, three of them collapsed on to sleeping racers. In the dark, we scurried to help each other and settled back down for a restless, watchful sleep. I lay awake for a long time, smelling the wet Earth and trying to ignore my nausea and bowel discomfort, which had returned in full force.

Day 6 – Coming home

50km

We were slow to the startline at on the Day 6, somehow lethargic from the rest. Ahead of us loomed another 50km of endurance, to be toploaded on to bodies that had already covered 180km of racing through a hell of sand, heat and pain.

About 23% of the field had already withdrawn. It was the highest number of withdrawals recorded in the 20-year history of KAEM. Alet had reported a record number of critical medical emergencies and had administered a greater number of saline drips than on any previous event.

At 8:30am, I set off together with Helen, Russell and Hylton. We ran hard out of camp and across the deep sand, with Helen chomping at the bit and pushing the pace.

Having neither the energy nor the mind to chase, I let them go.

To my surprise, I arrived at Checkpoint 1 just as Helen left. Around 20km, shortly after Checkpoint 2, I caught up with her again. She was walking.

"Are you okay?" I asked and slowed down to walk with her. The feeling between us was pleasant and collegial.

"Yes," she answered curtly – not because she was unfriendly but because she spoke little. Her candid brevity was most appealing.

On the flats and hard-packed sections, we jogged together, and in between the long silences, Helen told me about her stellar career in triathlons, and how, in 2010, she had become one of the top 10 Ironwomen in the world. She had taken the podium together with triathlon greats like Chrissie Wellington. I understood that she had come to the desert to rest from the chase and the pressures of the leader board, as well as some other heartaches in her life. In some way, we all went to the desert to heal.

We trotted side by side, enjoying each other's company, and entered into Checkpoint 3 where the volunteers welcomed us: "Looks like the two of you are on an easy training run."

Helen sat down.

As always, I refrained from taking a seat. In long-distance racing, nowhere poses greater danger than checkpoints, where there is shade and the temptation of chairs and the beguiling care of volunteers. The moment one sits down, four minutes can flash by in a wink. On a stage with five checkpoints, that amounts to 20 minutes foregone! Good transition discipline can secure a win against far stronger competitors.

My strategy in every race is to remove the lid of my hand-held bottle well before I get to the checkpoint, then immediately on arrival, fill it, while gorging on as much water as my stomach can onboard. I try to do this pretty much without breaking my stride. I then pour some water over my head and neck and immediately head out while thanking the big-hearted volunteers. This process burns less than 25–30 seconds.

As I left the checkpoint, I offered: "I will trot slowly. Catch me."

Helen never caught me again. I believe it was on purpose.

Multi-day desert racing is so much more than just a duel to the finish, it is a pilgrimage of the heart. Compared to other sports, like triathlons and tennis and golf, it is a small and obscure sport, and it is for many of us more than just a public stage for athletic performance. A desert race is a place of making deep connections along the way and of learning about oneself at the edge of endurance. It is a place of becoming so quiet within that one gets perspective on one's life and what needs to be done. Sometimes, the quietness inside is so spacious that one gets a glimpse of a memory of ancient times, and of ways we used to be and how we used to live in the beginning.

When I run in the Kalahari and imbibe on litres of water at the checkpoints, it feels oddly familiar, like some primordial ways are coming back to me. Sometimes I collect a long stick from the veld and run, carrying it like a spear in my right hand. Maybe my body knows this stance from what feels like a long time ago. It is the stance of the Bushman hunter on the run. Bushmen were accustomed to the natural cycles of famine and feast. They had the ability to consume vast amounts of food and water, and their stomachs were even able to stretch sideways to accommodate this eating cycle. As with water, so it was with the hunt.

Deep in my heart I feel like a */Gwikwe*[64]. I love running at midday when the sun is at its zenith. Who knows? Perhaps some old part of me remembers that this is the best time of day to hunt. I eat sparsely throughout the day, and at night, I can put away a meal that would put a competitive eating champion to shame. I have eaten like this for most of my racing life, long before intermittent fasting became a thing. It is the way of the hunting Bushman clan.

With every day we stayed in the Kalahari, my body and my soul felt more and more at home.

Helen arrived in camp 30 minutes after me. She held aloft one shoe: "I shouldn't have changed my socks. My feet are killing me. Not a good day."

For all intents and purposes, Helen had won KAEM, because ahead of us lay the final stage of only 23km to the finish line. It was far too short a distance for me to erase the one-hour gap that remained between us. It did not matter. Helen was a worthy champion and I felt proud that I had not failed myself and given up on the second day when I lost the race in Death Valley.

What matters, in racing, as in life, and as in love, is that we accept that sometimes the path will be hard. What matters in the end, whether it is going our way or not, is whether we are able to remain committed. It is only by staying in that we can build something meaningful in life. It is only by persevering across the rocky path that we can grow and become better. Such is the worthwhile journey. One will never reach the highest bar in a spirit of ambivalence or half-heartedness.

Helen came to rest next to me. We sat under the hot canvas and shared a portion of my goji berries while enjoying the animated banter around us. The atmosphere in camp was jovial, for the worst was behind us. There was also a palpable sadness because we knew it would soon be over.

We sat together in little clumps, laughing and chatting, wishing to somehow draw out the hour and hold on to the beauty and simplicity of the experience; to take home with us those feelings of community,

64 The "/" sign indicates the click sound.

belonging and camaraderie, and to hold on to the friendships that had been formed in special moments on that great sand face of the Kalahari.

And above all, we wanted to hold on to that feeling of belonging in the wild.[65]

Irish Fergus asked me at the beginning of the race: "Are you a writer who runs or a runner who writes?" If I had had the presence of mind then, I would have said that I am a modern-day Pied Piper who writes to remind our civilisation about the necessity of remaining connected to Nature, of living simply, and of having a deep reverence and relationship with the life in all things.

I would say to Fergus that, like him, I have retained something of the Kalahari Bushman spirit, and that I have come to tell our children, and their children, a story of a far-off place where a human and a gemsbok can still have a decent conversation.

Day 7 – Lorraine's Crossing

(FINISH LINE)

Morning came. They set us off one last time in a staggered fashion. Lorraine, Edward, Phil and Ayob left at 5am.

Three hours later, I set off together with Helen and Russell, running hard, swift and strong. The dirt road opened before us like an invitation.

Helen ran ahead.

The desert physios had massaged my colon the previous night, which brought great relief. It was the first time since the beginning of the race that I had run without feeling pregnant and on the brink of throwing up. Home beckoned, and thoughts of Thandi made my heart beat hard with anticipation. I increased my speed. The lover and the warrior in me gleamed tall, swift and sharp-edged.

After 6km, I caught Helen and we ran together. She looked tired, but I couldn't say that it was from racing. "I have six jelly babies.[66] Do you want

65 Scientists describe this human tendency to seek connection with Nature in the *Biophilia Hypothesis* (Wilson, 1984). "Biophilia" literally means the love of life and living systems.

66 Not my usual choice of food, but my beleaguered stomach insisted that I trade my raisins for jelly babies.

some?" I offered. She didn't and started walking. I slowed down to stay with her.

I recognised that she didn't want to race, that she didn't want or need the win or the publicity, and that all she wanted was to be left alone and to have the time and space to deal with her own stuff out there in the desert.

After a while, we picked up the pace and ran together into Checkpoint 2. She sat down and I galloped through the checkpoint, as is my way.

I passed Lorraine 10km before the finish line. She was walking and flinching with every step. She had three more hours of pain to endure, but smiled and waved regardless. I saw the steel in her gaze. In her mind's eye, she had already tasted the finish line and there was nothing in the world that would stop her from getting there.

Less than an hour later, I spotted a troop of baboons where the three giraffe had greeted me on the first day. "Until next year, friends," I called. The big male barked after me. I felt heard, seen and known. Boesman was finally home.

I crossed the finish line of the 20th Kalahari Augrabies Extreme Marathon as the second female home and fourth overall.

Helen came in 10 minutes later. I had shrunk the two-hour gap between us to 52 minutes. It was a valiant effort, given my illness and the calibre of my competition. I was grateful, relieved and above all, I felt a glorious sense of hope. I had overcome my silent fear that menopause and the natural processes of aging had brought an end to my racing life. A woman can run for as long as her heart is in it. When I crossed that finish line, that knowing had irrevocably settled in my body and in my bones.

We cheered the remaining racers in. Edward flapped his long, scarecrow arms around me, and Ayob came over the line and brought me a rusk as a parting gift.

When we heard that Lorraine was about to arrive, we lined up on either side of the home strait. Lorraine turned the corner, waving her walking poles aloft and beaming. We cheered, whistled, and clapped, tears welling in our eyes. There before us, in Lorraine's crossing, we recognised the victory of the human spirit, the highs and lows of our own challenges, the bitterness, sweetness, euphoria, camaraderie and the love.

I left immediately after the race, just as I had the previous year, skipping prizegiving to get back home. But a sadness as big as the Kalahari Desert had settled in me. Sometimes one knows long before a bad thing happens.

"I know you are tired but come, this is the way."

RUMI

16

PARADISE LOST, PARADISE FOUND, 2020

"Refuse to fall down. If you cannot refuse to fall down, refuse to stay down. If you cannot refuse to stay down, lift your heart towards heaven like a hungry beggar and ask that it be filled. It is in the middle of misery that so much becomes clear."

CLARISSA PINKOLA ESTÉS

After KAEM, I underwent a battery of tests and was diagnosed with a chronic case of a leaky gut. My small intestine had become permeable, allowing harmful bacteria and poisonous substances through into my bloodstream. The disastrous consequence of this condition, especially for endurance athletes, beyond the headaches and compromised immunity, is that the gut lining is unable to effectively absorb nutrients. No matter how much or how well one eats, one is, in fact, starving.

It was a strange doctor's visit. She asked a few pointed questions, and then held me for most of the consultation while I cried. At the end of it, she noted on her computer: "Chronic intestinal permeability, most likely due to persistent stress at home."

Grief can remake us. Remorse can cut deeper than a surgeon's blade. I was about to come through the greatest damage of my life, and in the process, gain something of incalculable value. I would learn through losing my family that I was not alone in the world, and that I was enough.

I had rushed back home from the Kalahari Desert, back to Thandi and Rhadi. But things were changing. Thandi's love was thinning. The more she withdrew, the more I craved her attention. She said she felt trapped. At the end of two years of love, we had fallen into a downward cycle of pursuit-and-withdrawal and the pain that goes with it. The more she needed distance, the more my fear grew and the tighter I held her. I became scared and controlling. In response, Thandi became angry and intermittently volatile.

Life at home had become unstable, our peace unravelling with increasing frequency and decreasing predictability. All it took was the slightest bit of grit in the system to set off a disproportionate malfunction. No matter what I did or didn't do, Thandi said I triggered her. My Thandi, who had said she would love to buy me a whole meadow of wildflowers, also said she couldn't have the life she wanted alongside me. We both suffered anxiety and devastating heartbreak.

In line with our increasing arguments, the signs of disinvesting accrued: All mention of moving in together ceased; there were fewer early-morning drops at race starts, and fewer family dinners out, until there were none. Thandi invited me over less and less, and when she came to visit me, the hours of togetherness shrunk to an hour or two of half-hearted drop-ins. The pain of her withdrawal became a constant, and my life started falling apart.

Without exception, my friends said: "Get out!" I made excuses and stayed.

I believe Thandi's friends advised the same. On the eve of the COVID-19 global lockdown, Thandi left.

South Africa implemented one of the hardest lockdowns in the world. Overnight and without warning, we lost all freedom of movement. We were not allowed to run, hike, swim or bike. We were not allowed in the streets, mountains or in the sea, or to leave our homes to see our loved ones – not family nor friends. No more work, no more church, no more social connection, and no more Run Club on the promenade. No booze, no cigarettes, no bars, no restaurants, no sport matches, restaurants or movies.

Suddenly we were each frighteningly isolated and alone – and for me, it was amplified a thousand-fold because I had also lost my family and my place in the world.

Stephanie at Run Club said: "Really, Erica, you should get a dog. The shelters are looking for foster parents during lockdown."

I couldn't possibly conceive of having a dog. What would I do with it when I went training and racing, and when I was running trips in Greece for months on end? Somehow, none of that mattered.

On the eve of lockdown, I met my dog at an overcrowded, out-of-town animal shelter. She was the most serious-faced, fudge-blonde Africanis girl without an inkling of a wag in her tail. She had been living in the same cage for six years, since she was a puppy.

"Her name is Kelly, apparently," said the clerk at the office after consulting the dog register. I put my hand through the chicken-wire fence and stroked her head. She leaned in for a brief moment, and then dropped back on to her paws, resigned to the six-year-long pattern of more boisterous dogs being led out of their cages to happy, new lives. The moment she did that, I knew she was mine.

I renamed her Roxie, for her beach-blonde hair. Roxie, gentlest of dog souls in all of the world, and as cautious as anyone with a broken heart, came into my house and filled some of the emptiness of Thandi's leaving.

I cried a river into Roxie's fur. She held me steady in her gaze, sometimes even in the dark of night, with a sad and tragic air, like Amy Winehouse, and with the same heavily made-up, oval eyes.

Roxie saved my life.

In the aftermath of the break-up, and during many hours of lockdown self-reflection, I saw my role, as much as Thandi's, in what had gone wrong.

I understood that pain is a part of relationships, as it is of life. We are all the inevitable and alternate victims and perpetrators of heartache. There is no benefit to bitterness and resentment, or in trying to make sense of the morass of rights and wrongs and who is most to blame. It is a dead-end game that leads to only more pain and entrapment. We are all fallible human beings, and we unwittingly hurt and disappoint each other, not because we don't love each other, but because we are imperfect.

I never lost hope that Thandi and I could grow soft hearts for each other's struggles and humanness, and that we would find our way back to each other. And by the grace of God, after a black abyss of six months apart, Thandi reluctantly agreed to try again.

My beloved Thandi came back to me "because you are a catch," she said, without a flicker of adoration in her eyes.

I went in naked and open, willing to change in whatever way Thandi thought I should. It was different for her. She came shrouded in a strange darkness, and with an aloofness that made me feel even more anxious than before. And more possessive. I turned it inwards, where it cut and quartered me this way and that.

Instead of the tender reunion I longed for, Thandi gifted me with an archive of rage, a few weeks of love-obliterating contempt and one final blow-up that went too far.

In that final eruption, two things happened. Its awful trajectory wiped out any hope I had of a future with Thandi. And it made me see the truth of how I stood in the world.

In a moment, my heart broke open as I stood before the little girl in the stinking, dirty chicken coop, so eager to please, and so quiet and brave afterwards. I realised that I was in adulthood, as in childhood, falling into the same sick pattern of fear and body-numbing compliance. And I realised that I didn't deserve it, and that I didn't have to, either.

The adult in me took the hand of that inner child and said: "No more."

That brief moment healed me more than a thousand hours of therapy or couple's counselling ever could. It made me accountable for my life.

On the day I walked away from Thandi, I realised that I am responsible for my own life, and that I have choice and agency. It is me who allows and disallows. It is me who draws the boundaries of what is acceptable and what is not. It is me who ultimately decides my life.

I never saw Thandi again; and in time, I came to count it a blessing.

The easy path is not always the most rewarding one. Sometimes heartbreak, whatever its cause, can be the greatest gift, because it offers an unparalleled pathway to awakening and profound personal growth.

Looking back on my life since childhood, I can't imagine that I would have been shaped and chiselled the way I have, had it not also been for the bad things that happened along the way. In a way, the heartache became the grit in the shell, and over time, the pearl.

Princess Anastacia, Billy, Sabelle, and Thandi – and all of the people I have loved in my life – have been my most instructive teachers. They were the ones who had filed down the rough and unhelpful bits of my character and who had awoken me from my habitual and unconscious early-youth, sometimes asshole-like behaviour. Each of my partners, by their presence, and later their absence, has made me in some way better than if I had not walked hand-in-hand with them through the dark valleys of paradise lost.

They taught me as much as my distance running did: That we are not fixed, and that we can grow and change, and always for the better, if we choose it. While one is still alive, there is always another chance and enough grace to do better.

Time has brushed over the most painful memories of Thandi. There is no blame. Instead, what remains is gratitude for the steep climbs and for the dark nights that made me. I finally learned that I am my own home and safety – I am my own Taj Mahal. I am my own big river and my own fat-trunked, dapple-shaded tree beneath which I can rest.

I had found my paradise within, and this time, it is mine for keeps.

"Out beyond ideas of wrongdoing and rightdoing there is a field.
I'll meet you there. When the soul lies down in that grass the
world is too full to talk about."

RUMI

17

THRIVE RUN CLUB, 2020

"One by one, voices will start
whispering, 'Me, too.'
And your tribe will gather.
And you will never
feel alone again."

L.R. KNOST

As COVID lockdown eased and we were allowed to run again in small groups, Run Club carried me through the stages of loss one painful step at a time. That merry band of thriving, lycra-wearing, COVID-masked, 10km warriors were the reason I got up three times a week before the winter sun and despite the winter rain, and despite the pain. They kept me going. They were the people who helped me move beyond the heartbreak of disillusionment and cajoled me back into the mainstream of my life.

We all need a tribe.

I have seen what running can do for people; how it can unite; how it can transform; how it can make a broken man walk tall and a floundering woman feel like she has regained a grip on her life. Every runner knows how the running juices spill over into the other areas of life. They become confidence, iron will and resilience. The sweat of consistent effort often mulls into a disposition of ingrained optimism. Running gives us something to be proud of: An aim, an identity and a discipline. It gives us something that nobody can take away from us.

Since the inception of Thrive Run Club years ago, I have stood as a midwife for many people's very first running kilometres, and in due course, I have witnessed the most remarkable personal transformations.

The first time Vernon and I ran together, it was just the two of us. It was a cold, grey, rainy day on the promenade, and at the end of 3km, Vernon collapsed next to his car, flat on his back in the drizzle, groaning and clutching at his heart.

Vernon came back for the remaining nine Thrive Couch-to-10km training sessions, and within 10 weeks, he had built up to running 10km injury-free and at a comfortable pace. Two years later, he still shows up three times a week for Run Club. There are no words to describe the joy when I see him, billiard-stick-straight, shoulders back, tall and light, his feet in quick cadence, and a look of pleasure about him.

That is how we all run at Run Club. We have learned the techniques[67] of how to run efficiently, without injury, and how to transform a slog of a jog into an experience of lightness and ease. Above all, we have learned to love running. The secret to loving running, especially in the beginning, is to run slowly.

Over time, many people have found a home with us. Three times a week, we run and talk – about our lives and our families, about our love and losses, and about the blessings and challenges of our day. We have become a Run Club family, and we inspire each other to show up week after week, rain or shine. For all of us, running has become so much more than exercise – it is a way of being, and a super-highway to feeling happy, or at the very least, happier.

There are many running clubs all over the world, serving the millions of people who identify as runners and who are motivated to train and to participate in the many races on offer. I started Thrive Run Club not for them, but for people who have never thought of themselves as runners – people who can't even imagine themselves running for the bus. I started Run Club for the woman reclaiming her life after remission from cancer, and for the new diabetic who believes he will never do long races again.

67 The full Couch to 10km Programme is available through the QR code at the end of this book.

Ask Alan Hardeker, a former Ironman who fell on hard times. He posted this message on our Run Club WhatsApp group:

I have struggled for many years to get back to running after a heart attack and being diagnosed with diabetes. Until I met Erica. I have worked with many top-end coaches and none of them were able to break the art of running down into simple lessons that would have an immediate and massive impact on my running performance. Run Club made me fall in love with the sport again, inspired me and encouraged me more than you can imagine. Listen to your Thrive Guru's gentle persuasion. You can achieve so much more than you imagine."

The spirit of Run Club is inclusive: Everyone is welcome, and every running achievement, whether 3km or 1 000km, is celebrated and respected. We encourage and inspire each other. We are kind, and we are fiercely non-judgmental – of ourselves and of others. There is space – to be and to run – without the pressure of "shoulds" and "musts".

We wear our Run Club T-shirts with pride. On the left sleeve, we have in large, brilliant-green letters: *"For the love of running"* and on the right sleeve, right next to our South African country flag: *"Run for unity"*. We understand that it is through our running that we belong to something bigger than ourselves, to a running family that reaches across the widest chasms of difference, and to an ideal of who we can be at our best.

When we are out there on the promenade doing our 10km runs, I am often overcome with a deep joy and love. I am doing the work I love. In my 20 years of wandering as free and as untethered as a tumbleweed, racing here and there and all over the world, I discovered that true happiness does not live in unbridled freedom and endless adventures. In the end, the home of happiness is in love and in serving others.

"Ask nothing of your running and you'll get more than you ever imagined."

CHRISTOPHER MCDOUGALL

18

SOMETIMES DREAMS COME TRUE, 2021

"Happiness is the ultimate inner experience of living with generosity, love, kindness, compassion and gratitude."

DEBASISH MRIDHA

Once a week, when we were children, my mom would drive my sister and me all the way to town for Sunday church service. Take-aways simply weren't done when I grew up, but on the rare occasion, my mom would skip the Sunday roast and concede to a 15-piece family bucket of Kentucky Fried Chicken (KFC). I remember holding the warm red-and-white Styrofoam barrel on my lap for the hour-long drive back to the farm and nearly passing out from the smell of the crispy-fried batter, greasy fries, and the deliciousness of dopamine-laden anticipation.

What I remember even more vividly than the happy-hungry journeys home, was the feeling I got in church when the reverend passed the final blessing: "May the peace of God that transcends all understanding be with you, now and forever."

I remember the feeling of my child's body softening into the hard church bench, and the warm glow that washed over me. It was a feeling that all was right in the world.

As I grow older, I have a sense of returning more and more to that place. I have found that in the moments when I shift my attention off worldly preoccupations – off gain and pleasure, and off competing, winning, striving, and achieving – the greater my peace and the more my life seems to right itself. It has made me still and content. Kinder, less self-centred and wiser.

I can't say exactly how it happened, but one day I discovered that I was happy. Just as I am. I have come to understand that a person can access happiness directly – that we do not have to detour there via anything else. It is a subtle ride to that place – as soft as acceptance, and as hard-cut as a choice.

I still race, but the undercarriage of my motivation feels different, and more spacious. I feel less driven and less compelled to run so very fast and so very far. I need it less. I have run 10 000 miles and more, and some through the desert. I think I am home, at last.

And yet I know that I will never stop running.

In a few months, I will be 50 years old. Spartathlon, race of races, is calling to me. As I write these words, there is a fluttering of great excitement in my stomach, and a premonition laced with macabre delight. When I finally arrive at that startline beneath the Acropolis in Athens to follow in the footsteps of Pheidippides and Yiannis Kouros, it will be the pinnacle of my sports journey.

Who knows what could happen? Who knows what a 50-year-old woman can do if she sets her heart and mind to it? I move towards it with the innocence of my earliest racing years, all the while knowing that as I get older, it gets harder to maintain the level of fitness and strength required for these long-distance feats.

Time is naturally switching my body into a new way of being in the world. It is a great deal more challenging to stay at race weight, and I no longer have the youthful abundance of performance- and feel-good hormones. My VO2 max is deemed excellent and top of the charts for a 50-year-old – but for a 24-year-old, it falls below average. In these later years, I have to race differently, have greater discipline and be more deliberate in my training. I also have to accept that the recovery period after a big race will consume more of my life than ever before. For the first time ever, the trade-off seems overly costly.

My focus has slowly been shifting away from racing for racing's sake. I am pouring my life's energy into building Thrive, into helping people off the couch and towards a healthy routine of moving, and into calling people back to spending time in the wild.

My greatest hope is that those who feel moved to join us will find us – and that they will bring their kids and their friends, and anyone in their circle of influence who needs a boost of heart, body, or soul.

And if you are a person who needs us, three times a week you will find us at Run Club early in the morning on the Sea Point promenade, where we are consistently putting in the hours, keeping the faith, keeping momentum, and sticking to our 10km practice. If you are so moved, run with us.

During the school holidays, you may find me on top of Table Mountain with a chattering group of kids who are in the process of learning the creative power of goalsetting; or you may pass me coming down the slopes of Lions Head at dawn with a group of divorcées who have all marched out to reclaim their lives; or in the vast Cederberg with a group of women on a Navigate course. They will all be holding compasses and maps and have the look on their faces of people who know where they are going in life.

In July, you may find me saying grace and dipping bread in olive oil in a rustic, Greek taverna with a band of kayakers who have become joyfully accustomed to thriving with only a shoebox of belongings in their boat, and who will go home inspired to simplify their lives and to tend to that which matters most.

On late afternoons, you may find Roxie and me strolling on the little trail below Signal Hill, under a dusk-pink sky and in deep, still communion with Nature and with that great, abundant, creative force that made the sunbird, the humpback whale, the dung beetle and the retina of the eye.

Or you may spot Helen-Grace[68], Malakai and me ambling along Kommetjie Beach. Malakai walks in the middle, holding both of our hands. He is full of six-year-old excitement and joyful chatter about the bluebottles and their sting. Roxie rolls happily in some rotten piece of red-bait, and then sprints across the beach, all upright tail, flapping ears, and panting tongue. The glossy surf rolls out on to the white sand. Helen and I

---

68 I met Helen-Grace through our shared love of adventure and the outdoors. We fell in love on the evening I broke a rib in the Cederberg – but that is a story for another time.

are silent and content, watching the perfect lines forming on the backline, knowing that we are both thinking to suggest a surf. Nothing needs saying.

Who knows what the two of us will still learn together, and how we will help each other grow, and what difficult paths may lie ahead of us? What is sure is that we are equally committed to the journey, and to the good that will come from it for us, and also for those around us.

The world feels calm and safe.

In the end, everything works out somehow – with hard work and conscious, consistent effort, while facing all of the risks, difficulties, and the stress of trying and often failing.

Sometimes our dreams come true.

One always has another chance.

AN INVITATION

"'What day is it?
Asked Pooh.
'It's today."
Squeaked Piglet.
"My favourite day."
Said Pooh."

A.A. MILNE

At the end of this book, I have included a QR code. It gives you access to *The Ten Commandments of Running* and the Thrive Couch to 10km in 10 Weeks training programme.

My wish for you is that you are inspired, and that these resources provide you everything you need to just start.

I will be there with you in spirit through the thin air of the climb as you begin. Just take the first step, and then the next, and eventually every next step will look after itself.

Just start.

And if you can, and if your heart is willing, dig in your ice axe and take someone with you.

Welcome to the Thrive Run Club family. We do it all for the love of running – for the love of life.

"Tell me, what is it you plan to do with your one wild and precious life?"

MARY OLIVER

JOIN
THRIVE RUN CLUB'S
COUCH TO 3KM/5KM/10KM IN 10 WEEKS
PROGRAMMES

Visit Thrive Run Club's Facebook page
(www.facebook.com/thethriverunclub)
to find out more.

* * *

Scan the QR code below for the Ten Commandments of Running and other runners' resources:

Made in the USA
Las Vegas, NV
05 December 2021

36183602R00142